understanding human behavior

An Illustrated Guide to Successful Human Relationships

COLUMBIA HOUSE / New York

Editor	Nicolas Wright
Deputy Editor	Susan Joiner
Senior Designer	Stewart Cowley
Art Editor	Mary Cooper
Art Assistant	Jeff Gurney
Editorial Assistants	Mundy Ellis
	Sarie Forster
	John Moore
	Michael McIntyre
Picture Research	Diane Rich
	Hazel Robinson
	Paul Snelgrove
Editorial Director	Graham Donaldson
Production Manager	Warren E. Bright

contents

introduction

Talking is an instantly obvious form of communication. But while you are talking to someone you are also communicating with him in another – and usually more meaningful – way.

This is through body language. Every movement of the head, every facial expression, every twitch of an eyebrow: each gesture says as much as the words we use. Volume Ten of *Understanding Human Behavior* will help you recognize these subconscious signals. Each has its own significance. Nodding, for example, when done slowly, means that we are interested in what a person is saying. We are, in effect, giving him permission to carry on. But, when we want to interrupt we nod rapidly, disrupting the other's speech pattern until he stops.

There are very few genuinely self-elected loners. All of us have a basic need for friendship. But how do we make friends? Where do we meet people? How do we approach and establish a relationship? Volume Ten gives you the answers. It also tells you whether or not there really is such a thing as a platonic friendship and warns of the outcome when friends come between husband and wife.

Attitudes towards crime have changed

(continued)

throughout history and vary greatly from country to country. Each time and each place has had its own method of dealing with the criminal. While one culture impaled the woman who murdered her husband, another transported its felons to colonize newly conquered territory. Volume Ten, in a far-reaching discussion, shows to what lengths society will go to deal with those who offend against it.

—The Editor

David Levin

Body talk

Next time you listen to a friend, analyze his movements—you'll find a nonverbal language.

In a crowded café in Mexico researchers watched two people deep in conversation. As they made points during their talk they reached out and touched each other—on the hand, the arm, the shoulder. In fact, in one hour 180 such person-to-person contacts were made. And when the researchers watched two Parisians chatting away 120 touching contacts were made.

But when they repeated their experiment in London it was found that the café conversationalists stubbornly refused to touch each other once during the whole hour.

Louder Than Words

It all went to confirm scientifically what people have known for a long time: that there are enormous variations between different races and different nationalities in the way that they use gestures and other body movements to augment and emphasize what they are saying.

Yet even though the British (and the Americans, Japanese and Scandinavians, too) seem very reserved in this respect, recent research has shown that each and every one of us indulges in an extraordinary variety of tiny unconscious gestures—like

almost imperceptible nods of the head, movement of our eyebrows and the eyes themselves—every time we meet someone or carry on a conversation with them.

In fact, these subconscious gestures "say" as much, if not more, about ourselves as the words we use. And this body language regulates conversation: with it we signal when we wish to speak or when we think it is someone else's turn. It also reveals how we feel about whom we are talking to—whether we feel superior or inferior, friendly or hostile, interested or bored.

In the last several years scientists have been discovering fascinating details about this silent "body language" and the role it plays in our lives. As one researcher says, "We speak with our vocal chords, but we communicate with our whole bodies."

There are two main ways in which this body language communication is carried on: through movement of the head and the use of facial expressions made by the eyes and mouth, and through "posture"—how and where we stand and sit when we meet or converse with others.

When two people talk to each other, they need some sort of cue to tell

Eye language is used the world over, but the "eyebrow flash" (illustrated right) is a recent discovery. In it both eyebrows are raised to maximum extent for one-sixth of a second. It is used as a friendly greeting.

them when to speak and when to listen. As one British researcher into this subject, Dr. Michael Argyle of Oxford University, says: "When people first meet it is unlikely that their spontaneous styles of speaking will fit together and there is a period during which adjustments are made—one person has to speak less, another has to speak faster and so on. This is all managed by a simple system of nonverbal signaling, the main cues being nods, grunts and shifts of gaze."

The head nod is the most basic of these signals. When we are listening to someone we give tiny nods of the head in rhythm with his words. These nods show that we are listening, that we are involved with what he is saying. They give him permission, as it were, to carry on talking. But when we want to say something, our nods become much more rapid, breaking up the rhythm of his speech, showing that we want to break in.

All conversationalists (even when they talk on the telephone) indulge in what Dr. Argyle has called this "gestural dance." But while head nods are important in regulating two-way conversations, it is the eyes which add so much more to this nonverbal communication.

American psychologist Dr. Julius Fast has made a special study of body language. He says, "Of all the parts of the human body that are used to transmit information, the eyes are the most important and can transmit the most subtle nuances."

Different Rules

However, when we are meeting someone or talking to them we spend most of our time not looking *at* them but looking away. The reason? Simply, it is rude to stare, because staring is an invasion of the other person's privacy. It is reserved for examining objects rather than people. Dr. Fast says: "With unfamiliar human beings, we must avoid staring at them and yet we must also avoid ignoring them. To make them into people rather than objects, we use a deliberate and polite inattention.

"We look at them long enough to make it quite clear that we see them, and then we immediately look away. We are saying, in body language, 'I know you are there' and a moment later we add 'but I would not dream of intruding on your privacy.'"

Of course, different societies and cultures have slightly different rules about eye contact. That is why we sometimes feel uncomfortable at being "stared at" by men from, say, the Arab world, where eye contact is normally a little longer than we are used to. And the rules of such behavior are not inborn: children have to learn them by experience. That is why young children often seem to stare at strangers who interest them. They are not being impolite; they just have not mastered the social techniques of body language.

We use our eyes to regulate conversation, too. Just before we begin to speak we look away from the listener—and just before we are going to stop, we give him a longish gaze, to indicate "It's your turn now." But even when we know people really well, we actually gaze very little into their eyes while talking to them.

Another researcher investigated how often people being interviewed looked at the interviewer. He found that the man who made the most eye contact still looked away 27 percent of the time—and the man who looked

away the most had his eyes elsewhere 92 percent of the time. And half the people looked away for half of the time.

The experts conclude that looking while listening indicates attentiveness and interest; while speaking, it is a measure of sincerity. We all recognize this, subconsciously, to be true. We call a rogue "shifty" because he shifts his eyes. And salesmen of all sorts (including politicians who want to "sell" their own policies) have long used the "sincerity signal" of good eye contact to help put their message across.

One of the most fascinating recently discovered signals of body language is the "eyebrow flash." In it both eyebrows are raised to their maximum extent for about one-sixth of a second.

The eyebrow flash was first reported to a meeting of body language experts at the Royal Society in London a few years ago. They were amazed. One of them reported: "Suddenly the members of the conference were made conscious of a gesture which they had been using many times a day without realizing it. From that moment on it became impossible to greet a colleague without a momentary mutual embarrassment as each realized he had used this commonplace gesture without meaning to."

The man who discovered the eyebrow flash was Dr. Eibl-Eibesfeldt of the Max Planck Institute in Percha, Germany. He has filmed its use all over the world, and he found surprising variations between different cultures. He told the Royal Society conference: "In central Europe, the eyebrow flash is used as a greeting to good friends and relatives, but if people are reserved, they do not use it."

Easily Misunderstood

In some cultures, however, the eyebrow flash is suppressed: in Japan it is considered an indecent gesture. But Europeans use it frequently, particularly "during flirting, when strongly approving, when thanking and during discussions—for example, when emphasizing a statement and thus calling for attention."

Dr. Eibl-Eibesfeldt added: "We are not normally aware that we use this signal but we respond strongly to it in greeting situations. We smile back and give an eyebrow flash. However, if we are not familiar with the person, we experience embarrassment."

Because there are wide cultural variations in this silent eye and eyebrow language, difficulties can arise. An American businessman, for example, might feel he was getting on

very well with a Japanese with whom he wanted to do business—and quite unconsciously begin regularly to use the eyebrow flash. But although he feels everything is going splendidly, he does not get the contract. The reason: the more reserved Japanese has been embarrassed by these, to him, "indecent" gestures.

Similarly, in some Mediterranean and Latin American cultures it is the custom for children to show respect and obedience by not meeting the eyes of an adult. So when they are accused of being naughty they will look down or away, even if they are innocent. In Western Europe, children will show their sincerity with a clear-eyed gaze. There have been cases where Mediterranean or Latin American children have been punished at school "because they looked so guilty." But in refusing to meet the teacher's eye they were only showing their respect.

Keep Smiling

There are problems about eye contact in sexual encounters too. It is curious that the Latin races, who are much freer in body movement and gesture than those in Western Europe, reserve prolonged eye contact for only the most intimate situations. These days it is quite permissible for English girls to look at men for relatively long periods without the signal being taken as "I'm available and amenable to further advances." But an even slightly prolonged glance in, say, Italy might be taken as a "come on." So perhaps the Italians' reputation for making unwanted advances to English girls is not entirely their fault.

There are dozens more ways in which we use our eyes, eyelids and eyebrows to enhance conversation. Knitting the brows or winking are other obvious examples. But for really strong signals about our true emotions, we use our mouths.

We can "lie" to people with words about our true feelings, we can even learn to "lie" with our eyes by, for example, consciously emphasizing the "sincerity signal" of eye contact. But it is much more difficult to lie with our mouths. We can pretend to be enjoying ourselves by smiling, but it is very difficult to keep it up—and often the type of smile we produce will give away what we are really thinking.

For researchers have shown that there are many different types of smile, which come through in different situations. The leading expert in this field is Dr. Ewan Grant of the Basic Medical Sciences Department of London's

Chelsea College of Science and Technology. He says, ''The lips are frequently used to express emotions and it is very difficult to disguise them.''

One of the reasons why we are so expressive with our lips is the way that man has evolved. Many mammals have long facial whiskers which need muscles to control them. Although man does not have these whiskers he still has the residual remains of the muscles, which gives him such precise control over his lips. There are hundreds of different smiles, but Dr. Grant has found that they can be grouped into five main categories.

First comes the ''upper smile,'' so

The most disturbing form of body talk – a girl crying.

called because the lips are only slightly open, uncovering only the upper teeth. Dr. Grant describes it as the ''how do you do?'' smile since it is seen briefly when people meet and shake hands.

This smile is also seen for longer periods in less formal situations— such as when children coming out of school rush to see their mother or when a wife welcomes her husband home from work.

We do not smile just when we are with other people. If we feel contented or happy on our own we will often smile to ourselves. When we do, we are most likely to use the ''simple smile,'' the ''I'm happy by myself'' smile. Here, while the corners of the mouth are turned upwards, the lips remain firmly together and none of

the teeth is exposed during the smile.

When we are expressing deep joy or excitement, especially in a crowd at, say, a baseball game where others are reacting in the same way, we use the ''broad smile.'' The mouth opens very wide, the lips are curled right back exposing both upper and lower teeth. This is the really uninhibited smile of sheer pleasure. It can be seen at its best in children unselfconsciously enjoying themselves in play.

One of the five groups of smiles is almost exclusively reserved for women and girls, because it conveys a feeling of subordination. Called the ''lip-in smile'' it is similar to the upper smile except that the lower lip is drawn in between the teeth. It is often accompanied by a slight cocking of the head to one side, and a shy, upward glance.

Marshall Cavendish

This is the coy smile of young girls and children, an expression of subservience and innocence.

The last smile is the one no one really wants to see. It occurs when the smiler wants to pretend that he (or she) is enjoying himself but really is not. They try to smile naturally but their true emotions show through and produce the "oblong grin." The lips are drawn right back all right, but instead of the mouth being happily open, the teeth are clenched. Dr. Grant says it is the sort of smile you can see on a secretary's face if the boss is chasing her around the office. Or you may see it in a wife when her husband asks her if she is enjoying watching the football on television.

Unconscious Gestures

As well as expressing approval or enjoyment, the lips can be used to signal the opposite emotions. If we disapprove of something or someone strongly, we set our lips in a hard, thin line. When we are sad we turn down the edges of our mouths. When we feel frustrated or we cannot get our own way, our lips begin to form into a pout.

It must be emphasized that all these facial gestures are usually done entirely unconsciously. They are true reflections of our inner feelings. We may be trying to express something completely different using words but our unconscious body language will often tell the true story. Of course it is possible to mask these expressions, to learn tricks for putting across sincerity, interest or pleasure which we do not feel. But in the long run the truth will out.

It may be wondered whether all these new facts about the hidden language of our bodies have any practical application or whether it is simply gathering knowledge for its own sake. We are still in the very early days of research, but it is already becoming clear that this new knowledge could be of great use in diagnosing and

c

d

f

A girl's mouth can register a wide variety of meanings. a. The top-lip or "How do you do?" smile seen briefly when people meet. b. The broad smile or uninhibited smile of sheer pleasure—lips curled right back exposing both upper and lower teeth. c. The false smile seen on a wife's face when her husband asks her if she is enjoying watching football on TV. d. The "I'm happy by myself" smile when we feel contented to be on our own. e. The subservient "lip-in" smile often accompanied by a slight cocking of the head and a shy glance—the coy smile of young girls. f. The pout—when we feel frustrated or cannot get our own way our lips begin to form a pout.

By teaching them a few of the "tricks" of body language—how to use their bodies, the gestures and their expressions to help in communication—we can help them to overcome these difficulties.

For the surprising thing is that as people begin consciously to use body language signals, they find that others react to their newfound confidence. This makes conversation and personal contacts easier. By consciously using the gestures which reflect relaxation and confidence, the inadequate communicator actually becomes more confident and relaxed. Such techniques are increasingly being used in group therapy sessions for patients suffering from neurotic and psychotic illness.

David Levin

treating some types of mental illness. Schizophrenics, for example, have noticeably different patterns of nonverbal behavior from other people.

One of the problems of many people, with mild as well as serious mental problems is their failure to communicate with others. Very often something seems to have gone wrong with their nonverbal signaling: it is "out of step," and so relaxed, flowing conversation becomes impossible.

Richard Hook

Eye for an eye

Man has tried many different ways of punishing criminals, but crime has never been wiped out.

Winston Churchill once said: "The mood and temper of the public with regard to the treatment of crime and criminals is one of the most unfailing tests of the civilization of any country." And it goes without saying that the attitudes of the law and the definition of the criminal should reflect the attitudes of the community, in any society laying claim to civilization.

Attitudes to crime change in the course of history and differ among nations. Only a few actions would appear to have been universally regarded as criminal—sacrilege, the violation of taboos, murder—and these have met with varying degrees of disapprobation. In Western society the majority of today's crimes are against property, largely because the majority of today's legislation is in defense of property, which for some

time has been held to be of supreme importance in our lives. In other societies, where property is less sacred, crimes in that regard are correspondingly fewer: the main criminal activity may be in an entirely different field.

What may be thought a crime in one country may meet with approval in another. Christians do not approve of bigamy, which is considered natural in the Moslem world. Nor do Christians approve of homosexuality—though in this field the law has begun to change—prostitution, adultery and a variety of other sexual "crimes," which at various times and in various places have been wholly acceptable to equally "civilized" societies.

In certain countries, such as South Africa, interracial marriage is "criminal," whereas in many parts of South

America it may be considered quite normal. On the other hand, it suddenly became "criminal" between 1920 and 1933 to drink alcohol in the United States. In China it is a crime to criticize the state; in so-called "free" countries, it is considered a fundamental right, even obligation, to do so.

The origins of every modern penal system go back to the need of the primitive community to protect itself from any element that might harm it. The difference in attitudes to crime depended on which aspects of life the community felt itself to be vulnerable. Early "laws" consisted of taboos; to break them was to offend the gods more than fellow members of the community.

But to offend the gods was to threaten vengeance against the whole community. Therefore punishment of the transgressor was the means to avert injury to the whole tribe. The Bellacosta of North America imposed the death penalty on any member of the tribe who made a mistake, however accidental, in the tribal dance, for fear of recriminations by the deity. Alternative expiations to appease the wrath of the gods were the slaughter of animals—bullocks, lambs, pigeons, goats, or whatever was suitable.

Incidents of private revenge, or vendetta, tolerated at first among many primitive tribes and still visible in the attitudes of such criminal organizations as the Mafia, were gradually replaced by the imposition of community retribution, which in turn led to repression of the "crime" by the organized state. This was the point at which laws became established and codes of common behavior were laid down. With the changing emphasis of attitudes to life, people and property, these codes themselves altered in the course of time, thus revealing that the law of man is really no more inflexible than the law of God as interpreted by man.

Trial by Ordeal

One of the oldest codes is that of Hammurabi, compiled in Babylonia, about 2000 B.C. Murder was dealt with by the family, except in the case of a woman who murdered her husband; she was impaled. This contrasts nicely with the attitudes of the Chukchee Indians, who apparently believed that anyone who was killed by his own relatives must have been so unpleasant that he deserved his fate.

In time, compensation replaced the eye-for-an-eye attitude of the Old Testament. In Ethelbert's English Code of about A.D. 600, certain basic compensations are laid down: a hundred shillings for the slaying of a man; twenty shillings for a thumb struck off; three shillings for a thumb nail; nine for a forefinger but only six for a ring finger; twelve shillings for an ear; and six for a front tooth. Of course, penalties varied according to the status of those involved, a condition that in fact, if not in theory, still prevails today. Among the medieval Germanic tribes, a serf's life was worth half that of a freeman's life, which in turn was worth a little over half that of the life of a noble.

Attitudes were such in the Middle Ages that once a person was held for a supposed crime it was virtually presupposed that he was guilty of it. Even if he survived one of the imaginative "trials by ordeal"—grasping a red

hot poker, walking on live coals, being immersed in boiling water or submerged in cold, undergoing trial by combat—and was considered free, he would often still be banished simply because it was judged that having been accused of the crime by his fellows he must anyway be a poor member of the community. If he *was* proved guilty, by that or any other more judicial method, he would lose a hand or a foot, suffer a whipping, be placed in the stocks or the pillory, or be branded for life.

Ducking stools, used to determine the guilt of witches (women whom today we might merely consider pleasantly eccentric), provided great public amusement. The accused was strapped to a chair and then thrown into deep water. In Europe witches were considered guilty if they floated and drowned if they sank, so they lost both ways. In Babylon and early Greece, the more humane reversal was practiced: if they floated, they were innocent.

Torture does not seem far removed from these ordeals. Christianity has much to answer for in this field of criminal treatment. The practice of torture in the Middle Ages was encouraged by the belief that it was necessary for the criminal to repent before being executed. The pains of hell, said the church, were so awful that it was worth any pain on earth in order to avoid them. If the church had on its conscience the salvation of the souls of the wicked, then it certainly should have had on its conscience the burning, stretching, flailing, pressing with weights, mutilations and breaking on wheels with which it indulged its idiosyncratic and cruel whim on the avowed behalf of the protection of society and the good of the criminal's soul.

Hide-all Cure-all

The only importance that imprisonment had in the retributional and restitutional scheme of early crime treatment was as a place in which to hold the criminal prior to punishment. Prison was never originally intended to be the universal hide-all-cure-all that it became during the last three centuries. In twelfth century England, jails were used for restraint until the case could be heard by the king's court. Only gradually did the prisons become punitive places of custody and to that end a great deal more disagreeable, despite thirteenth century instructions that "the law wills that no one be placed among vermin and putrefaction, or in any

horrible or dangerous place, or in the water, or in the dark."

Whatever the law willed, it willed in vain. Prisons became a convenient place in which the inconvenient could be forgotten. In 1545, Henry Bricklow wrote that prisoners' "lodging is too bad for hoggys, and as for their meate it is evil enough for doggys, and yet, the Lord knoweth, thei have not enough thereof." Almost two centuries later, another observer noted that the prisons were "a noysome, stinking hole . . . full of vermin, wherein is neither chimney nor easing house." Starvation and fever carried off many inmates unable to afford the bribes necessary to obtain better conditions from the private controllers of the prisons, who grew fat on the desperation of their charges.

Place of Correction

What cure there was took only the form of correction aligned with strict discipline, cramped quarters among unsegregated fellows (women, children, murderers, debtors, witnesses, all together) and some hard labor. When the Bridewells (prisons of the seventeenth century) were full, new ways of coping with the criminal were looked for. Transportation was the answer. It was not a new idea. The early Greeks and Romans had sent criminals to the mines and quarries or to the galleys and penal colonies. England sent her criminals first to America and then to Australia, on which route they endured intolerable suffering. France used Africa, New Caledonia and French Guiana. Russia still makes use of Siberia—a convenient expanse in which to lose the unwanted.

In the United States, the prison system became highly organized and took a variety of forms, from the solitary confinement of the "separate" system of Eastern State Penitentiary in Pennsylvania, founded in 1829, to the more humane principles of the Quakers. "Solitary" was a treasured concept of eighteenth century rationalists, who believed that it encouraged penitence and hence reformation. The rival "silent" system, instituted in Auburn, New York, did at least allow prisoners to work together and slowly replaced the "separate" system. Credits for good behavior went toward an earlier release in the "mark" system, introduced in the English penal colony of Norfolk Island, off the coast of Australia. And in the Irish system of the 1850s, the prisoner progressed through a series of stepping stones, from isolation, through communal

work, to "intermediate prisons," in which he was fitted for the return to the outside world.

As principles, these various attempts appeared to the eighteenth and nineteenth century conscience as if they were trying to do something for the criminal, but when the real conditions inside many European and American prisons were investigated they were found to be so bad that no conceivable chance of improvement in the prisoner's life or attitudes could have been hoped for. Resentment, revenge, apathy or death were more likely.

Writing at a later and marginally more enlightened time, George Bernard Shaw had some sharp words to say about the contemporary system: "To punish and reform people by the same operation is exactly as if you were to take a man suffering from pneumonia and . . . stand him naked at night in the snow . . . while engaging a doctor to administer cough lozenges, made as unpleasant to taste as possible so as not to pamper the culprit."

He did not blame the eighteenth and nineteenth century reformers, only their followers. The chief reformers deprecated the silence, solitude and squalor that they found. During the latter part of the eighteenth century John Howard traveled through Europe and Russia and revealed to his contemporaries the ghastly nature of the prisons they ostensibly condoned. He was followed by the Quakeress Elizabeth Fry, equally appalled by the condition of the prisoners and equally determined to help them regain their dignity and their hope.

Prevention, Not Cure

There were theoretical reformers as well, whose influence, in time, was also deeply felt. The Italian nobleman Cesare Bonesana, Marchese di Beccaria, who died in 1794, argued for prevention in preference to punishment and remarked wisely that "no punishment for a crime can be called strictly just—that is, necessary—so long as the law has not adopted the best possible means in the circumstances of a country to prevent the crimes it punishes." He further warned against trying to force "a multitude of intelligent beings" into "the symmetry and regularity that only brute and inanimate matter admits of." He might well have agreed with the

Three ways of dealing with offenders: torture by the Iron Maiden (top left), death in a Mafia vendetta (top right), and an English country prison, with a modern approach.

English philosopher John Stuart Mill, who stated firmly that "the only purpose for which power can be rightly exercised over any member of a civilized community against his will is to prevent harm to the others."

Another nineteenth century reformer was Jeremy Bentham, who attempted to make punishments fit crimes with scientific exactitude. As with Beccaria, his penalties were not intended to be any harder than was needed to deter the criminal. Unfortunately Bentham spoiled the humanity of his argument by admitting the pleasure obtained in exacting vengeance on the criminal. And the vengeance was indeed savage. A boy of 13 was hanged in 1801 for stealing a spoon, and seven years later two sisters of 8 and 11 were executed for something equally trivial.

Physical Traits

The Scots essayist Thomas Carlyle cried that revenge was a correct and "even a divine feeling in the mind of every man." In outrage he described the criminals as "these abject, ape, wolf, ox, imp or other diabolic-animal specimens of humanity."

His argument appeared to be backed by the findings of the Italian Professor Lombroso, who published his theory on "delinquent man" in 1876. In the postmortem examination of a notorious bandit called Vilella, Lombroso expounded his theory lyrically: "At the sight of the skull I seemed to see all of a sudden . . . the problems of the nature of the criminal—an atavistic being who reproduces in his person the ferocious instincts of primitive humanity and the inferior animals. Thus were explained anatomically the enormous jaws, high cheekbones, prominent superciliary arches, solitary lines in the palms, extreme size of the orbits, handle-shaped or sessile ears found in criminals, savages and apes, insensibility to pain, extremely acute sight, tattooing, excessive idleness, love of orgies and the irresistible craving for evil for its own sake, the desire not only to extinguish life in the victim but to mutilate the corpse, tear its flesh and drink its blood." Small chance that there should be any attempt to "cure" a criminal so envisaged.

Lombroso's theory was quickly disproved by the English prison doctor Charles Goring, who compared the physical proportions of three thousand convicts with a university group and found them little different. But Lombroso's scientific interest in the criminal prompted others to try

the field. The inquiry expanded from the purely physical. An Austrian, Ernst Kretschmer, concluded that certain kinds of temperament seemed to be associated with certain physical types: the "leptosome" (lean and angular) would display different personality characteristics from the "pyknic" (short and round), or so he thought. But the answer is not quite so simple.

All reformers believe that they have the answer to the problem of how to deal with the criminal. The argument in this regard is heated, because treatment of the criminal involves many of the community's most cherished superstitions. Until recently, prison seemed clearly the simplest and safest solution. Reform was merely a matter of improving the conditions of prison. But "merely" was a slow process that has not been completed even yet. And the prisons have done little, so far as the evidence demonstrates, to "cure" the criminal.

Boys' reform schools appear to have done little better. They were intended to develop responsibility in the younger criminal and provide him with specialized training and treatment. To this end, they made use of the recreational, educational and employment facilities of the outside world. But nonetheless they tended to institutionalize the criminal, not re-adapt him to community life.

At the turn of the century, probation seemed to offer the best hope of rehabilitation or "cure" for the criminal. First begun in 1841 by a cobbler called John Augustus, who lived in Boston and offered to stand bail for and look after a man accused of drunkenness, the experiment was a success. Within 18 years Augustus stood surety for 2,000 offenders. In 1907, the Liberal Government in England introduced probation as an alternative to prison sentences.

Loss of Dignity

This was only the beginning of changes in many countries throughout the world, changes that have accelerated in recent years despite the apathy and reactionary instincts of the bulk of most communities, changes aimed expressly at helping the offender to regain his dignity and his sense of worth in the community and so contribute to its well-being. Today's reformers have as hard a battle ahead of them as any of the eighteenth century reformers and agitators but at least their philosophy seems more in tune with the "civilized" criteria laid down by the more enlightened thinkers.

Don Lawrence

Peeping Tom

The world is divided in two—those who participate and those who prefer to observe. In spectator sports, those who stand on the sidelines are well catered for, but there are other kinds of games which people play and any onlookers had better watch out.

As a striptease dancer bumps and grinds, as her garments slide seductively to the floor, men in the audience loosen their ties, wipe the sweat from their faces—and keep a pretense of disinterest by coolly discussing the finer points of her anatomy.

In everyone there lurks a possible sexual response to seeing others nude, to watching others make love. For most people this is a minor and natural part of their sexual make-up —for the voyeur, *looking* is what sex is about.

Most people can understand something of the voyeur's passion. Men who turn to watch a pretty girl walk down the street, perhaps with un-brassiered breasts bouncing, girls who eye a bronzed beach boy working out, and people excited by an explicit sex scene in a movie are all incorporating a visual sensation into their sexual life. The couple who occasionally enjoy watching themselves make love in a mirror are extending their sexual repertoire rather than indulging in a perversion. And others who accidentally come across someone sunbathing nude—or even making love—will look before passing on. These episodes may enrich the ordinary person's sexual imagination and so complement a normal sex life.

But the voyeur goes further. He compulsively seeks out situations where he can view the sexual organs or sexual activities of others. In some circumstances this may be little more than casually positioning himself so he can glance upwards to see a flash of thigh or underwear as women climb some convenient flight of stairs or standing over a seated woman to peer down her neckline.

More seriously, the voyeur may search out a vantage point which guarantees a "view"—perhaps an apartment that overlooks a locker room, or a park bench from which he can surreptitiously watch courting couples on the grass. In the most severe cases he will prowl around buildings at night, trespass in gardens, climb balconies or trees in order to peer through a bedroom window at a couple undressing and making love. The compulsive voyeur haunts public places and clings to darkness.

The voyeur distances himself from sexual contact. He prefers the anonymous link of watcher and watched to the personal interrelationship of love-making. As he watches an unknown woman undressing or a couple making love, he masturbates or records the image in his memory to replay as part of his sexual fantasies. The voyeur may be frightened of sexual inadequacy—many are partially impotent with women—and prefers voyeurism because he dominates the situation. He sees without being seen. But his gratification is vicarious. Looking at others having sexual intercourse can never bring the two-way interaction that forms much of the excitement of making love. For the voyeur, sex is a one-way scene.

"You have no idea of the pressure I'm under," Frank confided. "It sounds so silly. I can't talk to a doctor—he'd just laugh or tell me to snap out of it. I live alone and don't have many friends—just one or two other guys who are interested in ham radio too. We've all got licenses and we compare notes on equipment and the other 'hams' we've contacted. I don't really have much time to spend on setting up a sexual relationship.

"It's at work that the strain begins. There are a lot of young girls in the office and they seem to wear next-to-nothing. Their blouses are so thin, more often than not you can see their nipples through the material. And they can be short, too, so that if they stand by your desk you're looking straight at their navel. And they're always bending over so you get glimpses of their breasts and their underwear. They're shameless really—and sometimes I think they're flaunting themselves at me. It's so difficult not to look and yet it's embarrassing if they notice you doing it.

"I know where one of them lives—she's called Susie—because I followed her home one day. I'm pretty certain she didn't see me. I go down there some nights, stand across the street and look over at her window—the road's on a hill so I'm almost level with it. Sometimes she doesn't draw the curtains right across—there aren't any houses up that way so I suppose she doesn't imagine anyone can see in. I've watched her undress several times now—I've got pretty good eyes—and once she was completely naked when she came over to the window to draw the curtains. Now when Susie's in the office I've got something on her—she'd curl up if I told her exactly what she looked like nude."

The influences that lead a person to voyeurism start young. Some parental attitudes to each other and to sex can misdirect the child's developing awareness of sexuality and lead to personality difficulties that voyeurism is an attempt to solve. An unassuming father, perhaps, reacting to a more dominant mother, may instill in the adolescent child a feeling of anxiety about his masculine role and a subconscious fear of women. These feelings may make communication with women difficult and, like the exhibitionist or even the rapist, the voyeur seeks refuge and reassurance through depersonalizing sex.

The voyeur is no modern phenomenon, as this "enthusiastic student of nature" clearly shows.

Mansell Collection

Parents who are themselves sexually repressed can affect the child's later sexual inclinations. The adolescent or young adult never progresses past the childlike stage of thinking of sex as naughty, and voyeurism becomes a continual game of "I want to see what you've got." The voyeur is often likely to be an exhibitionist too, exposing himself to others in a reversed version of this game.

Keyhole Kates

Most voyeurs in this compulsive sense are male—as are most sex criminals. Alfred C. Kinsey considered voyeurism to be limited solely to men. But in the United States, the 1971 commission on pornography and obscenity decided that women responded to visual stimulation—pictures of nudes—in the same way as men. The pupils of their eyes enlarge (this also happens when they are shown pictures of a mother and child and demonstrates heightened interest) and other signs of physiological arousal appear. But, unlike men, women do not rate themselves as aroused, and it may be that by responding to social assessments of sexual roles women repress any tendency to overt sexuality, including voyeurism. Certainly the reaction of women spectators at pop concerts and quasi-sexual, sadistic wrestling matches suggests the impulse is there to be released.

That parents who are unable to talk openly about sex may be one of the influences leading to voyeurism is confirmed by researchers who have found that voyeurs tend to acquire their sexual knowledge at a later age than average. Unlike the teenager who gradually learns about sex and comes to accept it as a natural part of an adult relationship, the voyeur learns little from his parents or his friends and finds himself suddenly confronted with—to him—an alarming

world of sexual involvement. Curiously the voyeur may not be attracted to striptease or pornographic books just because he never had the opportunity to learn about them while his sexual personality was being formed.

"When I was eight," said Gary, "my mother caught me with Eleanor. She'd taken her pants down and was letting me look at her. My mother really thumped me. I didn't find a girlfriend until I was 23 and I was 25 before I had sex—although I'd been masturbating pretty regularly from the age of 14. Even now that I'm married, you know, I like to masturbate still. I can dream, you see, but when I'm with my wife, well, that's it, isn't it?

"I began looking out for women about the same time I started masturbating, I guess. The local swimming pool was the place. I'd lie and sunbathe with my eyes half open watching girls climb out of the water. As they lean forward at the top of the ladder their swimsuits sag forwards so's you can see their breasts. Then the superintendent caught me feeling myself and wouldn't let me in.

On Display

"Then it was the park in the summer. Some of those girls don't mind what they do with a guy right out there in the open. Even now that I'm married I'll take the dog down to the park on a warm evening when it's still light out. Get off the path into the trees and it's better than a sex show. I'm not a pervert—I make love to my wife as often as the next guy—but it just does something to me seeing up a girl's skirt when she doesn't know I'm looking."

Another component of the voyeur's psychological make-up may be a conflict between his falsely simplified view of what masculinity entails and the realities of his own life. Like many sexually inadequate men, the voyeur believes unceasing virility—a virility he himself knows he lacks—is essential to masculinity. Also he may cling firmly to the notion of sex-linked roles in everyday life. Perhaps despising an ineffectual father, he will build a picture of the manly man as totally concerned with male pursuits of sport and entertainment, trampling unthinking over the weaker sex's emotions and never giving help with "female" domestic tasks.

Irwin Yalom, a psychologist, has found that this false masculinity leads to underlying components of sadism and a desire for the forbidden in the personality of the voyeur, who perverts the ideals of strength and bravery into forms that he can handle

without fear. Indeed the voyeur is often a frightened man, usually timid, and violent only when he fears capture. His sadism, operating impersonally on his "victims," may be turned emotionally on women in his life or even on animals. His desire for the forbidden, for overcoming danger, leads him to prowl public and regularly patrolled parks or to trespass in private gardens. The voyeur experiences the thrill and domination of a symbolic rape—but in the majority of cases is far too timid actually to attempt a sexual assault.

And, in addition, the voyeur may enjoy the intoxicating excitement of revealing his presence and relishing the consternation that results—and may even be stimulated by the notoriety and attention brought about by his eventual arrest.

"I've been beaten up once and almost arrested," said Brian. "I don't mean to do it but I'll begin to feel restless. Once I get into that state I have to go out, and however much I try to resist, sooner or later I'll be working my way to somewhere I can see into a bedroom window. It's quite an adventure getting into a garden or up a fire escape without being noticed and then moving close enough to see through a window.

"The time I was caught I didn't realize the window opened down to the ground. I knocked a flower pot onto the ground and the guy came right through the window and began beating me up. His wife was screaming her head off but she managed to call the police on the telephone. I twisted away and ran off down an alley behind the houses as the police were blasting their sirens up to the front.

I spy with my little eye. His urge to peek may stem from childhood fears of involvement, and now the only way he can work off sexual frustration is by prying.

Heinz Bogler

"The local paper called for a vigilante squad to patrol the streets after dark—and printed the guy's description of the man he'd nearly caught. Apparently I'm nearly six foot six with muscles like a gorilla. I actually volunteered for the vigilantes and we roamed around for a few nights. One of the funny things, though, one of the other guys on the squad said he'd seen some woman flaunting herself, you know, walking around naked with the lights on and the drapes open. With people like that around it's a crime not to take the opportunity."

Face at the Window

The voyeur's "victim" as often as not does not know what is happening and so is unaffected. But for a couple courting in a public place to realize they are being watched can be unpleasant—even if they shrug it off as just another dirty old man. And if people suspect their bedroom is being watched, or if a whole neighborhood realizes someone is prowling by night, paranoia can reach fever pitch.

To be watched while making love is bad enough—but to this is added the fear of the unknown. Who is out there? What does he want? The single woman who sees a face at the window will be rightfully frightened because she cannot tell whether it is a potential rapist or a timid voyeur. And even when there is no physical threat the shock can be disturbing.

"One day my boyfriend was looking out the window after we'd made love when he saw a naked man watching us through binoculars from the building across the street," said Pat. "It was really creepy. We have the blinds down all the time now."

People who think they may be victims of a voyeur can notify the police and take all possible steps to avoid calling the attention of a voyeur or of providing gratification for him. By ensuring the curtains are always drawn before making love or undressing, by avoiding provocative dress or behavior in areas that can be overlooked, people can counter the threat of the voyeur.

And the voyeur himself, particularly if he seeks psychiatric advice, can learn to develop a more adult attitude to sexuality in which he draws pleasure from sharing sexual relationship with another instead of looking on.

Behind the trees the secret watcher lurks, getting his kicks from seeing others do what he himself cannot. Here, certainly, is a case where nonparticipation is a crime.

David Levin

Black box

How are you? Maybe all you need to find the answer is a pendulum and line.

Nowadays, if a newspaper headline refers to a "Black Box" it is safe to assume that the box in question is an instrument of the kind used in aircraft to monitor conditions.

But this is a recent development.

From World War I until the 1960s, the term "Black Box" was used for a contraption which could do for extrasensory perception what the radio does for ordinary perception.

When tuned, the Box was designed to pick up or transmit telepathic messages, in such a way that the information could be used, usually for diagnosis or treatment of disease. This process was named radiesthesia.

It was born during the nineteenth

century, the offspring of a union between water divining and spiritualism. Instead of a forked hazel twig, some water diviners preferred a pendulum which, they felt, was more sensitive—as many do to this day.

Every diviner has his own code, but the general principle is the same; that the pendulum "bob," if suspended from a thread between finger and thumb, does not remain still.

It will begin to swing back and forth, or round and round; and the way it moves can give the answers to questions that the questioner himself has no sensory means of knowing.

The water diviner, for example, may walk over a field with the question in his mind, "Is there an underground stream below?"

A Swinging Success

If the answer is "No," the pendulum will rotate (or swing) in one direction; but when the answer is "Yes," the direction or rotation of swing will change. He can then consult the pendulum on further issues, like how far down the water lies, and whether it is fresh or brackish.

Not everybody has the ability to make use of the pendulum in this way. But it is easy to try it out, and some people employ it as an everyday aid to living—for example, to find lost keys. The expert pendulum user can go through the list of possible places where the keys may be, asking "Is it in that room?" When he gets a "Yes," he narrows down the search until the keys are found.

When the spiritualists realized this a century ago, some began to use the pendulum for their own purposes, asking it questions in much the same way as they asked questions of the ouija board. The pendulum also had the advantage that a single person could use it—provided, of course, that he is a "sensitive."

The first person to realize that this method might be adapted to assist the diagnosis and treatment of illness appears to have been a Frenchwoman, Mlle Chantereine. And it was a Frenchman, the Abbé Mermet, who popularized it in his *Principles and Practice of Radiesthesia.*

The basic principles, Mermet suggested, were that, firstly, all bodies are constantly emitting radiations. Secondly, the human body enters these fields of influence, becoming the seat of nervous reactions, and a kind of current flows through the hands. Finally, if an appropriate object, such as a rod or a pendulum, is held, the invisible flux is made manifest in the movements of this object, which acts as a kind of indicator.

Mermet commonly used a pendulum of his own ingenious design. The "bob" on the end of the chain was hollow, and the top part was a cap which could be unscrewed from the rest. Into the bottom part, Mermet put a small quantity of whatever it was he wanted to find.

If he was looking for water, for example, he would put water in the bob, as if to forge a better mental link between himself and the water below. And when he came to use the pendulum in diagnosis, this was easily adapted; he put something belonging to the patient, or a drop of the patient's blood, into the bob, then asked questions designed to discover the cause of illness.

A further refinement, which came later, was the use of a chart made out in the form of a compass, with the names of diseases spaced around it in place of east, northeast, north-northeast—and so on. Holding the pendulum over this chart, the radiesthetist waits for a swing, indicating what disease is attacking the patient.

The same technique can be used to indicate lines of treatment, the pendulum recommending some drug or change of diet or rest.

A few radiesthetists, Mermet in particular, showed such consistently good results, even under test conditions, that skeptical investigators were impressed—Dr. Alexis Carrel, for one, a Nobel Prize winner from the Rockefeller Institute in New York.

Drum the Tum

The physician, Carrel argued, must not think only in terms of known diagnostic techniques; he ought also to be trying to detect in every patient his individuality, his resistance to the cause of the disease, his sensitivity to pain, the state of all his organic functions, his past as well as his future. He must keep an open mind free from personal assumptions that certain unorthodox methods of investigation are useless. Therefore he should remember that radiesthesia is worthy of serious consideration.

But by the time Carrel was expressing this opinion—in the 1920s—the tide of medical opinion was strongly against considering unorthodox methods of any kind. And it happened that radiesthesia had become the most resented form of unorthodoxy because its latest manifestation—the Black Box—seemed to be masquerading as "scientific."

The Black Box was the brainchild of a Californian scientist, Dr. Albert Abrams. Born in 1863, Abrams had a brilliant academic record, and he embarked upon what at first promised to be an outstanding career as a physician. But one day, when he was examining a patient by tapping his stomach and listening to the sound given off—"percussing," as it is called—he noticed a change in the percussion note. Investigation showed that this occurred whenever a nearby X-ray set was switched on or off.

The outcome was radionics, practiced with a gadget which, Abrams claimed, was capable of diagnosing what was wrong with a patient. Its nearest present-day equivalent would be the electroencephalograph, by which it is possible to detect brain disorder from the picture it gives of a patient's brain waves.

Mystery Box

Abrams made a further claim. It was not necessary, he asserted, for the patient to be present. The patient might be hundreds of miles away. A drop of his blood would suffice; the gadget would find the necessary information in that sample.

What was worse—so far as the medical profession was concerned—Abrams began manufacturing the Black Boxes, as they now came to be called, selling them for $300 a piece, plus tuition fees. It was bad enough, his medical colleagues felt, for Abrams to be relying on what to them seemed a transparently bogus contraption. But to encourage unqualified practitioners to prescribe with its help was unforgivable. Nevertheless, Abrams continued to use (and sell) his Box until his death in 1924, and by that time there were hundreds of his Boxes in use all over the United States.

And all over Europe. Intrigued by reports about the Box, a number of doctors had experimented with it in other countries, and some had perfected their own versions, including one which was to become standard, where the diagnosis was given by the "feel" of a piece of rubber. To the medical profession, this only made the Boxes seem more bogus; to outward appearances they still looked as if they were electrical gadgets but electricity was no longer involved.

In the year of Abrams' death, a committee of British doctors and scientists was set up to investigate and discredit the Bos—in this case, a machine made by a Glasgow practitioner, Dr. W. E. Boyd. The committee had Sir Thomas (later Lord) Horder as

chairman, and included well-known doctors and scientists.

The first batch of tests, as described by Beverley Nichols in *Powers That Be*, was relatively simple. Abrams had claimed that among the things his Box could do was give a "sulphur reaction"—indicate when sulphur was present, even in minute amounts. Horder agreed that this would suffice for the preliminary inquiry. The operator would be given a series of powders wrapped up in such a way as to make it impossible for him or anybody

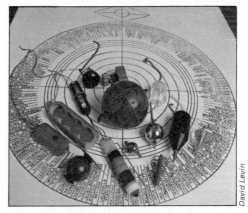

David Levin

David Tansley, a respected modern practitioner of radionics, with the pendulum that belonged to Mermet. Given a sample of a patient's blood or hair, the pendulum can apparently diagnose the cause of an illness. The practitioner can then broadcast healing vibrations to cure the patient. Left: Some of the pendulums that are also used for the same purpose together with a calibrated chart showing homeopathic remedies which can be used in healing the patient.

David Levin

else to ascertain what they were. Some would be sulphur; some would be other substances. Boyd's task would be to find which was which.

The method Boyd adopted was to put his Box on a table beside the subjects—Horder, and one of his colleagues—who were connected to it by a length of flex, leading to a metal disk attached to each subject's forehead by a rubber band. One by one, the specimens—25 of them—were then placed in a small hatch in the machine, and the subject's body

David Levin

The Black Box, a sophisticated version of the simple pendulum and line, is used in the practice of radionics, a modern offshoot of radiesthesia. The complex dials are used with the pendulum to tune in to extrasensory frequencies to diagnose and treat illness. Every pathological state is thought to have its own vibrations. Once the trouble is ascertained, appropriate "healing vibrations" are transmitted from the Box, through a blood or hair sample, to the patient.

"percussed." The machine duly registered the tone from the percussion, which was found to change with different specimens.

If the percussion note was dull, the machine operator would indicate that sulphur was present; if the note was resonant, that sulphur was not present. At the end of the 25 tests, the seals on the specimens were opened, and they were compared with the machine's predictions. The Box had gotten all 25 right. The odds against such a result being achieved by chance (somebody calculated) were 33,554,432 to 1 against.

No Mumbo Jumbo

The result, in fact, seemed too good. It must have been achieved by sleight of hand. So further tests were arranged, this time under the supervision of Dr. Eric Dingwall, a member of the British Society for Psychical Research, with a reputation for his skill at nosing out fraud of any kind. But again, the machine (or its operators) scored 25 out of 25—the odds against such a result happening becoming astronomical.

Despite his misgivings, Horder was convinced. He was impressed by the fact that Boyd and his assistant appeared to be going about their task in a workmanlike, almost casual, fashion, without mumbo jumbo. And he could hear for himself the change of note which the machine registered whenever a specimen was inserted into its hatch in the Box or taken out. Even more striking, he felt, was the fact that he and Dr. Heald, while they were acting as the guinea pigs, "could definitely feel an alteration in the abdominal muscles as specimens were inserted or withdrawn through the hatch without their knowledge." In other words, they could themselves feel the symptoms which the percussion was designed to detect.

In his report, Horder conceded that certain substances, when placed in a certain relationship to the machine, were capable "beyond any reasonable doubt" of producing changes in the abdominal wall of a kind which percussion could detect. And this meant that Abrams' thesis must be considered to have been established "to a very high degree of probability."

Never, perhaps, in the history of medical science had there been such an overturning of accepted medical dogma. But, Horder pointed out, it remained to be discovered how the Box worked; and that would require further research. That research, however, was not undertaken.

And without this research the medical profession remained unmoved. There were also some notable failures. When an American Black Box operator, Dr. Ruth Drown, submitted to testing in Chicago, her diagnoses were wildly inaccurate. And in Britain George de la Warr, who became the most active practitioner, was never able to produce really convincing results under test conditions.

But he frequently produced striking results in his ordinary line of business, notably in a case where some cattle had been dying mysteriously and nobody could find out why. De la Warr took his car down to the farm and rigged up a gadget like a radar scanner on the roof, from which he could direct the Black Box's attention to the surviving cows and to the pasture.

He then asked the machine what was the trouble with the cows, and its reply indicated "fluoracetamide." Sure enough, it was found that waste matter containing that poison had been disposed of down a drain near the field, enough to kill off the cows eating the grass.

Many cures have been credited to the Box—including, surprisingly, a considerable number of racehorse ailments. For a time there was something of a craze for the Box in racing circles. In 1962 the London *Observer*'s racing correspondent described how Scotch Delinquent, a promising but temperamental horse, had suddenly become listless and almost crippled.

Horse Doctor

The vet could find nothing wrong with him, and somebody suggested trying the Box. A local practitioner, diagnosed that the horse had what, in humans, would be described as a slipped disk. It was treated (also by the Box) and promptly astonished its stable lad by behaving once again like a bucking bronco. Soon, it was back under starter's orders again.

Is it possible to account for radiesthesia by any rational theory? In its manifestations, it appears to be a combination of telepathy and mind over matter. The mind, it suggests, may be capable not just of perception at a distance, but also of action at a distance.

Historically speaking, this is a very ancient belief. In his study of the Kahunas in Hawaii, *The Secret Science Behind Miracles*, Max Freedom Long described how they have traditionally demonstrated a similar kind of power. He gave their explanation of it—they believe in the existence of a force comparable to magnetism, or gravity, which the mind can activate.

By analogy—just as it is possible for man to control the flight of an aircraft hundreds of miles away by means of a radio beam which gives orders to the aircraft's automatic pilot, so that the aircraft can be made to go faster or slower, to climb or to dive—so the vital force, "mana," can be exploited to diagnose or treat patients at a distance. The transmissions themselves may be weak; what counts is their ability to arouse the appropriate response in the patient.

Given that there is such a force, what part does the Black Box itself play in broadcasting or receiving its transmissions—if that is what they are? De la Warr was convinced, as Abrams had been, that it should be possible to manufacture a box which would be both transmitter and receiver in its own right—the operator's task being simply to turn the knobs or perform whatever other tasks are required, as a mechanic does.

Diviners Galore

But de la Warr was endlessly thwarted in this ambition. It would seem to him that some refinement he had thought of was going to do the trick. But then, tests would reveal that the Box's results were inconsistent.

The most likely explanation is that the Black Box is nothing more than an elaboration of the water diviner's hazel twig, or pendulum. A pendulum hung from a hook does not respond in the same way as it will when held *by* somebody; nor does a twig, merely carried over an underground stream on a tray. There must be interaction between the operator and the gadget, whatever the gadget may be. And the operator must be a "sensitive."

It seems very probable that far more people are capable of becoming water diviners, or radiesthetists, than is generally recognized. But it is also true that even experienced sensitives cannot guarantee success at any given time and are often unable to get results at all, when they are under pressure. They are frequently unlucky when they are particularly anxious to get results as they naturally are when being tested.

As Dr. Aubrey Westlake—himself a practitioner of radiesthesia—has observed, this does not necessarily discredit their claims; they may make strikingly accurate diagnoses at other times. But it presents a difficulty, because belief in their own method is often a psychological necessity to them, and once their confidence is shaken, their work may well suffer as a result.

All you want to know about...

FOOD & HEALTH

Zio Art

Q WHAT DOES THE BODY DO WITH ITS FOOD?

A The two main functions of food and the nutrients it contains are to build the body and to maintain it. The two processes have a good deal in common, but clearly the *growth functions* are the most important until the individual is physiologically mature (at about the age of 20), after which the *maintenance and repair functions* become paramount. The main constituents of the body are worth cataloging for they help us to understand just why no single food, other than special diet compounds, is adequate to maintain a healthy human being, let alone grow one up from scratch. An average man aged about 25 who weighs, say, 150 pounds will, in physiological terms, be made up of about 95 lbs. of water, 25 lbs. of protein, 20 lbs. of fat, 8 lbs. of minerals and 2 lbs. of carbohydrate. During the period of most active growth, very considerable amounts of protein, minerals, and so on must be supplied in the diet in order to build up bones and muscle and nervous tissue, and if these are not available signs of malnutrition with stunted growth and a serious liability to sickness appear. Even after the individual is fully

grown, the need to ingest nutrients of various kinds does not come to a full stop, for most parts of the body are in a constant state of running repair and replacement. For example, the inner lining of the intestine is totally replaced—that is, completely new tissue cells are substituted for the old ones—*every four or five days.* The life span of red blood cells is about four months—which means that we get a complete turnover of blood three times a year. The same rule of change even applies to the microstructure of the skeleton, which is constantly being dismantled and reassembled (in very small bits, fortunately) throughout our lives. It is a rather exciting fact that the body has mechanisms, some of which are built in and some of which are actually supplied within a balanced diet, which sort out the dismantled constituents of bone, blood and so on, and reuse them in one or other of a wide variety of roles. In other words, the body is a magnificent recycling system employing techniques and principles which the world's most advanced ecologists would envy. On the other hand our bodies are only partially self-sufficient and must import, at very regular intervals, supplies of literally hundreds of different nutrients —proteins, carbohydrates and fats, minerals, vitamins, trace elements and

of course vast quantities of water and roughage to keep the machine in good working order.

WHAT IS PROTEIN AND WHY DO WE NEED IT?

The simple answer to this is that we need protein because it is one of the most basic and essential constituents of all body cells—whether blood, bone, nerve or muscle. This is the stock answer given, but like so many other stock answers it is only a very partial one. To go into the topic a bit more deeply we need to know that there are in fact many types of proteins, all of which are highly complex molecules, themselves composed mainly of substances known as amino acids. The amino acids—there are 22 different kinds of these—are the really active parts of the proteins and, by combining with each other in various ways, they can effectively convert one kind of protein into another. The importance of this flexibility will be clear if one realizes that deficiencies in one part of the body can be remedied by making use of "spare protein" available in areas where a surplus exists for one reason or another. Vast amounts of protein are needed by the body—for example muscles contain about 30 percent protein and liver about 25 percent. Even higher proportions exist in less watery parts of the system such as the hair, teeth and bones.

HOW MANY DIFFERENT KINDS OF PROTEIN ARE THERE?

Fifty years ago diet experts, while understanding the importance of protein for the growth and restoration of living cells, tended to view it as one specific substance which acted as a kind of general purpose foundation for the cell. Now we know that there are a very large number of different proteins, some of which have names which may be familiar—collagen, keratin, albumin—but the most useful classification to help understand their role is to group them according to their function. There are in fact four kinds of proteins which are generally known as *structural, contractile, transport* and *catalytic.* The structural proteins, as their name implies, are the building blocks of large parts of the body, including the skin, nails and bones. The contractile proteins, again as their name implies, can change shape and feature prominently in muscles and also in the stomach and intestine. The transport proteins, some of which are also known as hormones, serve to carry things throughout the body and act as chemical messengers delivering substances from one cell to another. From the point of view of understanding food, health and diet however, easily the most important type of proteins are known as enzymes —the catalytic proteins. These are in fact the most common, and their principal significance is the way in which they are involved in the final process of digestion, when they act on food, breaking it down into its constituent amino acids and subsequently dispatching these to wherever they are needed in the body.

COULD WE DO WITHOUT PROTEINS?

Although this appears to be contradictory, the answer is technically Yes—provided that we could supply ourselves with all the necessary amino acids which are contained in the proteins. Proteins themselves are only important because they contain the amino acids which make up the really fine structure of the body's physiological mechanism. Incidentally all proteins that we consume were themselves once part of other living systems, either animal or plant, and for this reason we can really look upon life on earth as a vast multitude of

living organisms steadily exchanging their component parts. In the first instance, of course, plants acquire proteins by synthesizing substances in the soil and atmosphere, aided by solar energy. Most animals are unable to synthesize their own protein, however, and must therefore capture it from elsewhere by eating certain plants or animals. Incidentally, not all foodstuffs contain equivalent amounts of protein and, furthermore, foods which may be rich in protein may not necessarily feature all the essential amino acids. In particular, vegetable proteins are often very short on one or more of the amino acids essential for good health, and for this reason vegetarians need to choose their own balanced diet with far greater care than do those whose diet includes meat and animal proteins.

WHAT ARE THE MAIN SOURCES OF PROTEIN IN THE DIET?

In a so-called balanced diet to supply the body with its complete range of amino acids, an ideal mixture would include animal and vegetable foods. In the United States and Western Europe, the average individual draws his necessary protein from six main types of food. The largest proportion —about 28 percent—comes from cereal foods, with bread being the biggest single supplier. Bread has been much maligned as a food, mainly by people who know nothing about diet. In fact, 1 ounce of bread contains about 2¼ grams of protein. The second most important source—about 27 percent in all—comes from meat, which on average contains 7 grams of protein per ounce. With increasing affluence meat plays a larger and larger role as a protein supplier in most people's diet and in most parts of the United States has replaced cereal foods as a main source of protein. The third major dietary source of protein is milk and cheese, making up about 23 percent of the total. Cheese is about as rich in protein as meat (7 grams to the ounce), while half a pint of whole milk contains 7 grams of protein. A fraction less than 10 percent of our protein diet comes from vegetables (including legumes such as peas), but with the soaring cost of meat, world dietary attention is being drawn to the soya bean, which is one of the richest sources of protein known to man. Nuts of various kinds also contain abundant supplies of vegetable protein. Allowing for regional variations, about 5 percent of the protein require-

ment of Western populations comes from eggs—the average egg contains about 7 grams of protein. Fish, offering about 6 grams per ounce, also contribute about 5 percent of the total protein requirement.

WHAT HAPPENS IF WE GO SHORT OF PROTEIN?

The amino acids which are the dynamic heart of most proteins are the essence of life itself and without them life ceases. In fact protein is spread so widely and is such a basic part of all animal and vegetable matter that it is almost impossible to eat and not take it in, in fairly substantial amounts. Nevertheless a low protein diet can lead to a lack of resistance to disease and even, in cases where individual proteins or amino acids are missing, to the onset of a disease itself. One of the most tragic and relatively common childhood illnesses, the hereditary disease known as cystic fibrosis, is known to arise when certain digestive enzymes are missing in the pancreas. Another hereditary disease, phenylketonuria, which leads to serious mental retardation in children, is caused because a particular enzyme, itself a protein, is missing in the tissue. With the exception of these hereditary diseases, however, the signs of protein deficiency are rarely seen in Western nations, though they are fearfully common in parts of Africa, India and Southeast Asia.

HOW MUCH PROTEIN DO WE NEED?

Protein requirements are at their highest during childhood and adolescence, when the body is not only repairing itself but also embarked on a gigantic internal construction program. After the age of 20 or thereabouts repair and replacement functions are the principal ones and as a general guide we could say that a safe level of protein would be a daily supply of 1 gram for each kilogram (a bit over 2 pounds) of body weight. Put into more easily conceived terms, this would mean that the average adult weighing about 150 pounds would need roughly 2¼ ounces of pure protein a day. This may not seem a lot, but it does require a fair bit of food bulk to contain it all. And of course we must not forget that we need a fair mix of different types of protein, both animal and vegetable, to ensure that a full range of amino acids are ingested. A good sized cheeseburger and two glasses of milk would, by the way, provide enough protein for a full day, though other important constituents essential to long-term health would almost certainly be missing.

WHAT ARE CARBOHYDRATES AND FATS AND WHY DO WE NEED THEM?

Most people believe that the only reason for eating is to acquire energy —that is to say, fuel to keep the body machinery in action. In fact energy requirements are only part of the reason for taking in food, and carbohydrates and fats are the principal nutrients used by the body as basic sources of fuel. Energy is needed not only for physical movement—walking, playing games or whatever—but also for all internal activity, including involuntary movements such as those of the digestive organs, the lungs and the heart. Even when we are in deep sleep, therefore, our body is slowly burning fuel, which is why we weigh a little less in the morning than when we went to sleep the night before. The energy is needed for two reasons —first to carry out the chemical reactions performed by the enzymes, proteins and various amino acids, which together make up the complex process known as metabolism. The enzymes and other proteins have a job to do and no work can be performed by any system, small or large, unless it has fuel to drive it. The second reason we need energy is to supply heat to keep the body at a constant temperature. This latter function is particularly important in mammals, including humans, who rely on maintaining a constant body temperature, irrespective of the conditions in the environment. Reptiles and other cold-blooded animals do not use up energy in this way and allow their body temperatures to drift up and down in tune with the world around them. This, incidentally, is why they can go for such long periods, if pressed, without eating.

WHERE DOES THE BODY GET ITS ENERGY?

The main suppliers of energy are carbohydrates and fats.
Carbohydrates themselves can be divided into two groups—sugars and starches, both of which come principally from plants. Sugar of the white, supermarket variety is known as sucrose, and it is extracted from cane or beet. Other kinds of sugars can be extracted from fruit and honey

(fructose) and even milk (lactose). The main sources of starch are flour, cereals, pasta, potatoes and legumes such as lentils and beans. Although sugars and starches may seem very different in the form that they appear to us on the table, they both have important constituents in common— molecular units known as saccharides. During the process of digestion enzymes go to work on the carbohydrates, whether sugars or starches, and quickly break them down into saccharide units, which then make their way into the bloodstream and are thereby passed around to every cell in the body. The total quantity of these saccharides in the system is known as the blood sugar level and is a very good measure of the amount of "instant energy" available to the organism as a whole. When we feel hungry it is because blood sugar is low.
Fats can come from both animals and plants—butter, lard, and meat fat on the one hand and olive oil, corn oil, and so on from vegetables. A certain amount of fat is present even in lean meat, eggs, and cheese and tends to be known as invisible fat for obvious reasons. The striking feature about fats is their tremendous source of calories—a gram of pure fat provides twice as much energy as a gram of pure carbohydrate. Fats are also relatively difficult to digest and, because they remain in the stomach longer than other foods, they give a greater sense of "satisfaction" and appeasement of hunger after they have been eaten.

COULD WE DO WITHOUT CARBOHYDRATES AND FATS?

At first thought the answer might seem to be categorically No, for without the fuel supplied by these energy sources our bodies would shrivel up and die. There is a curious and slightly misleading way around this, however. By means of its own marvelous mechanism of transmutation, the body can, if it runs short of fats, make use of any surplus protein by converting it into glucose. In this way an individual *could* therefore subsist on a largely protein diet, free of the more traditional sources of energy. There would be very little point in doing so however, because the process of converting the protein into glucose is a very inefficient one—enormous amounts of raw material are needed to produce quite small amounts of energy. Since protein is contained in basically expensive foods, and carbo-

hydrates and fats are cheap, there is nothing to be gained by striving to get all our energy from protein.

WHAT ARE THE MAIN SOURCES OF CARBOHYDRATES AND FATS?

In the Western world most people find that carbohydrates provide the greatest proportion of the energy value of their daily food, and in Britain and the United States they offer on average almost 50 percent of our calorie intake. Fats provide about another 40 percent, with the remaining 10 percent coming from the protein foods. Ounce for ounce the fats are the most concentrated forms of calories, which means that it is easier to acquire surplus energy by eating fatty food, whether animal or vegetable, than any other. This might seem to be a good argument for eliminating the fats from the diet altogether, but it so happens that they contain rich sources of some vitamins and minerals, and in the case of vegetable oils substances known as the "essential fatty acids" are supplied. These latter, which sound as though they ought to be avoided at all cost, are actually needed for satisfactory growth and also for the health of the skin. Fats also tend to be exceedingly good to taste.

HOW MUCH CARBOHYDRATE AND FAT DO WE NEED?

Provided the mixture that we take in offers the appropriate selection of other nutrients, such as vitamins and minerals, the answer is that we need only enough to supply the energy necessary to keep our body alive. This varies of course according to a number of factors, including age, body size, and the amount of physical activity which we take. There are fairly good rules for deciding exactly how much energy in calories is required for any individual, but as a very rough guide a man aged 35 with a "normal" weight of 160 pounds and in good health will require about 3,250 calories (or kilocalories to be precise) every day. A woman of equivalent age and with a "normal" weight of 135 pounds will require about 2,250 calories per day. These figures would have to be raised or lowered to take account of such factors as the amount of physical activity engaged in. It is a sad fact of life that if energy intake regularly exceeds the appropriate amount for age and build, a person will inevitably and remorselessly put on weight.

Camera Press

A friend indeed

A man without friends is a man alone. And on the road of life, who can do without a fellow traveler or two—someone to understand our weaknesses and reflect our strengths.

Almost all human beings—certainly those we like to call "normal"—form attachments to other human beings. The range of emotional bonds which are forged between people is infinite in variety and complexity. After all, there are as many idiosyncratic facets and subtle nuances in these two-way relationships as there are unique personalities contributing to them. As each and every person is unique, so every relationship has something that is individual about it.

It has been said of personality that "every man is in certain respects like all other men, like some other man, like no other man." The word "relationship" can be substituted for "man." When the social scientist studies human relationships he is trying to find out in what respects every relationship is like all other relationships or like some other relationship. His search for the common factors, the general principles

underlying human attachments, seems ponderous and dull when compared with the brilliant insights of the poet or novelist who deals with particular cases.

We have only to think of Shakespeare's exploration of the characters and interactions of Hamlet and Horatio, Anthony and Enobarbus, or Othello and Iago to question the worth of the solemn journal articles and monographs on "interpersonal attraction" as it is called by social scientists. Nevertheless a good deal of valuable information is beginning to emerge, concerning the "how," "when" and "why" of human relationships, from the plodding but systematic investigations of the scientists.

Knowledge is crucial in this area, as the ability to form deep, lasting and rewarding relationships is crucial to man's physical survival and his psychological well-being. Indeed, it is the very core of his existence as a

moral and social being.

Of all the human relationships which have been studied—parent-child, family, sexual, group and two-person friendships—the last has received least attention. This scientific neglect is strange because the bond of friendship has been highly valued and idealized throughout history.

Aristotle believed that a friendship based on virtue was the most permanent and stable relationship possible between two persons. The names of David and Jonathan have become part of our everyday language because their relation—embodying love, altruism, dependability, loyalty and mutual support—has become a metaphor for friendship. It symbolizes these values which are highly prized in our society. The concept of friendship is idealized, perhaps, because it is one of those rare human institutions where values are honored not in the breach but in the performance, not so much in the form of lip service as in a real and meaningful sense. Thus the betrayal of a friend and the perversion of the idea of friendship—by simulating friendliness for personal gain or to bring harm to the "friend" —are among the cardinal sins in our value system.

What is meant by friendship? When used loosely it may refer to a casual acquaintanceship. Generally, however, it describes a deep, long-standing confiding relationship between people (usually members of the same sex) who are bound by common purposes other than the reduction of sexual drive. In other words, friendship involves a relationship that serves no ulterior motives such as sexual, economic or political gain. It is felt by the members of the pair to be a result of free choice.

Status Symmetry

The distinctive feature of a bond of friendship is what is called status symmetry; there is a relationship of mutual respect as opposed to unilateral respect. In the latter, *one* person does the controlling, advising, persuading and influencing. He carries most weight in giving opinions and judgments and in making decisions. Where there is mutual respect, as in a friendship, there is not this huge gap in status between the members of the pair. In relationships of mutual respect, discrepancies of this sort are bound to arise in particular situations but there is an overall symmetry or balance in the influence of each of the two participants. Does this mean that individuals of different status cannot be friends? The answer depends on whether the differences in status intrude upon the relationship. If they are not allowed to get in the way friendships can be formed.

Friends then—and some people have many lifelong, staunch friends— are those for whom we have a deep affection. We know them intimately, the relationship is lasting, and we are inclined to make the sort of allowances for them (and the sacrifices) which we would make for members of our families. Our liking for others and their feelings toward us, the sharing of interests and experiences, the relaxed and undemanding association with certain chosen friends—all these things and many others produce a sense of warmth, identity, security and well-being in what is only too often a rather cold and inhospitable world.

Given these desirable qualities in a friendship it can be said that we all need friends. Although books on

mental health and positive "psychological adjustment" attach great importance to how well we get on with our parents and sexual partners and how we relate to various social and work groups, they have paid less attention to the ability to make and keep friends. However, there is evidence that without friends people can experience an intense sense of deprivation and loneliness. According to the psychoanalytic theorist Karen Horney, the neurotic personality sees himself as essentially isolated and helpless in a potentially hostile world. She viewed much of the neurotic condition as being due to failures in the types of interpersonal relationship and social skill that most of us take for granted.

Most of us have a deep-seated need for people to appreciate and love us, people on whom we can depend in times of crisis, people to whom we can give gifts, individuals with whom we can share experiences and in whom we can confide, others who will allow us to "be ourselves" without criticism or interference. Some rare individuals do not need these things and hence are quite "complete" or "fulfilled" without friends. They may deliberately isolate themselves and dwell as hermits in some far-flung corner. There are others who also seem no worse off for the absence of friends; perhaps relationships arising from marriage and family life provide all the emotional and social nourishment they require. Others, probably most of us, even with the benefits of other kinds of relationship, feel the need of the special advantages of friendships.

Mythical Figure

Why should this be? In listing the features of a good friendship, we have given part of the answer. But it goes deeper than that! The notion of the friend goes deep in the "universal consciousness" of man. It is such a central aspect of our social existence that the philosopher-psychiatrist Carl Jung considered that friendship is an *archetypal image*. Archetypes are innate ideas residing in man's "collective unconscious," representing universalities, significant aspects of his existence. According to Jung we see these universal archetypes reflected in dreams, folklore, literature, art, myths and visions. The image of the friend, the helper, guide, and supporter can be traced among widely differing peoples; from the Greeks of the classical period to the North American Indians of the present day.

Over and over we can find a record of a helpful figure on the other side of consciousness. The figure is called by different names: it is Hermes, the messenger of the gods; it is the "daimon" in which Socrates placed his trust; the figure of the "genius" known to the Romans; the "guardian angel" of Christian belief. Mithras, the god of light of the ancient Persians, later protector of the Roman legions, originally meant "friend."

Shock Absorber

Modern men and women, particularly those engaged in some form of creative or dangerous work, often seem to meet this figure—as with the "one more than could be counted" that at times accompanied the Shackleton expedition to the Antarctic; and the "friendly companion" to whom Francis Smythe, climbing alone at 28,000 feet, went so far as to offer part of his food. Above all, dreams, visions, and voices reveal this figure—a figure that gives comfort, support, assurance, helping to show the way. Even a figure of the stature of Jesus Christ felt the need of a friend in his hour of tribulation. At the Last Supper he placed John, his closest friend and the disciple whom he loved most, by his side.

Here, then, is the essential supportive or "therapeutic" ingredient of friendship: meeting the occasional need for help and moral support, crises which are common to most people and which can be overcome by the possession of sympathetic friends. The reason why most of us do not need to discuss our sexual, social and family adjustments and maladjustments with a psychiatrist is because we have friends and under relatively "normal" conditions they provide a supportive, sympathizing and complementary function which is at times crucial to the stability of sexual, social and family life. They are "shock absorbers" and restorers of confidence.

A study of 40 same-sex pairs of college-aged friends produced responses to the question "What does a best friend do for me?" which showed the importance of ego support. There were such replies as: "I am important to him," "recognizes my abilities,"

How do we make friends? Perhaps we live in the same district or we went to the same school. Or perhaps we have an interest or hobby in common. Or could it just be that we like being together? The important thing is that we see eye to eye.

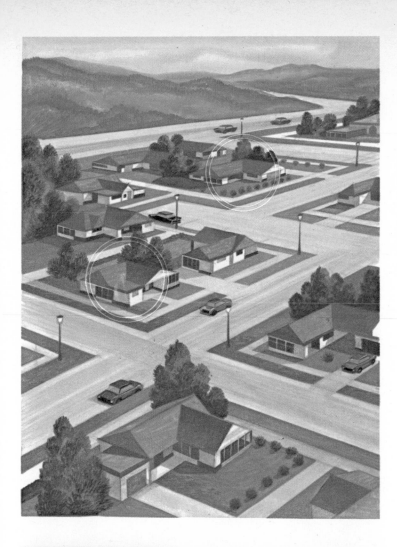

Ron Embleton

1113

"seeks my advice," "thinks my ideas important," "praises me," and "remembers me." Almost equal in frequency in mention were answers that emphasized the protection of the friend's ego: "Keeps me from loneliness," "defends me if someone gossips or criticizes," "calms me when I'm excited or worried," "shares my depressions," "keeps up my courage," "makes me feel secure."

The researcher Dr. Sanchez-Hildago characterized friendships in general as *symbiotic,* meaning that each friend found some of his important life needs met by the other. One friend may find strength and certainty in his relationship with the other person, while the other might find a sense of relaxation in the gentleness and retiring nature of his friend's personality. It is doubtful whether (despite our belief in purely altruistic friendships) a one-sided contribution that meets needs for one friend but not the other will prove viable. In symbiosis, there is value for both partners.

Act Naturally

There are many kinds of friendship —those of childhood, those of old age, the friendships between business acquaintances, those between men serving in a battalion of troops seeing active service, the relationship between struggling artist friends, the democratic friendship between equals, the leader-follower friendship, and many other variants. The common characteristic running through all of them is this: true friendship is a relationship of *mutual* need-satisfaction and mutual respect.

Individuals who are immature, in the sense of being self-centered, exploitive and narcissistic, find it hard to keep friends because they find it impossible to give of themselves. While many clinicians would agree that the emotionally isolated individual is often immature—indeed, perhaps a victim of some form of mental disorder—it is necessary to draw a distinction between people who *cannot* establish such contact and those who *do not.*

The excessively friendly "hail fellow well met" person—the individual who tries to be popular with everyone— may well be compensating for serious psychological deficiencies. These considerations make it difficult, if not impossible, to measure the "capacity for love" in any very accurate fashion. The position is further complicated by the hypothesis of many investigators that extreme social isolation is a *cause* of mental breakdown and not

Jesus' betrayal by Judas. Even beautiful stained glass doesn't take the sting from this ugly act.

merely a sign of its presence. In this way it has been linked with such problems as suicidal behavior and neurosis. Causal factors are notoriously difficult to establish in any study of behavior and this criterion of social isolation, increasingly stressed in modern Western societies, is very difficult to apply in the individual case, except where the isolation of the individual from his fellows is extreme.

Friendships are stable or unstable depending on how much mutual satisfaction of needs is provided and how permanent the needs are. The old adage "old friends are the best friends" is true only if the needs and the mutual capacities to satisfy them remain the same. Some people who make friends lose them easily. Samuel Butler, the seventeenth century satirist, said that friendship is like money, easier made than kept. And Dr. Johnson, the eighteenth century essayist, put his finger on one of the problems

when he said that the most fatal disease of friendship is gradual decay or dislike hourly increased by causes too slender for complaint and too numerous for removal.

Friendship is one of the most valuable of human relationships. One of the greatest advantages of a good friend is that we can drop the mask we assume to face the world; we can be completely honest. A friend knows us and accepts us—there is no need for disguises. A friendship is ruined when we assume our friend understands but he does not; when we think he accepts when he is unable to accept.

Perhaps this is why the friendships forged at high school and college (in early and late adolescence) are deepest and most likely to continue through life. They tend to be honest relationships, evolved before we assume our many adult defensive mechanisms and role-playing masks. The following case history is an example of a successful friendship.

The friendship has developed between two university students who are roommates, attend the same courses and play for the university women's tennis team. Both are extroverted and sociable and enjoy parties and having people in for a snack and a chat. Jane is inclined to be a bit dominant and suggests activities, organizes the chores in their rooms, and so on. Priscilla is happy to be led on small issues. They discuss their problems with each other and often go out with their boyfriends on dates as a foursome. Both women are religious but not churchgoers. They have struggled to get to university, both coming from a lower-income background in which they had first-hand knowledge of financial struggle. Both work hard and separate their existence into clearly demarcated work times and play times. There is lighthearted rivalry between them with respect to grades, but the competition is always mild. They know each other's faults and are tolerant of them. They enjoy letting off steam to each other when they have experienced some failure or frustration. The friendship has lasted two years; it is warm and affectionate but not sentimental. Each can afford to speak her mind to the other without giving offence.

In the words of one psychologist: "The process by which persons are initially attracted to each other and finally become *friends* can be represented by a funnel with a series of filters in it. Each person has a funnel with filters designed to fit his particular criteria for a friend." Priscilla and Jane have successfully passed through the four filters in this funnel.

Factor of Proximity

The topmost filter in the funnel is the factor of proximity, and this determines the people upon whom the other filters will work. It may be obvious to point out that, apart from pen pals, direct face-to-face contact is necessary for the formation of a friendship, but it is often forgotten. Priscilla and Jane pass through this filter, because they live in the same house.

The second filter operates on the principle that like attracts like and is reflected in the popular saying that "birds of a feather flock together." Although there is some evidence that opposites attract, the similarity filter is supported by most of the studies of

friendship. Priscilla and Jane have similar individual characteristics; they are of the same age and similar intelligence. People who, in the end, choose each other tend to have such similar characteristics as age, intelligence, sex and athletic ability.

Although individuals first tend to be drawn together because of shared attributes, their friendship, as with the two students, is more likely to persist if they have common interests, values and attitudes—the third filter. There is a tendency for choices to be influenced by similarities in social background, religious and political affiliations, and racial group membership. When friends are members of similar groupings, it means that their values and attitudes will often be alike, because they have both been exposed to similar "norms" and ideals in their formative years. Not all friendships, however, follow directly as a consequence of similarity. People who do the same things are certainly likely from the outset to share similar attitudes and interests. Thus the similarity between friends may be directly related to factors which made the relationship in the first place, that is, simply the factor of nearness rather than similarity of attitudes as such.

The fourth filter is the similarity of personality. Although the evidence is still somewhat conflicting, studies of personality generally show that we choose as friends those people with desirable characteristics such as high intelligence and special abilities. There is also a tendency to choose those who are described as sharing our positive traits, that is, our best characteristics. On the other hand, those who share our negative traits are usually rejected as friends. But the really significant influence is the *belief* that another is similar to ourselves; this counts for more of our attraction to the person than whether or not he is *actually* similar. There is evidence that individuals choose others as friends when they have characteristics desirable in terms of their social group. In a study of a small college for women, where the climate of opinion was liberal and where the girls were really concerned about national, political and economic issues, those who were most frequently chosen as friends were usually the most liberal.

Some people are attracted to others whose needs complement their own. Thus a dominant person may become friendly with someone who is predominantly submissive. Researchers have shown that some people choose

others because the others have chosen them. In the same way, a person likes others whom he believes are fond of him. The satisfaction of needs seems to be related to the question of friendship—studies show that people tend to be attracted to others who can help them attain their own personal goals.

Semiconscious Strategy

The actual process of making friends —the choice and then the strategy of following up an acquaintanceship—is largely a semiconscious one. Some attempts at creating a friendship are deliberate, highly conscious processes, but many "just happen," a consequence of circumstances and unconscious choice. The majority of our friends pass through the "friendship funnel," as with Priscilla and Jane—our friends are usually similar in personality, background and interests. But of course there are exceptions. A mean, unpleasant character is unlikely to choose a similar friend. We also choose some of our friends to complement our own character.

It is after the age of 11 or 12 that social standards and attitudes begin to assume a much greater importance in the formation of friendships. At this stage children begin to select their friends in the same way as adults. They tend to choose friends who have parents of the same socioeconomic status as theirs. The importance of living close to their friends is no longer quite so influential. Friendships are about equally divided between those made at school, those made through home contacts and those formed in the neighborhood.

Friends must also meet certain standards of social presentability and have acceptable attitudes as well as similar interests. During adolescence small select friendship groups, or cliques, are very influential in the individual's life. The members of these cliques generally come from the same socioeconomic background, tend to be alike in personality and interests, and share common values.

Some of the factors which influence adult friendships are already evident in the evolution of friendships during childhood. It is important to distinguish between popularity—that is, general attractiveness to others—and *specific* friendships between individuals. Popular people may have many admirers but few friends. Perhaps this is due in part to admiration being an isolating factor in the complicated process of making friends. "It's lonely at the top" is no idle comment.

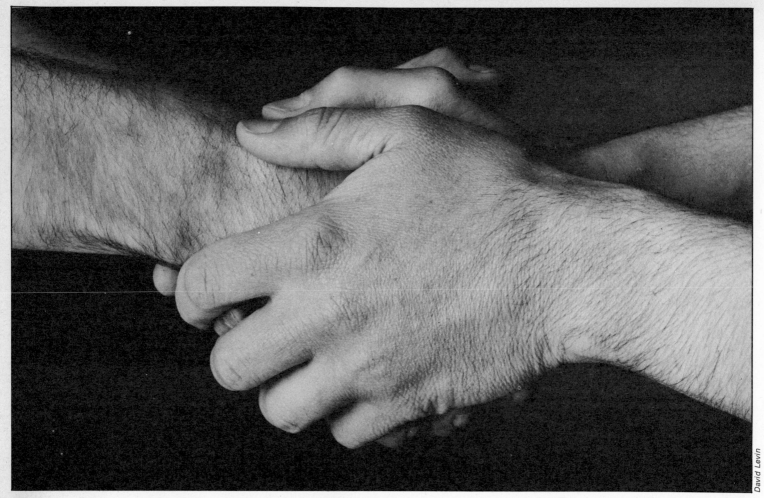

David Levin

Be a pal...

A new friend is as new wine; when it is old and mature drink it with pleasure.

Is there *really* an art in making friends? This frequently asked and heartfelt question can be answered with an unreserved ''Yes!'' Furthermore it is an art which can be taught. While the forming of friendships is a matter which comes naturally—and without effort—to some privileged individuals, there is a component of skill to the art which can be learned. Like the other arts, what can be taught will be circumscribed by the ''raw material'' of native talent—in this case the talent for making relationships in general brought to the learning situation by the ''pupil.''

What is this talent? It is more accurate to describe it as something acquired *very* early in life, rather than being innate or inbuilt. The capacity to express different forms of affection, to have loving feelings, to care for others, to feel for them and to be affected empathically by them varies from individual to individual. And the

ability to love is acquired by everyone in earliest childhood. It evolves out of the nurturance, attention and expressed love of parents, siblings and other family relations, and this immensely subtle and complex learning process culminates in a mature assessment of oneself and others, and the social-emotional commitment (made up of sexual, spiritual, caring feelings) one is able to give to others.

Sigmund Freud has demonstrated how, concealed within all our adult relationships, lies the imprint of our earliest family relationships. He pointed out that the relationship with our father shapes our attitudes to those in authority. The capacity for friendships, and the pattern that friendships take later on in life, are conditioned by our early experience of siblings, the number and sex of siblings and our ordinal position in the family. And they are particularly influenced by the self-love and self-

confidence parents have instilled.

Parental love for the child is a giving love. The child's love for his parents begins because they gratify his needs, but as he matures he comes to need them because he loves them. Love in the family setting forms a backdrop for the evolution of other forms of love. Brotherly love, for example, begins within the family but extends to the love of friends. The period during which the child's first attachments are formed is a sensitive one; interference with these emotional bonds may have serious repercussions.

A child who has been brought up in a home where he is unwanted and neglected, where he has never learned to trust and to love, and where he has experienced little in the way of nurturant care will be at a great disadvantage. His behavior is self-defeating and involves him in a vicious circle: he wants attention so he behaves in the only way he knows will gain attention, *any* attention—in other words, abominably. This invites more rejection; he feels more unwanted; he increases and performs variations on the theme of his attention-seeking behavior, and so on.

A child's reaction to rejection depends, of course, on the severity of the circumstances. Much depends upon whether both parents are involved, the degree of affection shown by the non-rejecting parent, the way in which the rejection is expressed, whether the child was accepted at first and rejected later, and other aspects of the child's total life situation. In general, the danger is that, in later life, rejected children will have difficulty in expressing and responding to affection and complete a vicious circle with their own children.

Self-esteem

A degree of self-love is essential to the formation of satisfactory relationships. The child assimilates from those around him the positive or negative feelings on which he bases his valuation of himself. His maturing personality is made up of the accumulation of self-judgments, and these assessments govern the way he relates to himself and thus the way he relates to other people.

If a person undervalues or deprecates himself he may fantasize about the perfect relationship. He is unlikely to fulfill his potential or to experience the loving relationship he seeks, because he is overly concerned with feelings of his own inadequacy. Because he feels unworthy he may be unable to believe that anybody with whom he might like to a form a friendship could find him likable. Or alternatively, anyone who *could* like him is not worth having as a friend. He may never form an attachment, or if he does he may become dependent —clinging to the object of his affection instead of sharing in a symmetrical exchange of affection.

Should, however, the individual come to overvalue himself, he may become narcissistic, compelled to love only himself. He may become self-centered and inconsiderate or even feel persecuted because others do not perceive his superiority. Although such a person may dominate, he cannot truly share a relationship.

Only if a person's self-image ·is adequate, related to reality, but allowing for the possibility of improvement; only if his concern for himself is submerged by his concern for others, his self-regard balanced by a regard for others, can he properly share in other kinds of love. The person who loves himself finds that he can love others.

People who are lacking in social skills, who are clumsy or shy, may lead very miserable and lonely lives. Millions of books have been sold on the promise that they will provide the magic formula of friendship. They usually neglect the vital skills of forming accurate impressions of other people—the foundations upon which personal liking leading to friendship are built. There is evidence, for example, that those who are the most effective leaders or the most popular or influential members of groups have more accurate perceptions and discriminate between people more sharply than other group members. The most socially competent individuals are particularly sensitive to *nonverbal* communications. Popular children are socially sensitive as can be gauged from the rich, complex and highly organized descriptions they give of other children.

Very often we have no prior information about the people we come into contact with; when we meet strangers we need all our social skills, experience and intuition about people to help us find out what they are like. In certain ways our role at a first meeting is that of the detective, looking for clues, piecing together fragments of information to obtain a picture of the other's personality and status. But, unlike the detective, much of this impression-forming, called *person-perception* by social psychologists, takes place at an unconscious level. In arriving at a first impression we automatically and almost unconsciously observe the other's actions, take note of his voice and accent, follow his words and how he says them, notice his mannerisms, and particularly notice the way he reacts to what we do and say. We, in turn, respond to his reactions. This cycle of action and reaction shapes the early stages of all the thousands of interpersonal events which occur in our lives.

First Impressions

Much of what is called "small talk" allows people to sort out their first impressions and to find areas of mutual interest. Complex social skills are always at work in the making of relationships. Some people are immensely skilled at person-perception, at making small talk and building up a pleasant, even if at first superficial, relationship. They do it largely automatically and with a relaxed and warm manner that puts the other individual at ease and engenders liking and a glow of self-esteem which comes when people think their company has been pleasing and stimulating to others. These skills can be acquired. For one thing, people can acquire a wide range of general knowledge by reading, so that they are informed and intelligent conversationalists.

It is surprising how much information and misinformation we pick up when we first meet people. The ordinary adult or child cannot clearly say how he interprets this information any more than he can describe articulately how he carries out other automatic acts such as reading or running. Yet we make extensive inferences about others' behavior, their thoughts, feelings, intentions, needs and attitudes. It is critical that we should make reasonably accurate interpretations. Being a good and sympathetic listener, with the ability to make *interesting* and nonthreatening comments, increases the accuracy of our perceptions and the likelihood of furthering the relationship.

Nobody Loves Me

How coordinated social interaction breaks down through misinterpretation can be seen in the case of the paranoid person with delusions of persecution. To him everybody seems hostile and rejecting; as a result he acts suspiciously or aggressively, in a prickly manner. The stranger, not surprisingly, reacts by withdrawing—which "proves" the paranoic's initial sense of persecution. This sort of self-defeating and vicious circle of events also takes place in less pathological examples of human interaction. Misunderstandings arise because generally a person reacts to what he *thinks* the other person is feeling and thinking, in addition to or instead of what the person is actually doing.

How do we form an impression of another person? One of the basic tendencies of people meeting others is to pull together a number of impressions, to make them into a unitary "whole" no matter how fragmentary the clues. When describing a stranger, most people make snap judgments about his character, simply from observing his physical appearance. We use all manner of clues for the interpretation of character—wide or thick lips indicate sensuality; fat people are jolly and friendly; domed foreheads and glasses indicate intellectual interests; pipe smokers are mature, wise and reliable. These are some of the many unreliable or totally misleading clues that most of us use in forming first impressions which may cause us to narrow the field of eligible friends quite needlessly.

Misjudgments about people in person-perception and other aspects of social skill may be fatal in the delicate period of moving from acquaintanceship to friendship. In a well-established relationship, of course, we do not have to be so "aware," so conscious of cultivating a friend by winning his interest.

We can also learn about the art of friendship from the familiar and commonsense idea that no social interaction will be prolonged unless it is rewarding to both participants. One of the most comprehensive theories based upon this idea is that of G. C. Homans in his book *Social Behavior.* His theory implies that we are in friendships for the profit we get out of them. Profit is defined as total gain or reward minus cost (a complex idea which includes the rewards that *might* come from doing other things). The nature of the profit varies from such intangibles as enhanced self-esteem, heightened morale and increased insight to financial help and material gifts. But not only must both participants derive profit; it is important that both feel that the profit is fairly distributed *between* them.

Social interactions are viewed as a social exchange somewhat analogous to economic exchange, in which people are influenced (consciously and unconsciously) by the ratio of "rewards" and the "costs" incurred in the interaction. Any activity carried out by one individual that contributes to the satisfaction of another's needs is termed a "reward." The term "cost" is applied to deterrents that may be incurred in contacts with another person—such as hostility, anxiety, embarrassment, and the like. If another reward is foregone because of engaging in a particular social interaction, this too is considered a "cost."

The term "outcome" refers to the ratio of rewards to costs—if the outcome of an interaction with a person is positive, it may be said to yield a "profit"; if it is negative, it is termed a "loss." For attraction to a potential friend to occur the reward-cost outcome must be above the "comparison level," a standard against which satisfaction is judged.

Psychologist Professor Paul Secord has analyzed friendship formation in terms of exchange theory as follows: when strangers meet—for example, at a party—they mingle, they sample interactions with other persons, estimate the profit obtained in each, and commit themselves to interactions yielding the highest profit.

Much of what is called small talk

Party time, and so the merry-go-round begins. At least that is until we home in on whoever turns us on. At first we make our way (follow the arrow) from group to group finding out who's there. Then we gravitate towards the group that seems most interesting. Then, perhaps, further selection follows. We may finish up chatting with someone with whom we have a lot in common. Throughout we are like gold miners, continually sifting through the guests in the hope that we can strike lucky and find gold. If so, it has been a good party.

Syndication International

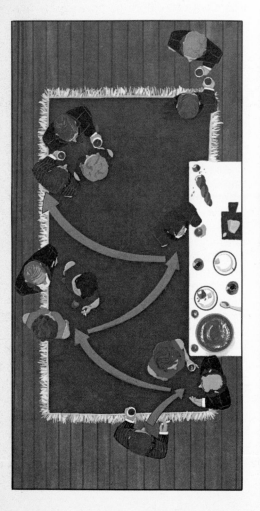
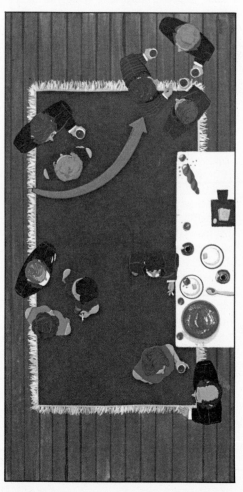

David Kinefield

serves the function of giving people time to sort out their first impressions and work out their social strategies. It also provides a neutral base from which to make conversational expeditions in the search for areas of mutual interest. Some people are skilled at these first meetings; others admit they are no good at them. This becomes a problem, especially in adolescence; an inability to make small talk, gauche movements and exaggerated gestures are all signs of deficient social skills and may be a hindrance to following up contacts and making friends.

You cannot always tell a book by its cover. The man on the left seems friendly, but he may only want to add you to his collection and bolster his ego. The man on the right withdraws but may be shy, not unfriendly.

On these first meeting occasions, individuals pick up a surprising amount of information *and* misinformation about each other. Nevertheless, they try to estimate the profit obtained in each contact, committing themselves to those interactions that yield the highest profit. Through "bar-

gaining" (not to be taken literally) they maximize rewards and minimize costs. That is, they avoid awkward topics which they see will cause another person distress or make him critical of them, and they say and do things which are likely to please him and maintain a congenial atmosphere.

After they have made a firm commitment, their previous sampling and estimation (that is, trying out various potentially friendly people) are reduced or eliminated altogether. Once a relationship has formed, it will last as long as the outcomes are satisfying to the participants. The rewards may be enough to prolong the bond throughout the party and even beyond, the two individuals associating on an increasingly exclusive basis until a final stage termed "institutionalization" is reached. This might be the beginning of an enduring friendship though many factors determine whether a relationship will last.

Give and Take

Although this theory makes it seem as if all friendships are exploitive—and of course some are—it must be repeated that the emphasis is on *mutual satisfaction of needs.* There must always be some give-and-take; friendships which are too one-sided, selfish, or exploitive are not likely to last. To continue with the economic analogy, when costs soar and the ledger is in fundamental imbalance, showing persistent losses, the friendship is likely to be in danger. The person who is worried about his inability to make or keep friends might carry out a small exercise in "accountancy," based on honest observations of his behavior with other people. Look at things from the *other* person's point of view. Are you being insensitive, too demanding, or disloyal? Is your company rewarding enough?

Immature and self-centered persons or aggressive and selfish individuals are not always able to manage the give-and-take of friendship. Among the many possible ways in which a person may act, only a few are appropriate to a given interpersonal situation. We have seen, when discussing "paranoia," how persistent misinterpretation of others results in the breakdown of coordinated social interaction. At a less significant level we all have biases in the way we look at the world; we all differ in the modes of analysis we apply to our impressions of others. This is particularly true in terms of the complexity of the concepts we use to describe them. Up to the age of about seven, children usually limit their descriptions to outstanding visible features.

In adults, complexity of description of others seems related to the degree of complexity of the observer's own personality. Most people have little problem with simple perceptions—another person's temporary moods, his approval or disapproval of particular topics, and his various reactions to themselves. Greater difficulty is presented by more subtle analyses involving other people's motivations and character traits. Here, personal biases obstruct perceptive interpretations.

Awareness of the more obvious errors we make in forming impressions of other people may increase our efficiency in social interactions. "Oversimplification" is a common source of error—life is simplified if we can pigeonhole people into "goodies" and "baddies" and situations into black or white. "Rigidity" is a bias due to the inability to see behavior which does not fit in with our conception of a person. Some people are remarkably impervious to contradictory evidence—information which goes against their prejudices and stereotypes. "Stereotyping" results in our viewing a person as a specimen of a certain group and therefore attributing to him *all* the characteristics of that group.

The individual as "detective" pieces together clues and fragments of information about his fellow beings in the course of his social interactions, trying to make accurate judgments about them to make sense of his social world.

We have to be very aware of the cues we emit which other people select and by which they judge (and perhaps misjudge) us. Psychologists call the first factor in this process *primacy.* Many observers believe that first impressions of a person are particularly important and lasting. One researcher obtained dramatic results when he presented information which suggested initially that a person was friendly; this impression "stuck" even if the initial information was followed by additional evidence that the same person was unfriendly.

Speech Patterns

Another principle, *vividness,* also makes us more selective in our impressions. Any cues that, for whatever reason, are striking or conspicuous are apt to be remembered and to determine impressions. An unusual dress may result in the person being noted as flamboyant or "eccentric."

The third principle is *frequency.* Cues that are frequently manifested by the same person are more likely to be noticed. Timidity or wittiness may not be noticed on first acquaintance unless they are manifested quite conspicuously—in other words, frequently.

These principles suggest reasons why repellent behavior and mannerisms or rudenesses and insensitivities do not allow us to get past first base in forming friendships.

There are two different types of cues or stimuli on which we base first impressions. Firstly, we rely a great deal on *what* is said. Secondly, research studies have shown that physical characteristics are important in our judgments of people. There is evidence that listeners tend to judge a speaker's personality by his speech pattern. The seventeenth century playwright Ben Jonson said, "Language most showeth a man: speak that I may see thee." In addition to his voice, the expressive movements, the gestures, the facial movements, and the postures of a stranger help to determine the impression he is giving. The man who gestures forcefully is perceived as forceful, the immobile speaker as cold and controlled.

Telltale Signs

Many people appear to make judgments on the basis of certain imagined associations: that a slumped posture indicates a dull, lifeless and depressed personality; a floppy handshake expresses a lack of warmth; jerky, erratic movements mean nervousness; sweeping, expansive gestures indicate force and vigor; while constraint of movement and stiffness of manner point to aloofness and reserve. While these associations will obviously apply in some cases, they are unreliable indicators for a reasonable judgment; sometimes they are totally misleading.

Many people believe (usually wrongly) in the value of facial characteristics as indices of character and let their interpretations of people be guided by them. The red-haired person is popularly considered to be quick-tempered; the individual with shifty eyes and thin lips is thought to be cruel. It is interesting to see that the "goodies" and "baddies" in the old films are typed on the lines of physical characteristics. Physical bearing and size are believed to indicate character and temperament, so the man who bears himself erectly is thought to be of upright character, and fat people are believed to be jolly.

Finally, we tend to like people when we are *prepared* to like them—it is possible to increase the probability of one person liking another simply by assuring him beforehand that he will. And if he is given evidence that the other person likes him, then this probability is greatly increased. The party hostess who goes to Mr. Brown and says, "I must introduce you to Mr. Smith—he has heard about you and really wants to meet you—and you'll like him, I know," and who then goes to Mr. Smith with a corresponding story about Mr. Brown, is acting upon a sure instinct.

Mary Evans

Up, up and away

Though we may be in the dark as to how it happens, to judge by the evidence, levitation is no fly-by-night affair. But these flights of fancy are brief. People with their head in the clouds always come back down to earth in the end.

Everybody has heard of Uri Geller, the young Israeli who claims he can bend metal objects by willpower alone. Certainly his television demonstrations convinced a great many people. But is Geller really doing what he appears to be doing? Or is he, as the skeptics suggest, merely a clever conjurer? The controversy still rages.

However, whatever the ultimate outcome of the argument, there are still those who believe that Uri Geller is the latest in a long line of men possessing what is now known as psychokinetic power—the ability to exert mind over matter.

The first serious scientific attempt to define psychokinesis was made in Britain a century ago by Sir William Crookes. His findings, which seemed to convince him that such power *did* exist, were published in *Researches in the Phenomena of Spiritualism*.

First, there was the movement of objects by human contact, but without pressure. ("The retort is obvious," Crookes notes, "that if people are touching a thing when it moves, they push it or pull it or lift it." But he was

sure that this was not always the case.) Second, he noted "percussive and other sounds," coming apparently from no human source. The commonest were the "rappings" always associated with spiritualism, but they came in many different forms, from delicate ticks to detonations. Third was the alteration in the weight of objects. Fourth, the movement of heavy objects. (His own chair had on occasion been twisted around, during experiments, when his feet were off the floor; at other times he and his colleagues had seen a small table move across the room, with nobody near it.) Fifth, the levitation of furniture off the ground, without human contact. (Why, skeptics had asked him, was it always tables and chairs which did such things? It was his business as a scientist, he would answer, not to reason why, but simply to observe and record; but as, in the ordinary room, the available heavy objects were furniture, it was not surprising.) And last but not least, the levitation of human beings.

"On one occasion I witnessed a

Above: The magazine *Punch* satirized the immense interest aroused in England by accounts of levitation. The string controls the altitude and the bell is the landing signal.

chair, with a lady sitting on it, rise several inches from the ground. On another occasion, to avoid the suspicion of this being in some way performed by herself, the lady knelt on the chair in such a manner that its four feet were visible to us. It then rose about three inches, remained suspended for about ten seconds, and then slowly descended."

This catalog, Crookes realized, was far from exhaustive, and he cited other examples which could be regarded as psychokinetic. These include automatic writing, where the medium holds the pen, but the pen, or some force working through it, appears to do the work on its own. Most baffling of all is what has since come to be known as translocation, where an object known to be in one place appears in another, having apparently passed not merely through the air but through a wall or a door to get there.

Crookes described such an event in his "miscellaneous occurrences of a complex character." While he was having a seance with a medium, he heard a hand bell in the room, as if somebody were wandering around ringing it; and eventually it fell on a table beside him. He was sure that he had left the bell in the room next door, and he found that one of his sons had actually seen and played with the bell after the seance had begun. Yet the door between the rooms had been locked, and he had the key in his pocket.

Miracles and Myths

At around the time Crookes was conducting his research, material was beginning to be collected to show that primitive tribes in all parts of the world took it for granted that certain men, witch doctors for instance, were able to move objects without touching them, to heal—and kill—at a distance. A striking example, which several Western observers have since reported, is the "calling" of fish by Pacific islanders, described by George H. Hutchinson in the *Geographic News Bulletin*.

The villagers in Samoa, he said, would gather on a point of land jutting over the sea to commemorate a prince and princess who had been changed into a shark and a turtle respectively. While they chanted, they beckoned; and in due course first a shark and then a turtle would come as if in answer to the prayer and swim around for awhile. Coincidence, the skeptics argued, or fantasy. But other observers have witnessed similar ceremonies, with similar results, since.

The literature of early civilization is also full of references to what could now be called psychokinetic events, usually ascribed to the intervention of the gods: Jove striking down upstart humans with his thunderbolts and other angry gods (or jealous goddesses) destroying those they dislike, or protecting those they love, by diverting javelins in midflight. The Old Testament has relatively few examples, though it could be argued that the trumpet call which flattened the walls of Jericho did so by virtue of some psychic force rather than by the resonance of the sound waves. But the New Testament provides several psychokinetic miracles, including Jesus' turning of the water into wine and his walking on the lake.

Later Christian holy writing teems with cases where saints and martyrs,

or their relics, have displayed such powers. Some continue to be believed by the faithful. The blood of St. Januarius is supposed to liquefy annually on his saint's day in a Naples church— though an eminent naturalist who was brave enough to taste the stuff pronounced unkindly that it was bat's urine. For other feats, however, there is more reliable evidence—notably the levitations of Joseph of Cupertino in the seventeenth century.

Joseph is an interesting case. His ecclesiastical superiors—he was a Franciscan monk—were far from impressed by his flights. Unnerved by them, they did their best to stop him. Partly this was because, at that time, extrasensory activities of any kind tended to be associated with witchcraft. And partly, no doubt, it was because of resentment that Joseph, who was what would now be described as mentally retarded, should have this gift from God—if it really was God, rather than the Devil, who was responsible.

Nobody could accuse Joseph of any lack of devotion to God in his daily life; and when, in church one Christmas Eve, he suddenly soared with a cry of ecstasy into the air and floated around by the High Altar, it was hard to believe that even the Devil would have had the audacity to sponsor such a flight. When Joseph went on doing it, however—in spite of himself—the authorities felt that he was setting a bad example, and for over 30 years he was banned from the public celebration of mass.

Yet the episodes continued. Walking with a Benedictine monk in the monastery garden, he suddenly flew up into the branches of an olive tree— only to lose courage and feel unable to fly back to earth: his colleagues had to come to his rescue with a ladder. When he was an old man, dying, the doctor brought in to treat him found him lying stretched out six inches above the bed.

Devil's Advocate

After his death, it was proposed that Joseph should be beatified. It happened that the Devil's advocate employed to sift the evidence was Prospero Lambertini, the future Pope Benedict XIV. Lambertini was interested in the miraculous; he was to write a perceptive treatise on the subject. He had assumed that the stories about Joseph were the product of overheated imaginations and objected strenuously to the proposal. But the evidence was too strong for him. Too many people had actually seen Joseph in

flight, including many individuals who could not be regarded as gullible. To maintain that they had all been deluded would have been difficult, as one eyewitness had been the previous Pope. Eventually Lambertini agreed, when Pope himself, to Joseph's beatification.

Joseph's feats of levitation are so well attested that it seems difficult to reject them even if he was a unique case. But he was not; similar reports by trustworthy observers were made about Teresa of Avila (who also was embarrassed about her levitations— she prayed to God to stop them) and a number of other saints. As more than one writer on the subject has pointed out, the historical evidence for levitation is considerably stronger than for many episodes which we accept as "history" without question. And the same applies to another form of psychokinesis which in spite of its familiarity for hundreds of years past has never achieved the dignity of a scientific-sounding name, or even an English name: the manifestations associated with poltergeists—noisy, or boisterous, spirits.

Table Turning

Until the seventeenth century, levitation, poltergeists and other varieties of psychokinesis created alarm, but no surprise. That saints or witches had access to occult powers was not in dispute. But with the coming of the age of reason, scientists began to question this assumption. And at the same time the number of reported psychokinetic episodes began to dwindle—perhaps because people were losing faith in God and fear of the Devil. Individuals continued to perform feats of psychokinesis—or claim to. But their claims were not taken seriously until, in the middle of the nineteenth century, spiritualism suddenly became a world craze.

Today, spiritualism is usually associated with visits to mediums to seek information from the spirit world; but its initial impact was made chiefly through psychokinesis—noises, such as rappings and drummings, and movements of furniture and household objects. "Table turning" became a popular home entertainment. A group of people would sit around the dining room table (after it had been cleared of the remains of the dinner), placing the tips of their fingers on top of it and waiting for it to move. Soon, the table turners began to read purpose into these movements: when the table jumped once, it was taken to mean the answer "yes," two jumps meaning "no," and so on.

This tended to confuse the scientific issue, which was primarily whether and how the table moved—not whether the force also represented some spirit intelligence communicating with mankind. And this was unfortunate, because orthodox scientists, however incredulous they were about table turning, might have been prepared to investigate it had it not been linked with spiritualism and occultism. And as a result most of them missed the opportunity to investigate the seemingly remarkable powers of Daniel Dunglas Home.

Home was unquestionably the most remarkable all-round psychic performer in history. He was born in Scotland in 1833, the illegitimate son —or so he claimed—of the Earl of Home, ancestor of the British politician, Sir Alex Douglas Home. From an early age he began to have psychic experiences, which grew more intense when he became an adolescent. When spiritualism became fashionable in the early 1850s, he was consequently in a position to exploit the publicity it attracted, and he became the most celebrated performer of the whole repertory of spiritualist exercises.

Levitation was his most spectacular accomplishment. Home "took off"

Right: Israeli Uri Geller—man or superman? As Geller strokes the spoon it begins to bend. Below left: A planchette, the automatic writing device supposed to allow the spirits a free hand. Below right: An example of automatic writing.

scores of times, in all kinds of surroundings, sometimes during spiritualist meetings, sometimes as if on a casual impulse. Many of the people who saw him airborne left accounts, of which the best known is the one by the Master of Lindsay.

"I was sitting with Mr. Home and Lord Adare and a cousin of his. During the sitting, Mr. Home went into a trance, and in that state was carried out of the window in the room next

to where we were, and was brought in at our window. The distance between the windows was about seven feet six inches, and there was not the slightest foothold between them, nor was there more than a twelve-inch projection to each window, which served as a ledge to put flowers on.

"We heard the window in the next room lift up, and almost immediately after we saw Home floating in the air outside our window. The moon was

Camera Press

Mary Evans

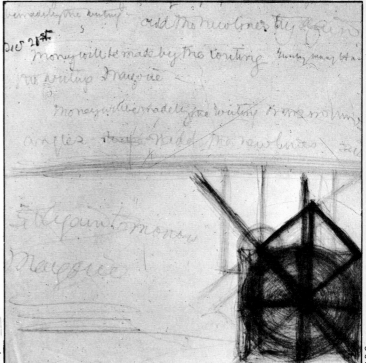

B.P.C.

shining into the room; my back was to the light, and I saw the shadow on the wall of the windowsill, and Home's feet about six inches above it. He remained in this position for a few seconds, then raised the window and glided into the room, feet foremost, and sat down.

"Home then demonstrated how he did it, flying out of the window—85 feet above the ground—head first, then returning calmly to the room."

Lord Adare and his cousin, Captain Wynne, subsequently confirmed the accuracy of the Master of Lindsay's description. And many other independent observers, in the United States as well as in Britain, testified to his making similar flights.

What makes Home's record all the more remarkable is that he seems to have been the only medium in history about whom there is no shred of evidence of fraud. A great many people believed him to be an impostor—including Robert Browning, who satirized him savagely as "Mr. Sludge;" but nobody who actually witnessed his demonstrations was able to fault them. According to one of those witnesses, Sir William Crookes, there were at least a hundred recorded instances of levitation.

"To reject the recorded evidence," Crookes felt, "is to reject all human testimony whatever; no fact in sacred or profane history is supported by a stronger array of proofs."

Home was far from being the only individual of his time who could apparently produce psychokinesis at will. Another noted medium of the time was William Stainton Moses—a respected minister and a schoolteacher, who suddenly found himself in possession of powers which, as he was a modest, retiring man, caused him great concern, so that he shunned publicity. Even those who could not accept the evidence of their own eyes when he gave demonstrations—which he would do only for friends—did not accuse him of fraud, so palpably incapable was he of deceit. All they could claim was that he had never allowed himself to be scientifically tested, so that his feats must be treated as not proven.

As public interest in spiritualism died down, reports of psychokinesis in its most striking forms, such as levitation and translocation, began to dwindle; but in more everyday manifestations it has remained common.

Dowsing is one example. Attempts have been made to account for the movements of a water diviner's hazel twig by attributing them to muscular spasm on the part of the diviner; but nobody who has felt the pressure, like an invisible thumb on the end of the twig, will find that acceptable.

Poltergeists appear actually to have become more common in recent years —occasionally in unexpected ways, such as Jung experienced, with Freud, when he asked Freud what he thought about psychic forces. Freud came later to believe in their existence, but at the time he was skeptical, and said so. As if to convert him, there was "such a loud report in the bookcase, which stood right next to us, that we both started up in alarm, fearing the thing was going to topple over us." Finding Freud still unconvinced, Jung promised that there would be another detonation—and there was!

Mary Evans

Sir William Crookes was a witness to Daniel Dunglas Home's remarkable feats of levitation. What stronger evidence could there be? he asked.

David Levin

Birds of a feather

Women who love each other aren't always the grotesque butch dykes of popular imagination.

Many women have experienced a sexual or emotional encounter with another woman. The crushes young girls develop on a teacher or older girl and the warm embraces between two friends are one end of a scale that stretches through a single exploration of a homosexual embrace to the spasmodic encounters of a bisexual woman who enjoys homosexual and heterosexual love-making to the long-term homosexual relations of the woman who makes love only with other women.

Bryan Magee, in his book *One in 20,* estimates that about five percent of women are lesbians, and other estimates suggest that the proportion of women who prefer homosexual love-making but find themselves trapped in a heterosexual existence may be 10 per cent or higher.

Women who are lesbian come from all backgrounds and may have any kind of personality. The exaggeratedly masculine "butch" lesbian or over-feminine "fem" lend a false image to others who are less flamboyant. Statistically there are fewer female than male homosexuals who have

1125

absolutely no sexual relations with the opposite sex. And it can be easier for a lesbian than for a man to maintain a heterosexual front and so contribute to the fact that lesbianism is not always noticed. Indeed, Sappho, the Greek poetess who lived on the Isle of Lesbos in the sixth century B.C. and whose poems dedicated to young women encapsulated lesbian love, was herself married and had children.

There can be, too, a greater tolerance of lesbianism than of male homosexuality—and it may even become a heterosexual masculine fantasy. At group sex parties men may urge two women to make love to each other while they watch, but it is rare for two men to become physically involved in front of others.

For most lesbians the first hints of their psychosexual preferences come fairly early. The family background may have some influence—although the fact is as yet unexplained. Some family groups seem to produce a high proportion of homosexuals. Or cultural suggestions may play a part—the desire to lead life as an active tomboy can sometimes be linked with later lesbianism.

During adolescence the lesbian's fantasies are mainly homosexual—unlike the masculine-oriented fantasies of heterosexual female teenagers—and many have their first experience of homosexual love-making in early adolescence. This first experience is usually part of a gradual progression towards life as a lesbian and not the mythical corrupting contact that forces a teenager into a lesbian existence despite her true underlying desires.

Many girls finding themselves attracted to women continue to go out

Some lesbian women find the overtly aggressive sexuality of men overpowering and turn away from men to their own, more gentle sex.

Les Edwards

with boys. Sometimes this is because they themselves are not yet totally aware of how their sexual personality is developing and sometimes because they hope to camouflage from parents forms of sexual involvement that might cause dismay.

As the lesbian grows into her twenties and thirties she may move into the gay world, openly acknowledging her sexual tastes and sharing her life with others who understand her nature. Some move in groups, organizing outings and parties that are a forum for promiscuously seeking new partners—but lesbians are more likely to form steady partnerships very similar to a heterosexual marriage, and the relationships between two lesbian women is likely to be as rewarding as any other strong and long-term commitment.

Girl Partners

"When I was a teenager, I didn't know what a lesbian was," said Charlotte. "My parents never talked about sex and somehow I was always a little apart from people at school who might have talked about it. I'd made up my mind I was going to win a scholarship to university so I was working while a lot of the other girls were just waiting for someone to marry. They used to chatter about boyfriends— which one had a car and who was going to take them to the spring dance. I went around with a boy sometimes, but we talked about exams and work, and I think he was more afraid of me than I was of him.

"It was after I spent nearly a year at university that I realized I was attracted towards Imogene, one of the other girls in my year. All the symptoms the others had when their boyfriends were around I had when I knew Imogene was nearby. I'd learned enough by then to know what a lesbian was—but I didn't think of myself as one. There was just this funny feeling . . . I didn't mind whether or not some boy had invited me out to the movies—but I did want to spend a lot of time with Imogene.

"One of the instructors helped me a lot. She sensed that I was unsettled and made me talk about what was involved. Nothing directly happened with Imogene—she's married now and for all I know was oblivious to what was going on—but that talk allowed me to examine my own feelings. By then I was mature enough to accept that this was the way I was made— no hysterics, no tears, just this is my life and I'm going to enjoy it my way.

"There were one or two false starts —I suppose there are in everybody's life—but a couple of years after leaving college I met Anne. She'd gone through almost exactly the same progression—I remember it was talking about it that developed a stong bond between us—and we've been living together as lovers ever since. My parents still insist on regarding us as 'sharing an apartment' but they've stopped trying to wish a good solid husband onto me so I suppose that even they have understood what we feel for each other."

For women who accept themselves as lesbians and who find that others share the same understanding, relationships can be a fulfilling combination of the emotional and the sexual. The relationship may be organized so that one partner plays a dominant role, taking day-to-day decisions and initiating love-making while the other responds passively. Or it may be a more equal relationship in which both share decisions and are equally likely to take the lead in love-making.

Love-making for lesbians has the same aim as for heterosexual lovers: it expresses love and attraction through sexual stimulation and release. The partners' sexual activity may range from kisses and cuddles to mutual masturbation, oral stimulation and pressing their bodies against each other. The idea that lesbians are dependent on a dildo or substitute penis is more a masculine assumption that penetration is essential to female satisfaction than a reality. Indeed for many women early episodes of lesbian love-making may be more relaxed and enjoyable than the equivalent initiation into heterosexual intercourse.

Emotional Ties

"Men always seem to worry about what we girls do together," said Angela. "It's almost as though they think they're missing out on something. What they don't realize is that a woman's body reacts to many kinds of sexual stimulation and it's not just a matter of pull here, push here and pop goes another orgasm. Sometimes Carol and I just lie close together and the sexual tension is as high as anything. Other times we may stroke and kiss each other. I know what pleases me but Carol is more than just a marvelous machine for my pleasure—we're deeply emotionally involved with each other, not seeking purely sexual kicks."

Many lesbian women have had sexual experience with men—sometimes while they were still unsure of their basic sexual tendencies, sometimes because of social expectations or even a near rape. Some find that they enjoy heterosexual lovemaking and reach orgasm with a male partner. Their lesbianism is an emotional commitment rather than a directly sexual imperative and they may happily lead a bisexual life. Other women may actively dislike heterosexual love-making.

A Woman's Touch

Social expectations may make it difficult for many women to recognize their own tendencies towards lesbianism and it is virtually impossible for them to escape from the parental pressures and economic necessities that lead to conventional marriage. Caught in a situation where the price of a secure home and of being able to bring up children—and many women who know they are lesbians would like children—is marital sexual intercourse, she may submit to joyless sex without ever realizing the possible explanation.

"I married young," explained Janet, "and my parents thought I'd made a good catch. David was certainly a good husband and father in the material sense—we had a comfortable house and we gave the children a proper start in life. But there was never any spark between us, we made love almost as a duty, because people in our position were expected to produce the regulation number of children. Taking a lover never crossed my mind. I didn't blame David for the lack of excitement. That was just the way it was. And I'd still be plodding along if Penny hadn't 'seduced' me—I suppose that's the word I've got to use.

"We met through our work for a local society and quickly began to spend a lot of time in each other's company. Then, right out of the blue, Penny asked me to move into her house with her—the children were grown up, David would hardly notice and we could just enjoy being women together. I decided to stay, right there and then. That first evening Penny put her arms around me as we were sitting downstairs and I felt more excited than I ever had with David— although I still didn't know what was happening.

"Now Penny and I live together and sleep together. David comes around sometimes—he's almost relieved now, although at first he didn't understand at all. We're both happier without having to keep up the pretense of being in love with each other."

Lesbianism, in some cases, happens

just because there are no men available. In a closed female community such as a prison, army unit, or convent, emotional ties can lead to sexual exploration. Some of these women are likely to be lesbian anyway, but others will take the attitude that sex even with another woman is better than masturbation and will be glad to return to a heterosexual life in other circumstances.

Secret Touch

Some women merely find that they are more comfortable with women than with men, even in a nonsexual way. But others are reacting strongly against men. Sometimes this stems from worries about pregnancy and abortion, and men are blamed as the instruments of these calamities. Sometimes it comes from profound distaste for being used as a sex object or even from fear of rape or a beating.

This hate can twist within the woman's personality to such an extent that it provides a justification for prostitution. The lesbian prostitute, and there are a number of them, takes money from men she "uses" and despises for their inability to arouse her. In other situations a similar feeling can drive a woman into proving herself better than men just to show that the world need not be male-dominated. This drive can take on a hysterical tinge if the woman is worried that her own girlfriend may be hired away by the despised yet still apparently attractive male.

The lesbian woman faces two main problems: the first is accepting her own nature, and the second is persuading others to accept and understand it. She may, for example, experience doubt and guilt because she feels sexual urges that are not "normal." For a woman who has little contact with others in the same situation, coping with conflicting forces—undeniable sexual attraction versus a mental picture of sexual propriety that does not allow its fulfillment—can be extremely wearing.

"I was close to suicide," confessed Elizabeth. "There I was, single, 24, no prospect of marriage and attracted to the students I was meant to be instructing. Classes were torture as I couldn't give any indication of how I felt for fear of losing my job. I'd go home in the evening and cry with tension and worry—all the time with a picture of one of the girls in my head.

"Finally I telephoned an advisory service I saw advertised. I didn't think of myself as a lesbian—I didn't think of myself as anything—but I certainly

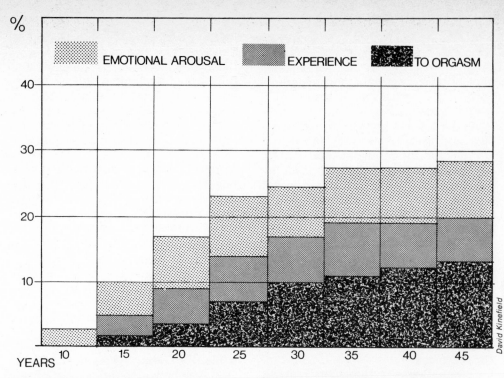

YEARS

was not doing myself any good as I was. The counselor was extremely sympathetic and suggested I went to one of their discussion groups. It was the first time I realized other people were having the same problems, and it was certainly the first time I realized there might be hope for me."

For others the problem comes in persuading other people to accept a decision that has been consciously taken. Many lesbians prefer to lead a "secret" life rather than confront the querying glances of work colleagues and acquaintances or the incomprehension or even rejection of parents and friends.

"I met Ruth when we were both working in the same hotel one summer," explained Sue. "She was a waitress and I was running one of the bars. I've known I was a lesbian for years, and I've led a very happy life with a number of partners. Taking the hotel job, though, was a reaction to the breakup of an affair. It was something to occupy myself with—and then I found Ruth and that was really a bonus. We spent the summer together and then she came to live with me for the winter—she'd been involved with women before but never to this extent.

"She wrote a letter to her parents trying to explain how she felt—she told me they'd understand although I was more suspicious than that. And of course I was right. Her father drove down here and smashed his way in late at night. He was raving. He accused me of turning his daughter into a dyke, he threatened to call the police —I thought he was physically going to drag Ruth away.

Above: A graph of the incidence of homosexuality in a representative sample shows how varied the experience is. Right: Gertrude Stein had a happy lesbian marriage with Alice B. Toklas (background) for more than forty years.

"He went on for two hours and then I think he expected Ruth to repent and swear she'd marry the boy next door. Eventually he left—just turned around and walked out. Ruth and he haven't spoken since then, although she writes to her mother. But when she describes what we've done—going for a picnic, things like that—she leaves me out. It's almost as though she goes around with a ghost."

Some lesbians have psychological problems that find a focus in their sexual lives—as can also happen with heterosexuals. Exhibitionism, overdependence on others, or a compulsive urge to dress in flagrantly masculine clothes can produce the kind of notoriety that forms a misleading public stereotype of the lesbian. While the majority of homosexual women behave much as other women in public and social situations, some are driven to the conspicuous behavior that can make it difficult for other women to admit to being homosexual. The duplicity of leading a "secret" life is a great strain.

When these problems can be overcome—and the purely practical difficulties of living as a responsible woman in a masculine-dominated society sorted out—the homosexual woman can hope for happiness and sexual fulfillment.

Language of love

Hey you! Keep your distance . . . or somebody will think you're much too close for comfort.

The concept of "territory" is a very strong one in the animal kingdom. All sorts of animals and birds stake out a little patch on this crowded globe which they regard as their own and which they will vigorously defend, especially against other members of the same species.

Man, too, is no different from the animals in this respect. People of every race and nationality like to have some space which "belongs" to them and their families—and where they enjoy special rights and privileges.

As well as this territorial "home,"

however, everyone also has another sort of individual territory, a kind of invisible shell of space a few feet around him. Wherever he is, whatever he is doing, he believes that this tiny piece of surrounding territory is his and his alone. If other people invade it he feels uncomfortable or threatened.

Because the world is so crowded, because we are going to meet or mingle with strangers every day, we have had to evolve a set of rules to enable everyone to preserve their own territory and to respect that of others.

We defend our territory not through words or through physical attack (unless the "invasion" is really blatant) but through the silent body language of posture and position: where and how we sit or stand in relation to one another.

Recently researchers have been making detailed studies of these silent communications and the different sizes of zones of space we create in various situations. There is even a name for such studies: the science of proxemics.

The intimate zone seen at three levels between lovers (1), friends (3), and strangers in a crowd (2). Social distance is observed between buyer and seller (4) and acquaintances enjoying a drink together (5). The banker (6) uses his desk to preserve far social distance from his customers. Close public distance obtains between lecturer and his students (7). The late Robert Kennedy (8) addressing a rally stands at far public distance from his audience.

Barnaby's/Camera Press

There are, for example, four distinct zones in which most people operate. They are called intimate distance, personal distance, social distance and public distance. There are variations in each category according to the degree of intimacy in the relationship between the people involved.

Take the *intimate distance* zone, for example. It can range from "close intimate"—actual touching—to "far intimate," ranging from 6 to 18 inches.

This is what body language expert Dr. Julius Fast has to say about it: "The *close* phase of intimate distance is used for making love, for very close friendships and for children clinging to a parent or to each other.

"When you are at close intimate distance, you are overwhelmingly aware of your partner. For this reason, if such contact takes place between two men, it can lead to awkwardness or uneasiness. It is most natural between a man and a woman on intimate terms.

Man to Man

"Between two women in our culture, a close intimate state is acceptable, while in an Arab culture such a state is acceptable between two men. Men will frequently walk hand in hand in Arab and in many Mediterranean lands."

In the Western world touching is equated with sexual contact. We cannot appreciate the touch of friendship. Nevertheless all animals, including humans, enjoy and seem to need some degree of mutual stroking and grooming, quite apart from sexual arousal. It has been suggested that love of animals is a channel for this repressed desire: we are not allowed to touch each other, so we have an animal to stroke and fondle.

In our crowded cities we always try to observe the far intimate distance. Watch people standing in a crowded train. They will strenuously try to keep their 6 to 18 inches distance. And if they do accidently touch each other they will rapidly draw away or tense their muscles to apologize silently for this intrusion.

In the next territorial zone—*personal distance*—there are *close* and *far* phases too. The close area is from about 1½ to 2½ feet. It is the shaking hands distance. But if you meet someone casually in the street and stop for a chat you will probably observe far personal distance. It is close enough for conversation but far enough away to preserve your privacy.

Close social distance ranges from about 4 feet to 7 feet. That is where

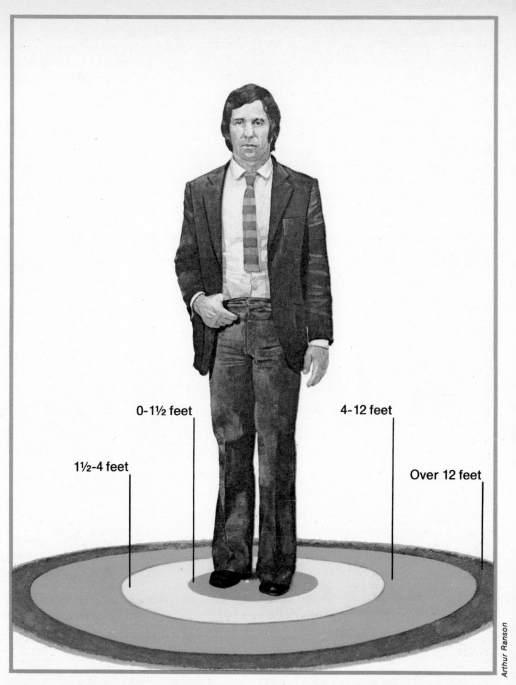

0-1½ feet

1½-4 feet

4-12 feet

Over 12 feet

Arthur Ranson

The four distinct zones in which people operate: intimate distance (orange), personal (yellow), social (green) and public (blue).

the housewife stands when she talks to the mailman or the delivery boy. *Far social distance*—7 feet to 12 feet—is for more formal social or business meetings.

Dr. Fast says, "The 'big boss' will have a desk large enough to put him this distance from his employees. He can also remain seated and look up at an employee without loss of status."

Finally, there are also two main phases of *public distance* as well. The *close* phase (12 to 25 feet) is for informal public gatherings, like a lecturer talking to a roomful of students. The *far* phase, over 25 feet, is for formal meetings, like an address

by a politician. Incidentally this distance is just about the same as many wild animals will let you advance before running away.

All these distances are only very crude approximations and there are wide cultural variations. In ordinary, everyday conversations, for example, Latin Americans and Arabs will stand much closer together than, say, the British or the Swedes.

Within any cultural group, there are variations between individuals. Dr. Michael Argyle of the Institute of Experimental Psychology at Oxford University has shown, for example, that introverted people insist on a greater than average conversational distance. This means that they can "withdraw" from a conversation more easily without suffering loss of face.

And there are intriguing differences

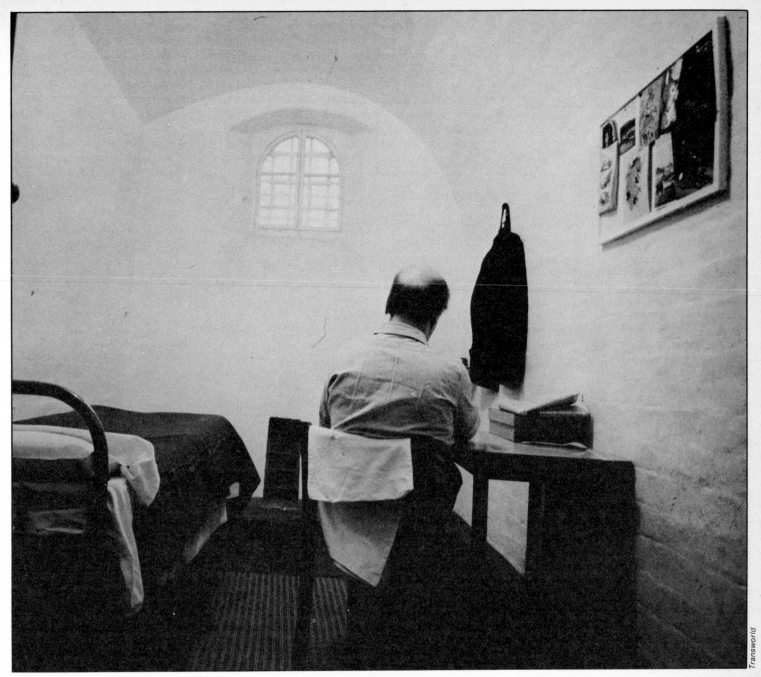

between the sexes. Tall men stand closer to people than small men but women do the opposite—the taller they are, the farther away they stand.

This seems due to the old concepts of male superiority: men want to look down on others when they are talking if they possibly can. By standing farther away, shorter men do not have to look up so much. Women, on the other hand, are expected to look up, so the tall woman moves farther away so she does not dominate.

The amount of personal territory we have is also related to status, and we can see this at work in a typical office situation. Generally the bigger the office, the more powerful the man. You can also gauge the relative status of business colleagues by how close they stand to each other. A junior going into the boss's office is ex-

pected to "keep his distance." But if the boss goes into *his* office, it is perfectly alright for him to lean over his employee's chair and even rest an arm on his shoulder.

Everywhere we go, we unconsciously divide up our surroundings and annex part of them as our personal territory. Take a man going into a restaurant to dine alone. If he is given an empty table which seats two, he will automatically divide its space in two. If another solitary diner joins him, he will be expected to keep to his half of the table. If he spreads out too much, by pushing his elbow, his plate or his cigarette pack across the invisible dividing line, the first man will begin to feel uneasy, under attack. His territory, his privacy, has been invaded.

One fascinating aspect of modern

The more violent the prisoner, the less he likes people around him. His "personal space" is very wide.

territorial behavior occurs in the automobile. Once behind the wheel, we extend our private territory to a shell around the whole car. If another motorist gets too close, we again feel that we are being invaded. Because the car has also given us a much bigger personal space, we also tend to feel more powerful when we are in our cars. This feeling of power goes to our heads: it is surprising how much more aggressive even the mildest-mannered man becomes when he gets behind the wheel of a car.

As the world, and particularly our cities, become more crowded, everyone's territory is increasingly invaded. Everyday, in the office, on the bus or train, in the restaurant or bar, we are continually having to make adjustments to our territorial concepts simply because there just is not enough space for each of us to have the territory we want. This, it seems, is one of the major factors which adds to the stress and tension of urban life.

The science of proxemics is still in its infancy but it has already given us clues about some of the reasons for antisocial behavior. Certain types of criminals, particularly those whose crimes have a strong antisocial element such as psychopaths, seem often to have a much stronger sense of territory than the average. If their space is invaded they tend to lash out violently to defend it.

Keep Your Distance

A New York researcher, for example, recently carried out an experiment with 15 volunteer prisoners—8 with a history of violence and 7 without. Each stood in an empty room while the experimenter slowly approached them. They had to cry "stop" when the experimenter came too close. The experiment was repeated many times and each man was found to have a distinct bubble of personal space.

But the violent criminals had body "buffer zones" which extended twice as far as those of the nonviolent men. When someone came too close, they felt as though the intruder was "looming up" or "rushing in." The researcher also said that these men went into "an unreal panic" when anyone invaded their larger-than-normal body zones. Such work is beginning to help us understand some of the reasons why violent crime is proportionately more prevalent in overcrowded areas.

Posture also plays a significant role in nonverbal communication. How people sit or stand or the position of their arms and legs also gives us clues about what they are thinking or feeling. It also explains how some people seem able to dominate a room without saying a word or moving a muscle.

This brand of nonverbal signaling is seen at its best in sexual encounters, in "boy meets girls" situations. Some men seem able to communicate their interest in a girl, to clear the way easily for flirting, much better than others. How do they do it? At the same time women may signal that they are interested and open to advances or that they are just "not interested." What are these signals?

The classic male sexual pose is called the "Western gunfighter." The man stands with his legs apart, his hips thrust slightly forward and his thumbs thrust into his belt, or pockets, with the fingers pointing towards his genitals. He is emphasizing his sensuality and masculinity.

But the true ladies' man, says body language expert Dr. Julius Fast, does much more than this. He has "an uncanny instinct for sizing up a woman's defensive body language and insistently breaking it down. Are her arms clasped defensively? He opens his. Is her posture rigid? He relaxes as they talk. Is her face pinched and drawn? He smiles and loosens his facial muscles."

When he has broken down her defenses "his next step is physical invasion, but physical invasion without touch. He cuts into the woman's territory or body zone. He comes close enough to make her uneasy, and yet not close enough for her to be able to logically object."

He follows this up by visual invasion as they talk: "What they say doesn't matter much. His eyes do far more talking than his voice. They linger on a woman's throat, on her breasts, on her body."

Until very recently it was expected that in sexual encounters, the man was the hunter and the woman the hunted. Women therefore had to attract the male, but at the same time society demanded that "nice" girls were not too blatant about displaying their charms or advertising their availability to men.

Sex Signals

Nowadays, with more equality between the sexes, women can use more overt sexual signals—like sitting with their legs apart, stroking their thighs as they talk, sitting "too close for comfort," thrusting forward breasts, pouting lips and so on. Many of these gestures are conscious and artificial—and if they are overdone, they can frighten off the sensitive male. Nonetheless, some of the old taboos remain, and many girls will exhibit the classic "I'm not interested" signals—tightly crossed legs and arms, for example—even though they do not really mean them.

Skilled interpretation is needed to see whether they express true emotions or whether they are just defensive reactions conditioned by society. The skilled ladies' man attacks with his own nonverbal signals to knock the defenses off balance and find out what the girl is really thinking.

As two people really begin to communicate, their body language becomes integrated too. They begin to unconsciously imitate each other's gestures and postures. If one has his legs crossed the other may follow suit—and they will probably cross their legs so that their knees are pointing towards each other.

Body posture is not solely about sex. We express other emotions too. It is intriguing how the words we use to describe feelings are in fact describing facts about the body. We say someone's nerves are "tense." In fact it is the muscles that are tense and this shows in the way they sit or stand and the position of their arms and hands. And an "uptight" locked-posture—where a person sits huddled up with arms and legs tightly crossed—often indicates a "locked-up" introverted mind.

The Busy Body

Knowledge of body language can be useful in helping those with mental problems which stem from their difficulties in meeting and talking to people. By teaching them to be more relaxed in their bodies, by explaining the techniques of physically "opening up," we can help to remove the tension and the withdrawal which is going on in their minds.

Knowledge about this nonverbal communication can be useful for the rest of us too. When meeting someone we can display our interest, our openness to their ideas, with the appropriate gestures to reinforce our words. We can show that they are truly welcome.

This is not done by artificially mimicking gestures or facial expressions. When we examine certain body signals we look at them in isolation, but body language is a complex amalgam of hundreds of different positions, postures, arm and hand movements, eye and mouth expressions. But if we begin consciously to use some of them to demonstrate our feelings, and if we genuinely maintain our interest in the other person, then all the other body signals will follow. And body communication will certainly make for a fuller more stimulating life.

The last word properly belongs to Dr. Fast, who has been delving into this fascinating subject for many years. In his classic book, *Body Language*, he says, "You've been playing the game of body language unconsciously all of your lifetime. Now start playing it consciously. Break a few rules and see what happens. It will be surprising, and sometimes a bit frightening and perhaps funny, but I promise you it won't be dull."

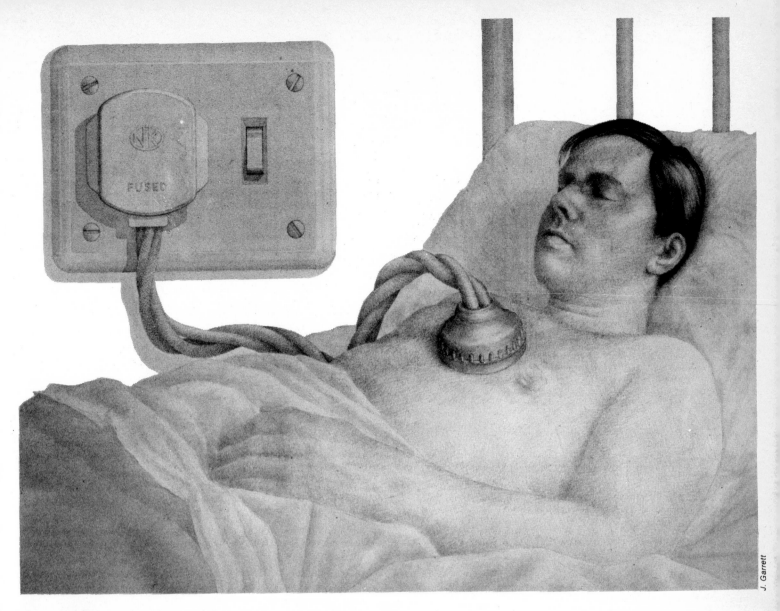

J. Garrett

Lifesavers

In this technological age, what could be more natural than keeping a man alive beyond his expected life span with the aid of a machine? But who is to decide when to switch off the life-support system that is holding a mere vegetable just this side of death?

Modern medical technology has given doctors enormous powers over life and death. With his sophisticated—and often very expensive—machines, a doctor can literally snatch back from the grave someone who, without the aid of such a machine, would undoubtedly have died.

He can maintain heartbeat, breathing and other vital body functions when, because of accident, disease or sudden breakdown, the patient's own life-support systems just cannot cope on their own.

Of course, machines do not give doctors absolute power over death.

Everyone still has to die sometime. But the machine can often help to postpone it or to support the body through an emergency until it has recovered sufficiently to take over on its own again.

Machines can play a vital role in three main areas of medicine. First is the rescuing of babies, especially those born prematurely, who are too weak or sickly to survive on their own. Machines like incubators can save and support them through their difficult first few hours, days or weeks.

Secondly, there are machines for people suffering from long-term prob-

lems, like kidney disease or the after effects of polio. The kidney machine, which washes the blood clear of deadly impurities, has to be used two or three times a week by sufferers whose own kidneys have failed. And the "iron lung" takes over the mechanics of breathing for patients whose own breathing muscles have failed.

Thirdly come the machines used in emergencies, especially those that can maintain heartbeat and/or breathing after a serious accident or heart attack.

The first category of machines pose few ethical problems, unless the baby is also born so seriously damaged that it has little or no chance of a normal life. The basic life-support system here is the incubator. The name comes from the Latin verb meaning "to hatch," and the baby's incubator works on the same principle as those warm boxes used to make eggs hatch into chicks. Basically the incubator is a device for maintaining a constant temperature around a newborn baby. For babies have much more difficulty in maintaining body temperature than do adults, because their surface area is much larger in proportion to their volume. And the body cannot go on functioning if the temperature drops too low.

Matter of Life and Death

Most babies manage well as long as they are kept warm, but weak babies just cannot cope. In the incubator, air is pumped in at a constant temperature: the smaller and weaker the baby, the warmer the air. The incubator is usually a "sealed unit." The air is pumped in over a thermostatically controlled heating element and the carbon dioxide is pumped out. The top is a clear plastic dome so that doctors, nurses—and parents—can see the child, and there are normally portholes in the side, with plastic gloves sealed into them, so that nursing can be carried out without opening the incubator. As well as being warmed, the air is also moistened, and sometimes babies who are having difficulty breathing or have poor circulation also have a little extra oxygen added to the air supply.

There is much more to incubation, however, than merely maintaining a warm air supply, and new techniques have been introduced which mean that hundreds of babies a year who only a decade or so ago would have had little or no chance of survival are now being saved. One recent case, for example, involved a three-month premature baby who was only a few inches long at birth and weighed just 16 ounces. Her heart and breathing stopped soon after she was born, but a nurse revived her and she was put into a high-oxygen incubator. She had been given only a one in ten chance of survival, but in three months she was fit enough to be taken out.

According to one leading pediatrician: "One of the great advances in recent years is in incubation. We can now, for example, control the temperature in incubators much more precisely to meet the baby's needs. We've evolved new techniques for

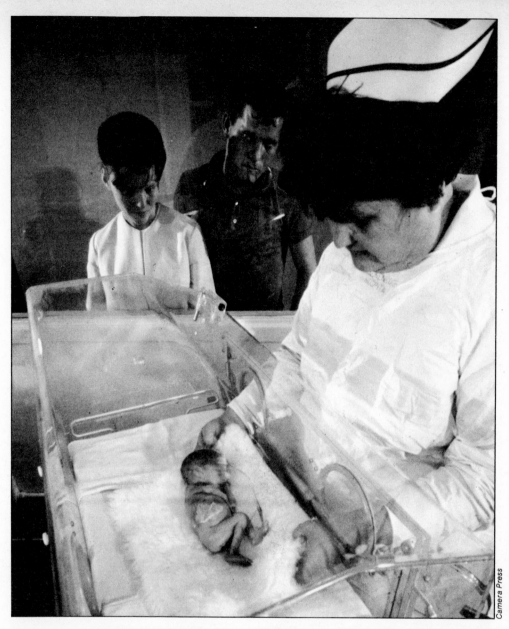

Camera Press

Every year incubators save the lives of thousands of premature babies who would be too fragile to survive on their own. The basic incubator works on the same principle as those warm boxes which are used to make eggs hatch into chicks.

clearing liquid out of the lungs and out of the stomach. And we've also got lots of monitoring systems which continually watch things like heartbeat and breathing. If anything goes wrong, lights start flashing and bells start ringing automatically."

British technicians have developed a special mattress which fits into incubators and moves slightly every time the baby breathes. If there is no movement for just 15 seconds, an alarm sounds—and the doctors and nurses can take swift lifesaving action. A new device also being tested could save the lives of most, if not all, of the thousands of babies who still die every year from a mysterious illness called

"respiratory distress syndrome," in which babies just stop breathing for no apparent cause. The device looks like a small spaceman's helmet and it fits snugly over the baby's head to provide just enough oxygen at the right pressure to maintain breathing.

Among the most distressing illnesses are those which cripple and kill healthy young adults. Poliomyelitis and kidney disease are two cases in point. But here, too, modern machines can save and maintain life. Due to mass immunization, polio is mercifully no longer the scourge it once was. In fact in the developed countries it is now very rare and only a few cases are seen each year. There are, however, still hundreds of polio victims who need support because of the after-effects of the disease. In its severest form, polio can paralyze the breathing muscles. For the unfortunate victims of this sort of polio, breathing must be constantly maintained with the help of an iron lung.

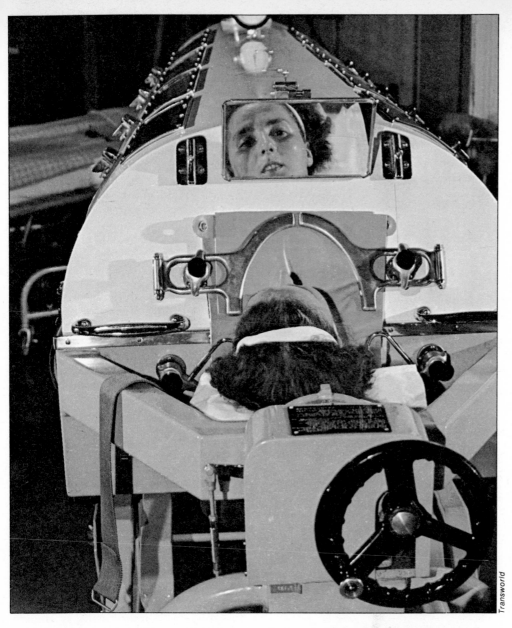
Transworld

They are much lighter and less bulky than iron lungs. The cuirass fits snugly around the middle of the body, with airtight rubber seals at top and bottom. The pressure between chest wall and the jacket is altered by a small pair of bellows. Because the legs and arms are free and subject to normal atmospheric pressure, blood does flow into the chest during the breathing-in phase. Unfortunately, however, cuirasses are not as efficient as iron lungs and their use is generally restricted to those with less severe breathing difficulties who may need help only at night or for a few hours during the day.

Iron Lung

In some conditions the patient's respiratory muscles gradually improve over a period of time. So instead of having to spend 24 hours a day in an iron lung, they can come out for increasing periods and, with the aid of a breathing jacket, sit in a wheelchair and be able to move around more.

Because of improvements in the iron lung, polio victims can live for many years but, of course, being "locked in" and wholly dependent on the machine creates enormous psychological problems. Many victims, however, show surprising degrees of courage and a capacity to remain cheerful and interested in life, despite their disabilities.

The most important job of our kidneys is to wash the blood free of impurities. If the kidneys are diseased, damaged or fail to function at all, these impurities will build up, poison the system and eventually kill the patient. We each have two kidneys and can manage quite well on one, so in many cases the answer is to transplant a kidney, either from a close relative or from a healthy person who has just died, say, from an accident. Kidney transplants are becoming more and more successful, but there are still many long-term difficulties to be overcome.

Many patients, however, are not suitable for transplantation or, because of the chronic shortage of donors, may have to wait a long time before a suitable kidney becomes available. For them the lifesaving answer is a kidney machine, also known as an artificial kidney or dialyzer.

There are many different designs of machine, but all work on the same basic principles. Blood is taken out of an artery and pumped through the machine which contains a special arrangement of plastic coils or plates in which the blood passes over a

Iron lungs were first developed in the United States in 1929, by Professor P. Drinker, a Harvard engineer. They are also known as tank respirators or Drinker respirators. The patient is enclosed in an airtight tank, with only his head protruding. Air is pumped out of the tank, lowering the pressure around the patient's chest and allowing it to expand. The lungs can then be filled with air breathed in through the nose or mouth. The pressure in the tank is regulated so that the chest expands just enough to allow the lungs to fill with air. Then it is increased again to the same as—or slightly above—the outside air pressure. The chest contracts, forcing the patient to breathe out. This "breathing cycle" is repeated at a rate of 18 to 25 times a minute—about the same as normal breathing.

The trouble with iron lungs is that the patient's life-style is severely curtailed and the machine is very cumbersome. It also poses long-term physio-

An iron lung is an airtight tank: Air pumped out of the tank lowers the pressure around the chest and allows it to expand just enough for the lungs to fill with air. When the pressure is increased, the chest contracts and the patient breathes out.

logical, as well as psychological, problems. Normal breathing also helps the circulation: during breathing in, blood is pulled into the chest. Because almost the whole body is enclosed in the iron lung the reduced pressure during the breathing-in phase affects the whole circulatory system and the extra blood does not get to the chest. And during the breathing-out phase, blood flow to the heart is actually reduced.

Because of these difficulties, medical researchers have developed new breathing-support devices which just fit over the chest and abdomen. They are called cuirasses (from the medieval chest armor) or breathing jackets.

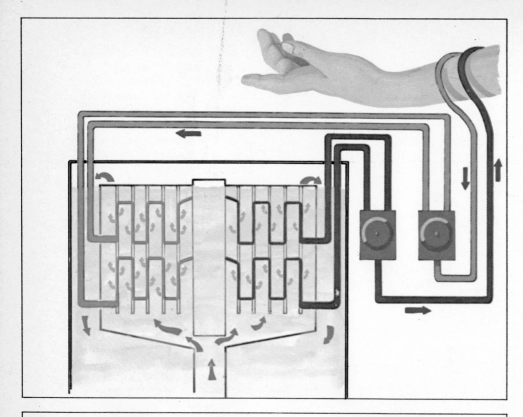

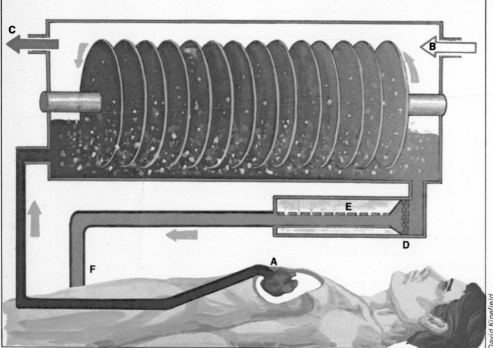

David Kinefield

Top: Cross section of a kidney machine. Blood is drawn from an artery and pumped through cellophane plates in sugar-saline solution. This process removes impurities and the cleansed blood is passed back into an artery. Above: Heart-lung machines oxidize the blood. "Used" blood is pumped from the heart (A). Oxygen is added to the blood (B) and carbon dioxide is drawn off (C). The blood is filtered to remove clots and bubbles (D) and cooled to allow a slower heartbeat (E). It is then returned to the body through a principal artery.

special fluid which washes out the impurities. The cleansed blood is then passed back into the body through a vein. The cleansing process takes several hours and many circulations of blood through the machine. Nowadays, kidney patients have special catheters (small plastic tubes) permanently attached to an artery and vein so they can easily link up with the machine. And instead of having to go to the hospital they can have their own artificial kidney at home.

There are still, however, problems with kidney machines, not least the risk of infection, through contamina-tion of the blood as it goes through the machine or because of the passage of germs through the catheters into the body. Obviously scrupulous hygiene has to be observed.

Nonetheless many patients with severe kidney disease who would otherwise have died can now survive many years because of their machine. They normally use it twice a week—either at home or in a special hospital unit—and each "blood washing" session lasts about 10 to 14 hours. The process is usually carried out at night while the patient is asleep, to cause the least possible disruption to his life. In fact kidney patients can live almost normal lives apart from their twice-weekly session on the machine. They have to be careful about their diets and to avoid injury or infection to the catheters.

Do-it-yourself Kidneys

One of the biggest problems, how-ever, is the shortage of machines and, of equal if not greater importance, of trained personnel to run the units, supervise the blood-washing sessions, and maintain the machine. Of course, more and more patients are treating themselves at home, using their own machines—and this substantially reduces the number of trained staff needed. But in a great many places where medical resources are already fully stretched, there just will not be enough money or manpower to pro-vide machines for everyone who could benefit.

So often doctors face the terrible dilemma of literally having to decide on life or death between two patients. How can they work out which life is more worthwhile? To try to help solve such problems one American kidney machine pioneer, Dr. Belding Scribner of Seattle, set up a panel of lay people to aid his assessment of patients. But few other units have followed suit. The doctors found there were so many medical and psychological factors to be taken into consideration that only they, with their intimate knowledge of the patient, could really make the best-informed and fairest decisions.

In the distant future we may well develop cheaper, more efficient, con-tinuously operating machines, per-haps even ones totally implanted in the body. But this is not going to be easy and such machines are unlikely to be developed for several decades.

With another modern life-support system, however, there are far fewer problems, because here the device *can* be implanted and it works con-tinuously. It is the cardiac pacemaker,

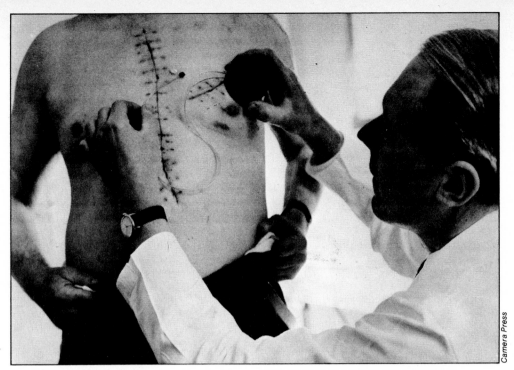

a device which gives tiny electric shocks, either to start up a heart that has stopped or to keep hearts which beat spasmodically pulsating regularly.

The first type is used in intensive care units to revive patients, usually after a heart attack.

The second type is an implanted device—about the size of a cigarette pack. It is used to treat a condition called heart block in which a patient's heart beats irregularly and flags easily; this can cause sudden fainting fits which could be fatal. There are two variations of this second type. In one, the battery-powered pacemaker sends out regular tiny electric currents at a rate of some 70 a minute which stimulate the heart muscle to expand and contract properly. In the other, the device picks up the patient's own nervous signals and makes sure they are delivered to the right place in the heart. So its electrical signals are regulated by the patient's own nervous system; this type of device is known as a "demand" pacemaker.

One of the problems, however, is that the batteries do not last forever, and an operation is needed every two years or so to replace them. New techniques are being evolved, however, to recharge the batteries from outside the body by radio waves. And smaller, more reliable longer-lasting batteries have been developed which are powered by a tiny pellet of radio-active plutonium—the nuclear fuel used in the latest atomic power stations. These should last at least ten years and further improvements may even last a lifetime.

A cardiac pacemaker is inserted into the left side of the chest. It "shocks" the heart into action with about 70 current impulses per minute. Thin cables transmit the impulses to platinum electrodes fastened to the heart muscles.

The most sophisticated lifesaving and life-support systems are brought together in intensive care units, which can now be found in many big general hospitals in the developed countries. The units, as the name implies, are merely areas where special care and attention can be concentrated on critically ill patients. Most often they are for those who have just had a heart disease crisis, but there are intensive care units for premature babies or severely injured road accident victims, for example, as well.

Many patients suffering a heart attack die before reaching the hospital and of those who do get there, 60 percent die in the first two days from another attack. A heart patient in an intensive care unit is connected to an oscilloscope which gives a continuous picture of the heart's rhythmic activity. Changes in the pattern can give early warning of trouble, such as complete heart block. Remedial action, like the use of a pacemaker, can then be taken.

A common emergency is ventricular fibrillation—when the heart muscles simply twitch rapidly and blood is not pumped. It can kill in three minutes. The constant monitoring of the oscilloscope means that prompt, life-saving treatment can be given with a machine called a defibrillator which passes a direct electrical current across the heart to restore normal beating.

As well as the oscilloscope, on hand by each intensive care unit bed are an outlet for oxygen, a suction point in case the lungs need to be cleared as in some respiratory diseases, and electrical points for such things as X-ray equipment or an electrocardiograph (ECG) machine, which gives a trace of the heart's changing electrical patterns as it beats.

Nearby might be a "resuscitation trolley" containing drugs and apparatus to restore normal heartbeat and breathing. These include the defibrillator and a "ventilator"—a machine for blowing air, or air enriched with oxygen, into the lungs.

There are many types of "breathing machines" which can be used in an emergency, but they are all basically very simple. The air is pumped (by hand or electrical power) through a tube which is passed down the mouth and larynx.

In cases where people have a long-term breathing difficulty, perhaps because of a serious accident, a tracheotomy may be carried out. Here the trachea (windpipe) is opened so that a tube can be passed directly into it to aid breathing.

The Price of Life

We now have a machine—the heart-lung machine—which can take over the vital tasks of both pumping the blood around the body and breathing in life-giving oxygen. But the heart-lung machine can be used for only a few hours because it damages the blood passing through it. So its use is generally reserved for "open heart" surgery when the heart *must* be stopped for several hours. The heart-lung machine is basically a pump, a device for mixing oxygen into the blood, removing carbon dioxide, and filtering the blood returning to the patient to remove clots and bubbles.

It is obvious, then, that modern machines can be wonderfully effective in saving and maintaining the lives of people who would otherwise have died. But in their turn, they create many long-term problems, particularly if they mean that a person is going to be dependent on a machine —like an iron lung or a kidney machine —for the rest of his life. There are difficulties, too, when machines maintain a semblance of life in people who, were the machine to be switched off, would never recover to anywhere near what we consider "normal," either mentally or physically.

J. Garrett

To fit the crime

Imprisonment for an antisocial act is all very well, but sooner or later comes the time of release and the moment of truth. For what has jail done to cure the criminal? If nothing, then the exercise has largely failed. Clearly it is not enough just to shut a man away.

"In order to reform a criminal, you must first break his spirit." That was the nineteenth century verdict of Elam Lynds, warden of Sing Sing, echoing the widely felt sentiment that prison was, first and foremost, a place of punishment.

George Bernard Shaw was one of the few enlightened thinkers who realized that there was no cure to be found in prison, and he accused so-called "reformers" of having "made the neglect, oppression, corruption and physical torture of the old common jail the pretext for transforming it into the diabolical den of torment, mischief and damnation, the modern model prison."

The self-congratulation and complacency with which the creators of the "modern model prison" have rewarded themselves have served

only to compound the chief disgrace of those institutions. All too often they provide a hide-all-cure-all for the public conscience and a scapegoat for public morality. Believing itself progressive, the enlightened community likes also to believe that the carpet under which it sweeps its problems is of the very latest weave.

In this context, no statement threatens greater evil within society than the comment delivered on the American 1966 Manual of Correctional Standards: "It permits us to linger, if we will, at the gates of correctional Valhalla—with an abiding pride in the sense of a job superbly done! We may be proud, we may be satisfied, we may be content." What the price of that content may be in terms of human futility it is difficult to guess.

A Government White Paper issued

in Great Britain lays down two criteria for the prison service, armed with which, it is to be supposed, the prisons may effect a cure of some kind. "First, it is the task of the service, under the law, to hold those committed to custody and to provide conditions for their detention which are currently acceptable to society. Second, in dealing with convicted offenders, there is an obligation on the service to do all that may be possible within the currency of the sentence to encourage and assist them to lead a good and useful life."

Society has never liked to inquire too deeply into prison conditions and even today there seems little doubt, from the volume of material wrested from the prison services of the United States and Europe, that they are not satisfactory. That is to say, conditions seldom appear to encourage the prisoner to take an interest in life—presumably a prerequisite to his rehabilitation. Nor do they eradicate the roots of his disaffection with society.

Gross overcrowding and unhygienic facilities are only a small part of a story often told and still in existence in many prisons. The latchkey image of the screws (prison officers), the school of criminality that prison provides, the sense of betrayal, the boredom, loneliness and sheer futility of prison, these are still the paramount influences of time inside.

Marked Man

The end result, for a variety of complex reasons, is that at the conclusion of his sentence, whatever his crime, the prisoner's punishment, cure, or whatever you may consider it is not itself ended. It is impossible for the prisoner to pay his debt to society and, as is implied in the theory of a prison sentence, wipe clean his slate. He will carry with him back to civilian life not only his experience of confinement, the nurtured resentment, acquaintance with other criminals, and sense of isolation, but he will meet in civilian life with the resentment of the community to which he returns.

As one ex-prisoner notes, the community, while quite prepared to take in an orphan or a refugee or pay visits to sick old ladies, will be a great deal more wary of someone who has been in prison. Clearly, then, society is well aware that the "cure" is unlikely to have been successful"; and, reciprocally, the reaction of society to the ex-prisoner, prompted by that awareness, ensures that the rehabilitation has little hope of being successful.

Aware of this problem, reformers are now making attempts to "open" the conventionally closed prison, in order to offer the prisoner something more than making mailbags or license plates. In order to fit the criminal for the "afterlife," San Quentin offers typewriting, dentistry and landscape gardening; in Britain, Coldingley prison offers some training in light engineering. The Helmut Ziegner Universal Foundation in Germany offers an industrial wage for factory work (which is strongly resented by the local community). Other prisons have followed suit, providing the prisoner with money for the upkeep of his family, to save for his release and, in certain cases, to repay his victim. Industrial interests fear the competition of these "subsidized businesses."

Weekend prison has been tried in West Germany, Belgium and South Africa. The offender serves his sentence in a series of installments, during which he is usually lectured on his misdemeanors. The advantage of this system is that the offender is not taken wholly out of the community—he can continue to pay his way and live with his family. But still the concept of "weekend prison" is almost laughable for many offenses. Yet —a more serious drawback—even part-time contact with prison inadequacies is enough to sour the offender on social institutions as a whole.

Other attempts to bring custodial treatment back into touch with normal life have included the use of work furloughs in the United States, whereby the offender is released during the day to pursue a job in the neighborhood and returns to detention in the evening. For longer-term prisoners at Tehachapi, in California, family weekends are arranged and special apartments are provided where prisoners can spend two or three weeks of summer vacation with their wives and children.

In Sweden, a prison has been built in the university town of Uppsala, to enable the prisoners to associate with the university and the students themselves to gain experience of and help with the prisoners. The American Project Newgate has similarities with this—offenders take part in the university and can earn a degree. These experiments, though inevitably meeting with the initial suspicion of the public, seem to leave hope for a reasonable degree of success.

Cost of Crime

At Ixtapalapa, in Mexico City, considerable attempts have been made to provide civilized accommodation for prisoners. In the prison for habitual offenders in Düren, West Germany, even these so-called hardened cases are given pleasant furniture and decoration for their rooms. At Malmö, in Sweden, therapy is provided by a team separate from those whose job is exclusively security; and Grendon, in England, provides professional medical and psychiatric care. At places like these it is possible to feel that positive action is being taken.

And positive action *is* needed to reduce the numbers of those in prisons. In West Germany, 83 in every 100,000 are in prison; in England and Wales there are something like 72 in every 100,000; in the United States there are nearly 200,000 prisoners, or 100 in every 100,000.

It costs $45 million a year in the United States merely to build the housing for the extra 4,500 anticipated prisoners and nearly half of those discharged revert to criminal careers within a year of their release—small evidence of any "cure." In Great Britain, it costs half an average year's wage to build a prison place for one man and an average week's wage to keep him for a week.

As well as human futility, there is financial futility in the prison system—an argument that might well carry more weight in the opinion of the reformers. In California, the counties are paid $4,000 for each offender taken off the prison list and maintained in the community on probation. These are real subsidies that are handed onto the probation service for constructive improvements. In Britain it may not cost more than the price of a half dozen packs of cigarettes a week to put a man on probation. It is reckoned that if the prison population of Britain were halved, something like £10,000,000 could be saved annually.

Radical Alternatives

At some stage or other, the public —that is, the individual in society—however reformist in principle has to admit that either they believe in reform only within the system of confinement, or that they are prepared to consider more radical alternatives. If the former, they will probably go along with such measures as parole, probation, detention centers, remand homes and so on; if the latter, they will probably quibble at what they consider to be the halfheartedness of such measures.

Still, parole is a well-tried system of rehabilitation and is recognized in most countries with a prison system. It consists of the early and conditional release of selected prisoners serving determinate sentences. Parole is highly sought after, and acceptance or refusal by the relevant parole board is a turning point in the prisoner's sentence. Great care is taken in the selection of those eligible.

Probation is another universally adopted system of rehabilitation. Begun in the last century in the United States—probation offers a chance for the offender to prove his ability to readjust to society under the care and with the help of a probation officer. A term of probation may be ordered by the court instead of a prison sentence. Sometimes the offender is sent to a special hostel, which provides a base for him and some kind of supervision; more often he may continue in the

community under the observation of the probation officer.

There are serious weaknesses in the system and it is argued that probation officers are too inclined to work solely with the individual, when they should be working equally with the community into which they are trying to reestablish the offender. The officer may also become too much like the prison guard, not the guiding hand; alternatively he may not be available when he is most wanted—in Denmark and Sweden, among other places, where the majority of the probation officers are voluntary, this could be an especial hazard.

Probation hostels, day training centers, homes of one sort or another, suspended sentences—in the United States, Britain, Germany, Holland, Scandinavia and elsewhere, these are attempts to base the offender within the surrounding community, with the idea that this temporary measure might provide a stepping stone for

San Quentin prison—an old-style jail where cell doors are opened by remote control for a count of heads while the guard stands safely at a distance from the convicts.

his rehabilitation into that community.

Holland has only 22 in every 100,000 in prison, and in 1972 had only 25 women in prison. It has achieved this comparatively low figure by its preparedness to experiment, the wide facilities it provides for the many different types of offender, and its realistic spending on the prevention of delinquency. The public prosecutor even has the power to waive proceedings against adults if, in his opinion, it will serve no purpose to bring them before the court. There is no bail system, no associated financial penalties, and damages can be awarded if it is proved that a person has been wrongly held in custody. Small psychiatric centers, such as the Van der Hoeven Clinic in Utrecht, are tak-

ing the place of the conventional prison.

In Copenhagen, they have gone a stage further. The Kofoeds Skole is a day center with voluntary self-enrolling attendance for the socially deprived—a sincere attempt to prevent crime by doing something about the prospective criminal before he resorts to the criminal act. Britain is still a long way behind other countries in its thinking, but there has been an attempt to create a clinic similar in function to the Kofoeds Skole in the form of the Inner London Center.

Britain has also fallen short on its vaunted "detoxification" centers. These were intended to provide facilities for those whose major crime is a drink problem, and as such they were a genuine attempt to provide a cure. Decreed under the 1972 Criminal Justice Act, nothing has as yet been done about them in Britain, while in California there are several centers already in operation.

Daily Telegraph

One idea that so far has not succeeded in the United States, because of the suspicions of the public with regard to it, is known as New Careers. This provides opportunities for offenders themselves to help in rehabilitating other offenders and applying themselves to a variety of social work called Community Service Orders in Britain. This program provides that anyone over the age of 17 can be given anything up to 240 hours unpaid labor in service to the community, as an alternative to custody.

More far-reaching in concept—and more hopeful in terms of "cure"—is the Neighborhood Council, which, in theory still, invests responsibility for the criminal in local communities. This concept leans toward the Chinese method of maintaining the offender in the community, which takes upon itself the burden of reconditioning its recalcitrant member. It is yet to be seen how this concept will work in fact in Western society.

But penal reform can be less harsh and more constructive. Here a prisoner is serving a sentence of community service and pays for his crime by helping out at a youth club.

One thing is sure—there are plenty of organizations eager to offer what help they can within the present penal system or determined to change that system in order to provide some sort of cure. For example, in Israel, where there is no serious stigma attached to the ex-prisoner, there is the League of Societies for the Rehabilitation of Offenders.

In New York, there are START (Short Term Adolescent Resident Training program) and STAY (Short Term Aid to Youth). In Los Angeles, there are RODEO (Reduction Of Delinquency through Expansion of Opportunity) and COYOP (Community Orientated Youthful Offender Program). Minnesota has community-based drug treatment programs.

Britain has NACRO (National Association for the Care and Resettlement of Offenders), concerned as much for the care of offenders as for the prevention of crime. It acts as a pressure group, a central agency for other interested bodies, and a public relations office to involve the public and overcome the community's suspicions with regard to the offender. Numerous other projects are also in existence and prisoners and ex-convicts have their own organizations.

Ultimately, the cure of the criminal rests with society—his cure can only be a two-way reconciliation. Nothing is gained by taking the offender out of the community, unless he is a danger to it. Wrestling responsibility from the judiciary and vesting it in the community ensures that the criminal is reconciled with those whom he has offended and that the society which has laid the grounds for his offense is made acutely aware that it can never hold itself totally blameless.

All you want to know about...

Zip Art

Q WHAT ARE VITAMINS?

A If any word in the vast topic of food and nutrition has been misunderstood it is the word "vitamin." Once again popular misconceptions about vitamins have led to hundreds of best-selling books which, in one way or another, play on people's basic ignorance of how the body works.

For two hundred years or so people interested in nutrition have realized that the health of the body is not dependent simply upon shoveling a certain amount of food into it every day. A "balanced diet" is needed. But what exactly constitutes a balanced diet? People responsible for supplying the crew of sailing ships in the eighteenth century, which would often be months away from port and fresh food supplies, realized that, even though there appeared to be ample food on board to keep the sailors free from hunger, many became subject to curious wasting diseases—scurvy was a particularly good example—which often cleared up as soon as the ship received fresh provisions on arriving at her destination. Naval doctors became convinced that there must be some substances present in land-based diets which were simply missing from a sailor's

provisions, and great efforts were made to try to discover what these substances could be. On his long voyage to New Zealand in the 1750s, Captain Cook supplemented his sailor's "beef and biscuits" diet with the juice of limes and lemons, which he had bottled before leaving port, and found that few of his crew fell victims to the dreaded scurvy. The discovery led to an increasing interest in the "hidden" constituents in food. Among the first essential constituents to be identified were the minerals—calcium, for one—but it was not until 1910 that a chemist named Casimir Funk identified another important set of "invisible" constituents—chemical substances known as *amines.* Realizing that there were a large number of these substances which needed to be taken into the body in food, Funk christened them "vita-amines," which soon became corrupted to vitamines. As chemistry advanced Funk's discovery was confirmed, but it was also found that they were not amines after all, but a variety of very different chemicals and the "e" was dropped.

WHICH ARE THE MOST USEFUL VITAMINS?

Shortly after Funk had made his first rather misleading discovery, as each new "vita-amine" was discovered, it

was labeled with a letter of the alphabet—A, B, C, D and so on. Presumably we should by now have got to vitamins X, Y and Z had chemists not in the meanwhile discovered that they were not really dealing with a large group of rather similar amines, as had been thought, but rather a huge range of chemically distinct substances. The first recognition of this was when the so-called B-complex vitamins were broken down and given separate numbers. Today many vitamins have been precisely described chemically and have their own names—vitamin B_1 is thiamine; vitamin C is ascorbic acid, and so on. Perhaps in due course this kind of identification will lead to the eventual disappearance of the word "vitamin," but we usually stick to the old lettering since this is how the substances are most popularly known. The most useful vitamins so far identified are vitamins A, C, D, E, K, and a number of the B vitamins.

WHY DO WE NEED VITAMINS?

It is one thing to know that we need vitamins and another to know *why* we need them. Proper understanding of their role in our body chemistry has begun to emerge only in the last few years. Though they each have a slightly different job to do, their chief function seems to be to act like the protein enzymes to assist in those microscopic chemical changes which constitute metabolism and which relate to the growth and repair functions of the system. The important point to recognize is that, while vitamins are essential to body function, they are not incorporated into the body as most proteins, starches and minerals are, but rather are used as aids to make the body work. A fairly useful analogy is to think of the body as being an enormously elaborate piece of machinery needing constant delicate adjustment to keep it in tune. The vitamins can be seen as the specialist wrenches and screwdrivers which allow this sensitive tuning to take place. These tools, then have very different tasks to perform—so different, in fact, that grouping them all under one collective noun "vitamins" is a bit misleading. Nevertheless most nutritional experts accept that we are stuck with the word and feel now that it is too late to change. One of the main differences among the vitamins —apart from what they actually do— is the way in which they are absorbed into the body, and here it is possible to classify them into two groups— water soluble and fat soluble. Water soluble are absorbed quickly into the bloodstream through the wall of the stomach after they have been ingested in the form of food; the fat soluble, however, cannot be extracted by the body from the parent food without the presence of fats of one kind or another. It is for this reason that a certain proportion of fat is necessary to our diet and that the role of fats is not simply to provide energy.

WHAT HAPPENS IF OUR DIET DOES NOT CONTAIN AN ADEQUATE SUPPLY OF VITAMINS?

If the diet is short of vitamins the system becomes progressively less efficient in the growing and repairing of its own tissue. This can lead to a number of symptoms and diseases, most of which can be cured dramatically by the administration of the appropriate vitamin. There are five major diseases of this kind, all of which were common in the nineteenth century, but most of which have been eradicated from Western societies and are now seen only in parts of the world where food is short. These are beriberi B₁ deficiency); pellagra (vitamin B); scurvy (vitamin C): xerophthalmic conjunctivitis (vitamin A); and rickets (vitamin D). It cannot be emphasized too strongly that these diseases, which are extremely un-pleasant, are almost completely non-existent in Europe and the United States these days, as almost all modern Western diets provide an adequate supply of vitamins. One of the few exceptions to this is the case of chronic alcoholism—a distressingly common Western affliction—which is often accompanied by a vitamin B deficiency due to the suffers' high intake of energy in the form of alcohol and their corresponding disinclination to eat solid food.

WHAT IS VITAMIN A AND WHAT DOES IT DO?

Vitamin A has a number of very important functions, which include the maintenance of the mucous membranes which line the internal walls of the stomach, the lungs and the urogenital system. The main function of these membranes is to protect the tissues from infection and, as the eye and eyelids are external organs which particularly depend on these membranes, vitamin A deficiency can lead to a specially dangerous type of conjunctivitis or eye inflammation. The interior of the eye—in particular the sensitive layers of cells at the back of it known as the retina—also depends on vitamin A, and for this reason people whose jobs require superacute vision—such as fighter pilots—like to make sure that their diets contain ample supplies of vitamin A. It is not difficult to achieve for it is present in large amounts in butter and margarine, fatty fish—such as sardines and tuna—milk, cheese and eggs. It is also found in orange and yellow vegetables and fruits in the substance known as carotene. This has led to the common folk myth that eating great quantities of carrots will enable you to see in the dark. In fact, eating a large amount of carrots will reduce any vitamin A deficiency that you have, but even if you ate a ton of them, you could not improve your vision beyond the normal.

WHAT ARE THE B VITAMINS AND WHAT DO THEY DO?

It was once thought that vitamin B was a single entity, but later experiments showed that at least 12 different substances are involved. They all have rather similar functions and tend to appear in the same kinds of food, and for this reason it is convenient to call them the "B-complex vitamins." The three most important of these are B₁ (thiamine), B₂ (riboflavin) and a third, which was identified chemically as niacin before it was given a number. Thiamine is particularly useful in transferring oxygen to body tissues, in the utilization of carbohydrates and also in the buildup of the important substance known as RNA (ribonucleic acid). Riboflavin is particularly useful in carrying hydrogen throughout the body. Niacin also acts as a carrier for hydrogen and oxygen as well. All three are absolutely essential to the dynamic metabolic processes of the body, and for that reason it is fortunate that they are so profusely present in readily available foods. One other in this family—B₁₂— is worth mentioning because of the important task it has in the formation of red blood cells. An interesting fact about the B vitamins is that, unlike almost all the others which have to be ingested in food, the body can supply its own vitamin B, at least to a limited extent, as the result of synthesis by microorganisms in the intestines. This is not a very reliable source of supply, however, and it is seldom enough to look after the complete requirement of the body. The B-complex vitamins are abundantly supplied in meat (in particular liver and kidney), natural brown bread, eggs and cheese.

WHAT IS VITAMIN C AND WHAT DOES IT DO?

Vitamin C is one of the most important of the body's "fine tuners" and a regular supply is essential—somewhat more so than is the case for others because the body does not naturally store it. Its main role is in tissue formation and the metabolism of individual cells, and principal sources of supply are fruits and vegetables. Of these the citrus fruits are easily the most potent sources, with green and salad vegetables, such as cabbage, watercress and tomatoes, following not far behind. Most fruits and vegetables, such as apples, plums, carrots, lettuce and celery, are, despite what most people believe, rather low in C —or vitamins of any kind, for that matter. Another interesting fact is that the vitamin C content of fruit and vegetables begins to decline immediately after picking and falls off steadily during storage. It is further reduced during washing and may be destroyed entirely in the course of cooking. An essential part of any normal diet, therefore, is a good supply of fresh fruit and uncooked vegetables. Vitamin C has been the center of a major nutritional controversy surrounding the dietary theories advanced by the eminent scientist

Linus Pauling. He has argued that estimates of the vitamin C requirements of a healthy human being are too low, based on the ancient assessment going back to the origins of the quest for vitamins of what was required merely to prevent scurvy. He holds that massive doses of C not only prevent the individual from being subject to infection but actually serve to promote a state of super good health. Hundreds of thousands of people have taken up Pauling's ideas and treat themselves to large doses of the synthesized vitamin without apparently suffering any ill effects. How helpful these doses are is very arguable, and most dieticians believe that any beneficial effects may be psychological rather than physiological.

WHAT IS VITAMIN D AND WHAT DOES IT DO?

Apart from the proteins, carbohydrates, fats and vitamins which are essential to a healthy physique, the body also requires certain minerals to maintain its microstructure. One of the most important of these is calcium—the building block of bones and teeth, and the primary function of vitamin D is in assisting the extraction of calcium from food and in its subsequent integration into skeletal tissue. For this reason vitamin D is so important in the diets of young people and nursing mothers. A shortage of it at a time of maximum body growth can prevent calcium from being utilized properly, with resulting weaknesses and malformation of bone structure—in particular the unpleasant disease known as rickets. Most healthy adults, on the other hand, seem to be able to do without vitamin D altogether, though there is some evidence that with advancing age, and the softening of bones which goes hand in hand with aging, vitamin D supplies may be needed again. This vitamin comes in all fat fish—herrings, sardines, and so on—and in dairy produce of all kinds. But there is another interesting source of supply—sunlight. The play of sun on the skin allows the body to synthesize vitamin D as the result of the chemical changes which take place in surface tissues. Sunbathing has evidently more to commend it than getting a good tan!

WHAT IS VITAMIN E AND WHAT DOES IT DO?

Vitamin E is involved in one of the latest in a series of claims for miracle substances which promise to revolutionize human health and happiness. These claims seem to be based on some curious animal experiments conducted a few years ago which showed that in rats a good supply of vitamin E is essential for the fertility of the male and for the ability of the female to produce a healthy litter. This has led to a predictable spate of articles and books in which huge supplies of vitamin E are recommended as cures for just about every one of the many hundreds of possible sources of failure in the human reproductive system—ranging from infertility to impotence, and even hypersexuality. There is, in fact, little evidence at this time that vitamin E plays any kind of role at all in human fertility or sexual behavior, and any improvements in the latter following vitamin E rich diets are almost certainly psychological. This serves as a useful warning, however, not to apply uncritically findings discovered as the result of animal experimentation to human behavior. Rats and people, while similar in many respects, are not the same kind of animal. In fact the amounts of vitamin E required by the body are very, very small indeed, and the job it has to do is somehow related to the health of muscles and skin. We literally never come across cases of vitamin E deficiency in Western societies, and it is freely available in all vegetable products, meats and eggs—in fact, in practically every food.

WHAT IS VITAMIN K AND WHAT DOES IT DO?

This vitamin is an interesting one to know something about, not because any properly fed human being is likely to suffer from deficiencies of it—it is present in almost all foods, most notably in spinach and green beans—but because it helps to remind us of what vitamins actually *do* in the body. They are *not* incorporated into the system in the way that many of the proteins, fats, and minerals are to serve as building blocks *within* the system, but they are functional aids to make the system work and assist with its machinery of operation. In the case of vitamin K, this action is directed to allow blood to clot at wounds. For this reason it is often injected into the body to counteract the effects of any overdosage of anticoagulants given in treating coronary thrombosis and other disorders involving blood clotting. There is some suggestion that vitamin K, like vitamin B, can be produced within the body by intestinal bacteria. Incidentally, these vitamin-producing bacteria are often killed in large numbers by antibiotics taken to counter infection, and for this reason many doctors prescibe therapeutic doses of vitamins when patients are recovering from diseases which have been treated with antibiotics.

WHAT IS THE VALUE OF VITAMIN PILLS?

Many people are still confused—quite understandably—about what vitamins are and what they do, and they are not helped to any understanding by advertisements and "fad" books. Vitamin pills are not pep pills which confer super energy or supply wonderful substances not available in ordinary food. Neither can they ensure glowing health and a superlative physique. Most vitamin pills sold by reputable pharmaceutical companies contain balanced supplies of synthetic vitamins, sufficient to provide the average daily requirement for a normal adult. They merely ensure that people on inadequate diets—perhaps because work pressures make it difficult for them to take suitable meals—do not suffer from a shortage of these important nutrients. The body does not store great quantities of vitamins and it is therefore prudent to make certain that we get a proper supply each day. On the other hand, surpluses of vitamins are of no value whatsoever. The body has few facilities for storing them and any that are in excess of normal requirements are simply passed out in the excreta. Present evidence therefore strongly suggests that the taking of large amounts of vitamins is one of our most wasteful hobbies. The reason most people who take vitamin pills seem so healthy is that, if they are concerned enough about their diet to take the pills in the first place, they are probably doing all the right things anyway.

CAN YOU TAKE TOO MANY VITAMINS?

The answer is most definitely Yes. Although excess vitamins can be expelled from the body, there is a limit to what the system can do to rid itself of waste products. Very large amounts of niacin can produce dilation of blood vessels and may even damage the liver. Huge amounts of vitamin D can also produce unpleasant side effects, but as no one could possibly ingest toxic amounts of these substances in ordinary food, the danger can only come about from overuse of vitamin pills and other fad diets. There is one exception by which you *could* produce vitamin poisoning—through eating natural foods. The liver of both seals and polar bears contains huge concentrations of vitamin A, as many Arctic explorers have found to their cost. Eskimos have long considered the liver of these animals to be taboo. You might think it unnecessary to warn people of the dangers of taking too many vitamins, but unfortunately there is good evidence that many people do get obsessively involved with crank vitamin diets and suffer as a consequence. One English chemist, who should have known better, recently treated himself to an exclusive diet of carrot juice supplemented by huge doses of vitamin A. He died of vitamin A poisoning, his skin and body tissues a bright yellow from the massive amounts of carotene he had swallowed.

WHAT MINERALS ARE ESSENTIAL TO THE DIET?

A properly balanced diet needs—in addition to proteins, the energy-supplying fats and carbohydrates and the functionally important vitamins — small quantities of about twenty inorganic substances known as the minerals and trace elements. Unlike all the other essential nutrients, the minerals are not living forms themselves but are elements and compounds existing in a natural state in the environment and which the body utilizes as part of its total life system. The most important single mineral is iron, which is taken up in hemoglobin, the factor in red blood cells that causes them to transmit oxygen. Iron is present naturally in meat (especially liver and kidneys), eggs, bread and fresh vegetables. Iron deficiency—fairly rare in Western societies—can lead to the condition known as anemia. The most common manifestations of iron deficiency occur in women during pregnancy and occasionally where there is a good deal of blood loss in menstruation. Other mineral elements required are calcium and phosphorous, both of which are important in a large number of ways. Calcium phosphate is the principal building block of bones and teeth and calcium is also required for blood clotting. It is liberally supplied in milk and cheese and also occurs in drinking water in hard water areas. The main function of phosphorous is in assisting the release of energy from digested food. This mineral is also present in practically every food that we eat. Other important minerals include iodine, which has a controlling influence on the metabolism; fluorine, which is an important constituent of bone tissue and also helps to prevent tooth decay; cobalt, which helps to manufacture red blood cells; and copper, which is present with iron in hemoglobin. The last four minerals are required only in microscopic quantities and, if taken in large doses, are in fact, toxic. Cobalt, for example, used to be employed by a leading beer manufacturer to give a good head to canned beer, until it was responsible for the deaths of a number of very heavy beer drinkers in one town in Canada. Other essential minerals include the salts, such as sodium and potassium chloride. These are needed to maintain the right concentration of body fluids, the correct balance of which is essento cell function.

WHAT ARE THE OTHER ESSENTIAL NUTRIENTS?

The two remaining nutrients, which help to provide a balanced diet, are water and roughage. Between 60 and 70 percent of the human body is made up of water, so it is not surprising that we need a constant supply of it. It is the most vital of the substances taken into the body, and most people can only live a few days if deprived of it. Roughage is not a nutrient as such and really consists of indigestible parts of common foods, particularly wholemeal cereal, root vegetables and fresh fruits. These contain the fiber cellulose, which provides bulk in the intestine that in turn promotes peristalsis—rhythmic movements of the intestine allowing the expulsion of waste matter in the feces. Dieticians believe that many intestinal disorders and the build up of toxic substances as the result of chronic constipation are caused by man's shift from foods containing adequate supplies of roughage to predigested "soft" foods such as white bread, mashed potatoes and the like. For this reason a regular intake of cellulose-based food, while not nutritive in the strict sense of the word, nevertheless contributes to a healthy food regime.

WHAT IS THE MAIN CAUSE OF MALNUTRITION?

The simple answer to this might seem to be a shortage of any of the vital nutrients. This is certainly true for large parts of the world where most human beings unfortunately have to make do on hopelessly inadequate diets. In affluent Western societies it might seem as though malnutrition had been eliminated. Unfortunately this is not the case for, while shortages of proteins, energy foods, vitamins and so on are now indeed rare in Europe and the United States, malnutrition is rearing its head from a totally different direction. This is in the form known as obesity. A gross surplus of food, surprising though it may seem, can be as damaging to the body—and also to the psychology of the individual—as is a gross shortage. There is even evidence that obesity can lead to as many illnesses and disorders as can undernourishment. Both are equally tragic symptoms of malnutrition.

Canned food may be quick and easy, but in the end there is no substitute for fresh vegetables, fruit, cheese, and wholemeal cereals to provide a balanced diet.

Marshall Cavendish

J. Garrett

Gay abandon

Any enclosed, single-sex life-style fosters homosexuality—and prison viewed as punishment still tends to fail. Indeed prosecution and imprisonment are likely to reinforce a man's homosexuality even if it had previously been rarely indulged.

Punitive attitudes toward homosexuality have been common in many civilized societies, although it has been tolerated in many primitive societies. Britain did not repeal anti-homosexual laws until 1967—it is now legal between consenting adults (that is, over 21) in private. Most of the United States still have punitive laws, as have West Germany, Austria, Finland, East Germany, Cuba and Russia. In France, on the other hand, the Napoleonic code made it legal; and it is legal in such Latin countries as Italy, Spain and Greece.

Where homosexuality is illegal, it tends to create associated crime and neurotic or psychotic conditions. Liability to prosecution lays many homosexuals—and some "innocent

> The word "homosexual" comes not from the Latin word *Homo* ("man"), as is commonly supposed, but from the Greek *homos* meaning "same" and is therefore correctly applied either to men or to women.

bystanders"—open to threat, blackmail, robbery or violence, either from unscrupulous homosexuals or from irresponsible policemen.

The homosexual is peculiarly vulnerable. Moral repugnance felt by prosecuting policemen, the courts, and the public has sometimes permitted unsavory methods of prosecution and persecution of homosexuals. Before homosexual law reform in Britain,

homosexuals who were arrested were often advised to plead guilty, whether or not they were guilty of the charged offense, to avoid unpleasantness.

For the lonely, promiscuous male homosexual, public lavatories are an exceptional temptation. There is no equivalent female or intersexual place of exposure: a secret yet public place designed for males to expose their sex organ in the presence of others. But any man standing at the urinal who does not keep his eyes directly in front of him may be accused by a watching policeman of trying to solicit the man next to him, and he may find it difficult to refute so nebulous a charge against him.

Prosecution and imprisonment are likely to reinforce a man's homosexuality, even if it had previously been rarely indulged. Any enclosed, single-sex life-style fosters homosexuality. And prison viewed as punishment still tends to fail.

It has been shown that if an act has two consequences—a rewarding consequence and a punishing consequence—ability to resist the act will depend on the *order* in which the two consequences occur. If the punishing consequence comes first and the rewarding one later, this is likely to act as a deterrent. If the rewarding consequence comes first and the punishing one later, as it would with homosexual gratification, there is little likelihood of inhibition. Indeed, with certain types of homosexual, the illegality of the act is known to increase the excitement.

Cause Unknown

Shortly after arrest, many homosexuals will declare themselves eager for therapeutic treatment—sometimes because they have suddenly become aware of the social consequences of their actions and feel a desire to be "cured"; sometimes because they feel that such a declaration will be in their favor in court or prison. Usually, though, homosexuals do not want to be "cured." Indeed, some disturbed homosexuals who need treatment for a concomitant neurosis or psychosis may resist therapy because they are persuaded that all psychology is bent on changing their sexual preference.

It is a mistake to assume that all homosexuality should or can be "cured." Homosexuality has been attributed to a great variety of oversimplified causes. It has been believed that a homosexual is on a calculated path of evil, that he is diseased, or mentally ill. Many believe that homosexuality is caused solely by "inadequate" parents. Some believe that it is the result of biological body errors.

Havelock Ellis wrote: "Several hypotheses concerning the possible innateness or direct constitutional causation of confirmed homosexuality have been examined, including the theories that it is genetically caused, is hormonally based, is directly connected with an individual's body build, is almost completely untreatable, is the result of brain damage, and is historically and culturally uniform in incidence. When critically reviewed, all these hypotheses are found to be distinctly lacking in any objective, confirmatory evidence of a scientific nature."

There is also a belief that homosexuals do not do manual work. But Kinsey found that although the incidence of homosexual activity appears to be less for rural than urban males, there is a generally lower total sexual outlet for farm-reared males. And there is evidence of considerable homosexual activity among lumbermen, cattlemen, prospectors, miners, hunters, and others engaged in outdoor "masculine" occupations. In fact homosexuality exists at all social and economic levels.

There is a possibility that some homosexuality may be "innate." This is the sort of thing that is almost impossible to prove or disprove. H. J. Eysenck and S. Rachman, in their book *The Causes and Cures of Neurosis: an Introduction to Modern Behavior Therapy based on Learning Theory and the Principles of Conditioning,* write that there is considerable evidence that homosexual patterns of behavior may be innate in many people, but that "there is also considerable evidence to show that in many people it may have been triggered off by a process of social learning and conditioning."

Conditioned responses may be positive or negative. A child learning to wake up in the night and go to the lavatory to relieve his bladder rather than wetting the bed is learning the appropriate conditioned response to a full bladder. If he fails to learn this, the conditioning process which would produce the socially desirable habit does not occur.

Traumatic Experience

On the other hand, there may develop a type of positive, appetitive conditioning which is contrary to the rules and laws of the society in question. "Thus, homosexual, fetishistic, or other perverse erotic behavior patterns may have become fixated through a process of conditioning in which these undesirable behavior patterns were in fact reinforced through orgasm or in some other way, so that the problem for the therapist is now one of breaking down the positive conditioning and of establishing in its place a negative conditioned response to these stimuli."

Homosexuality may have begun at puberty—when both boys and girls tend to turn away from the opposite sex for a time. Sexual development may then be arrested at that stage. A traumatic experience may lead to chronically maladjusted conditioned responses. Family circumstances or behavior may have aroused either hos-

tility or overattachment to one parent or the other. Isolation from the opposite sex or long and close association with those of the same sex may predispose someone to think with ease and warmth of his own sex and with fear and strangeness of the opposite sex: the appropriate social skills may simply never be learned.

The enormous variety of beliefs about the cause of homosexuality, about its correct treatment, and about the *aim* of the treatment makes it difficult for the disturbed homosexual who seeks therapy. In the journal *Diseases of the Nervous System* there were recent reports of the efficacy of group psychotherapy in overcoming the homosexual's "defense mechanisms of isolation, rationalization and denial."

Cottaging Activity

Homosexual patients remained in the group treatment and continued to work on their conflicts rather than retreating from therapy as is frequent in individual psychotherapy. Group treatment of 30 patients, compared with 20 untreated "controls," resulted in a considerable reduction of neurotic symptoms, improved social relations, increased insight into the causes and implications of homosexuality, and some increase in heterosexual orientation and decrease in homosexual preoccupation.

The journal *Behavior Therapy* reports a "behavioral analysis" which assisted a recently married man who had a long history of "cottaging"—homosexual activity in public lavatories—and was continuing these activities in spite of his marriage. Following heavy drinking bouts, he would go to one of several "cottages" known to him and indulge in mutual masturbation there with another man. This would occur several times a week. He usually had difficulty with the chosen man afterwards—he was unable to "assert" himself. He loved his wife and had no difficulties or inhibitions in making love to her. But his "cottaging" activities were badly affecting both his relationship with his wife and his work.

Behavioral analysis showed that a central element in his "cottaging" was the reinforcement he got from putting himself at risk of being caught—and then succeeding in getting away with his "night out." It was found that he "did not even erect to homosexual sexual situations."

He did not however want to stop his activities completely—only to put them under control and "just go into public conveniences and play around occasionally.'' And this situation would be apparently acceptable both to him and to his wife.

In therapy he was taught how to assert himself with his male sexual partners and was accompanied on his ''cottaging'' visits by therapists, who neutralized the danger-intrigue element by treating the procedure with indifference. The ''cottaging'' dropped

This prison cell scene from the controversial film *Fortune and Men's Eyes* shows how a confirmed homosexual — the tattooed, casually smoking youth — can influence a waverer, who is likely to succumb to the temptation because he has no other outlet for his emotions.

to one visit a month, and there was a dramatic improvement in his work. He became able to assert himself, and his relationship with his wife became much more satisfactory.

Probably the majority of the knowledge of homosexual practices and relationships is based either on spectacular newspaper accounts of criminal cases or ''gay clubs'' or on the study of homosexuals in prison or under psychiatric care. None of these reflects the attitudes or experiences of most homosexuals.

Judgment about the comparative promiscuity of homosexuals is difficult. Most heterosexuals are bound by law to marriage partners; and they have children. Even so, infidelity, desertion and separation are plentiful.

Without such bonds, it is impossible to say how enduring heterosexual relationships would be.

Many homosexuals form a lasting emotional attachment, and probably a majority desire to. Failure to do so may be caused not so much by the ephemeral or promiscuous nature of homosexuality as by its categorization in most societies as illegal or abnormal. Even where law reform has legalized homosexuality to some extent, there are many occupations in which it would be punishable by dismissal or at least by nonpromotion. A jealous or dishonest or sadistic homosexual partner in a long-term cohabiting relationship could be a constant threat. It may be fear that makes a homosexual confine himself

Joel Finler

Marshall Cavendish

to ephemeral sexual contacts.

Even where homosexuality is totally prohibited by law, most homosexuals do not come into contact with the law. Of those that do, a majority are likely to be poorly educated, and a possible quarter or a third are likely to have been convicted for other, nonsexual offenses in addition to their homosexual convictions. Michael Schofield, interviewing convicted homosexuals in London prisons shortly before the 1967 Act reformed the law, found that of the 50 men in this group, 20 (40 percent) had also been convicted of a nonsexual offense, 19 of them more than once. Of the remaining 30 men who had not been convicted of a nonsexual offense, 14 had more than one conviction for sexual offenses. So only one-third of the group were first offenders.

Precarious Position

"Most prison officers assume that homosexuals operate largely in criminal circles and it is not difficult to see why they make this assumption," Schofield writes. He also notes that it was unlikely that any of these men were capable of a long-term emotional relationship.

Undoubtedly the precariousness of the homosexual's social situation contributes to promiscuity and callous behavior even towards a long-standing sexual partner—in ways that only the most brutal heterosexual man would practice on his wife.

One of Schofield's homosexuals said, "It's hard to understand how it happened. We spent every moment together, and there were no signs of a breakup. Then suddenly he brings this other person back and they stayed the whole night together. From then on things just broke up."

It is often suggested that female homosexuals form more stable and enduring relationships than males. Some researchers infer from this that either it is "in the nature of" women to maintain stable relationships, as it is not in men; or that women are conditioned to dependence on a sexual partner, and this obtains even in deviant situations.

In any case, female homosexuals

A homosexual relationship is not necessarily a promiscuous one: this gay couple settles down to watch TV like an orthodox married couple. Generally male homosexuals are attracted to other men (not to a "queen"—an imitation-woman), and female homosexuals tend to avoid butch caricatures of men.

are rare—simply because there may not be the same number of contacts as male homosexuals are likely to have. Kinsey found the incidence of homosexual responses and contacts to be much less among females than among males. He also found a definite correlation between increased educational level and the incidence of female homosexuality (24 percent of graduate-school-educated females).

Adolescent Experiments

Homosexuality among schoolgirls is less common, as masturbation is, if only from ignorance. A boy's erecting penis immediately teaches him his area of sexual arousal and the way to gratify it. A young girl's vagina is concealed and covered, her clitoris unnoticeable. In order to experience orgasm, she needs to know a great deal about her body.

Girls are more likely than boys to experience "crushes" on women teachers or other girls and to experience vague sexual longings. Some mutual bodily fondling, not necessarily leading to orgasm, is probably commoner than mutual masturbation, which is fairly widely practiced among boys. In single-sex schools, especially boarding schools, homosexual practices are to some extent inevitable. The English "public school" system is famous for its fostering of male homosexuality, although such practices may be abandoned at the end of school days.

Even in fee-paying girls' schools, girls are usually so strongly conditioned towards marriage, and the acquisition of suitable male partners beforehand, that there is little attraction for a homosexual relationship even with the most brilliant girl in the school. Female homosexuality is rarely considered exciting.

For boys, on the other hand, there is the ancient Greek idealization of homosexuality and its associations with art, intellect, and romanticism. Among intellectual or artistic boys—or those with ambitions to be so—there is knowledge that there are many more intellectuals and artists among men than among women: and sexual associations among men may therefore be considered on a higher plane than those between men and women.

Sexual practice among homosexuals varies greatly: lying together and caressing each other may be all that happens; mutual masturbation is common, and so is fellatio. With many males, full anal intercourse may never occur. A minority do not indulge sexually at all. And people who ask for therapy—without any compulsion—are frequently those who have never practiced homosexuality at all but have recognized that their sexual impulses are not heterosexual and are disturbed by this.

Rigid Roles

Where a homosexual's sexual practices do not interfere with his personality development or with his ability to work, and where they do not deeply disturb him or harm other people (like his wife or children if he indulges in homosexual acts after marriage), there is no real cause to disturb him.

But where a homosexual is persisting in overt illegal acts or on a course of behavior damaging to others, or where he suffers neurotic or psychotic symptoms, then therapy is indicated. Therapy is, however, difficult, even where there is willingness to change. If there is the slightest unwillingness to accept therapy, it will be virtually impossible.

If rigid male-female gender roles are allowed to dissolve in the near future, and coeducation made obligatory, it is quite possible that the incidence of homosexuality in our society will radically reduce.

Britain repealed antihomosexual laws in 1967—it is now legal in private between consenting adults over 21. Much of the United States still has punitive laws, but the Gay Liberation movement seize every opportunity to declare themselves.

Transworld

Dave Smith

Mind over matter

Who can put limits on the power of thought? The possibilities are positively mind-bending.

The earliest recorded scientific tests of the physical manifestations of spiritualism were in the mid-nineteenth century in France, by Count Agenor de Gasparin.

With some friends, he carried out a series of experiments which showed, time after time, that certain individuals were able to move objects without touching them; and the forces at work were measured by the same means as were used by physicists to measure gravity. It even proved possible to estimate the psychic power of the individual involved.

Up to that time, the tendency had been to think of levitation—the ability to lift objects or lift oneself in apparent defiance of the laws of gravity—as supernatural, and therefore a sign of divine or diabolic intervention, disrupting the natural law. But de Gasparin felt sure, from his observation, that there was a more rational cause. In certain conditions, he suggested, the human will can operate at a distance, on inert substances.

De Gasparin's report, published in 1854, was followed a year later by another survey of the phenomena by Professor Thury of Geneva, giving the very similar results of his own researches and coming to much the same conclusions. There must be an undiscovered force at work, Thury argued; and he described it as "ectenic," from the Greek for extension—a term which would very probably have remained in use, had the British scientist, Professor Sir William Crookes seen it before he came to describe his own researches.

Look, No Hands

But Crookes, not knowing of ectenic's existence until somebody pointed it out to him later, adopted the term "psychic," which is still in use today.

By virtue of his academic standing —he was a fellow of the Royal Society —Crookes was able to get his reports published in the *Quarterly Journal of Science*, and in 1871 he described

Levitation is a supernatural power that moves objects by other than physical means. Should it ever be proved to exist, one thing is certain—it will begin by raising an eyebrow or two.

how he had tested the medium Daniel Dunglas Home for his ability to move objects and to play tunes upon musical instruments, without touching them. He had heard that Home could perform these tricks, but it was not until he had observed him doing them half a dozen times that he had became convinced that the phenomena were genuine. And he had set to work to devise ways to convince other scientists.

Home was brought to Crookes' house and sat down in front of a wire cage in which there was an accordion. The cage was so constructed that Home could insert his hand and touch one end of the accordion. But he could not reach the keys, and his hand could be seen by the observers, who included an eminent physicist and a lawyer.

By Crookes' account, "Very soon the accordion was seen by those on each side to be weaving about in a somewhat curious manner; then sounds came from it, and finally several notes were played in succession. . . . We heard distinct and separate notes sounded in succession, and then a simple air was played. As such a result could only have been produced by the various keys of the instrument being acted upon in harmonious succession this was considered by those present to be a crucial experiment. But the sequel was even more striking. For Mr Home then removed his hand altogether from the accordion, taking it quite out of the cage, and placed it in the hand of the person next to him. The instrument then continued to play, with no person touching it and no hand being near it."

Card Games

Even more impressive, so far as Crookes was concerned, were Home's feats in altering the weight of objects. Crookes had rigged up a board attached to a balance; simply by touching one end of the board, Home could make the balance oscillate, as if the board was losing or gaining weight. Yet the board had been so placed that the simple pressure of Home's fingers could not have moved it. Even when Crookes jumped on it, it registered only very slightly.

But Crookes found that others were more difficult to convince. He invited the cooperation of scientific friends to undertake a more systematic inquiry. "But I soon found that to obtain a scientific committee for the investigation of this class of facts was out of the question and that I must be content to rely on my own endeavors."

And it was not just the orthodox scientists who were skeptical towards the idea that mind could influence matter. His fellow psychic researchers became disillusioned by the discovery, in case after case, that the mediums who were producing the phenomena were cheating—not all the time, admittedly, but occasionally. And once somebody had been caught in the act of cheating, or trying to cheat, all their past achievements tended to become suspect.

Research into the subject continued, but became piecemeal; and it was not until the 1930s that it was taken up again seriously.

How this happened has been described by Louisa Rhine in her *Mind over Matter: Psychokinesis.* Her husband, J. B. Rhine, had been appointed to the psychology department of Duke University in North Carolina; and in 1930 he had begun to test students there to try to discover whether the mind could pick up information other than through the five senses.

The method he adopted was not new; the subjects were invited to guess the numbers on cards in envelopes. But the technique developed to assess the results was new; the subjects went on guessing and guessing in long "runs," and their final total of "hits" was then compared with chance expectation.

Anybody may guess correctly—Rhine's reasoning was that a coin is lying "heads" up six times out of ten, when chance expectation is five times out of ten. But if somebody guesses "heads" correctly six hundred times out of a thousand, that is different. It suggests that he may be being fed with correct information which way the coin has fallen, often enough to make his guessing significantly more consistent than chance.

At first it was assumed that the information came by telepathy—that the successful subjects were reading the mind of the experimenter sufficiently often to score better than chance. But then, it was found that some subjects could guess the cards in this way even if neither the experimenter nor anybody else knew which card was being guessed—in other words, that the guessers were clairvoyant: they could "see" hidden things around them. And some subjects could actually guess not only the card which was the actual target but also the next card which would come up in the test.

Gambler's Dream

One subject, Hubert Pearce, appeared to be able to score consistently above the chance expectation level in tests both for clairvoyance and for precognition.

What Pearce was doing was the equivalent of guessing correctly not merely which way a penny had fallen, six times out of ten, but also which way it was *going* to fall, six times out of ten—the gambler's dream. And as it happened, it was a gambler who took the Rhine saga a stage further—as Louisa Rhine recalled.

A young man came into her husband's office at Duke, sat down on his desk, and said, "Hey, doc, I've got something to tell you I think you ought to know." The something was a discovery the young man claimed to have made in the course of his gambling activities, shooting craps. He had found that he could control the fall of dice—*by willpower.* At times, he said earnestly, when throwing dice in gambling, he could get the faces of the dice to come up as he wanted them to. He was certain of it. He could not do it all the time, he admitted, only when in a particular mental state. But, then, the dice seemed to work for him.

Soon Rhine and his visitor were on the floor in a corner of the office, throwing dice; and though the results were not recorded, they were apparently good enough to persuade Rhine that this form of psychokinesis must be taken seriously.

Against the Odds

Rhine began to experiment with psychokinesis in much the same way as he had previously experimented with telepathy, clairvoyance and precognition, using dice in place of cards. The results were striking. Twenty-five subjects—students at Duke University and friends—"willed" the dice to fall with a certain number uppermost over a series of runs. The proportion of times which the dice fell right for them was, in statistical terms, significantly high—the odds against chance being responsible were over a billion to one against.

Since that time, experiments in many other parts of the world have repeated the pattern; and they have been conducted with a variety of refinements, to make sure that human elements other than the mind are not involved—electrical machines to throw the dice, for example.

More recently the experiments of the physicist Helmut Schmidt, originally of the Boeing Corporation but later Rhine's successor at Duke, have provided additional confirmation. Quantum physicists regard certain events in connection with radioactive decay as unpredictable: "nature's most elementary source of randomness." Schmidt asked subjects to predict which of four lights would be turned on, the sequence in which they were going to be turned on depending on that unpredictable random source. The odds against chance producing the results which Schmidt's subjects were able to produce turned out to be two thousand million to one.

But perhaps the most striking of recent experiments into psychokinesis have been conducted by Colin Brookes-Smith and some friends in Britain. In 1972 they held 57 sittings designed to explore

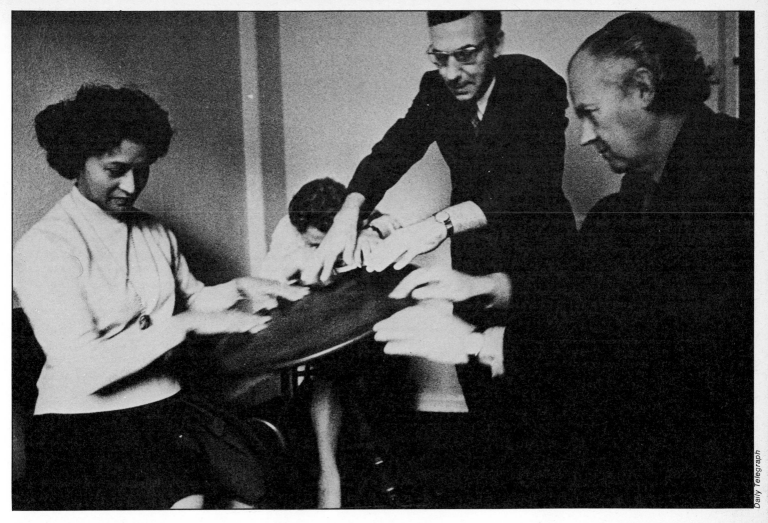

Daily Telegraph

scientifically the forces at work in the Victorian pastime of "table turning."

As originally conducted, a group of people would sit around a table in the dark, placing their fingertips on it, and wait for it to begin to move—sometimes to make noises, sometimes to rock, sometimes to rise off the ground. Often the antics of a heavy table would be so striking, and indeed alarming, that it would be clear to those taking part that some occult (as they assumed) force must be at work.

Lift-off

But skeptics invariably pointed out that there was no way of being sure that the table was not being pushed or lifted by one or more of the group around it. If, however, elaborate pains were taken to prevent cheating, like tying up the participants' legs, the tables ceased to cooperate: proof, the skeptics maintained, that it was all absolute nonsense.

The psychic researchers disagreed. What was needed, they felt, was some way to leave the table turners their freedom, so they would not be inhibited, but at the same time to monitor their behavior, so that they would be detected if, consciously or unconsciously, they added their own

Table turning is a phenomenon as yet to be explained. A group of people with just their fingertips on a table have seemingly caused it to rise from the ground. Is this an occult force at work?

force to whatever the psychic forces might be which were working on the table. And this was done in Brookes-Smith's experiments by using the latest scientific aid available, "data-tape recording."

The principle is much the same as ordinary tape recording, but there is more than one track, each recording some different aspect of what is happening: so that while one tape is collecting the sounds of an experiment, another can be collecting a record of the movements of the table, and so on. By this means it is possible not merely to register the movements, but also to tell where the force is being applied. So when the leader of the group tells the table to rise, tapes are recording the reaction of the table and the pressures put upon it. If, for example, one member of the group is assisting the table to rise by pushing or pulling it up, the data tapes can disclose the culprit's identity. At the same time, they can actually

measure the strength of whatever force is involved.

In his report to the Society for Psychical Research, published in their *Journal* in June, 1973, Brookes-Smith was careful to insist that the experiments his group had undertaken with the help of data-tape recording had been exploratory and that the results obtained should be regarded as no more than an encouraging indication that this line of research is worth pursuing.

But those results, he felt, had been sufficiently consistent to show that "by adopting suitable procedures, paranormal forces can be made available 'by the pound' in repeatable experiments almost at any chosen time." As it is this kind of repeatability which has for so long eluded researchers, these experiments in psychokinesis may constitute a decisive advance.

The Russians have also been experimenting with psychokinesis—notably with a Leningrad housewife. Nelya Kulagina was a teenager in Leningrad when the Germans invaded. She fought in the Russian army, becoming a sergeant in a tank regiment before being wounded and discharged. Subsequently she married

1155

Titbits

and had children and grandchildren.

William A. McGarey, an American doctor who went with a team to investigate psychic research in the Soviet Union in 1970, arranged to see her, by which time she had already been carefully tested in laboratories by Russian scientists and filmed in the process. She demonstrated for this American team quite casually, at a table in their Leningrad hotel dining room.

"While many of us crowded around the table where she was sitting, she obligingly caused several small objects to move across the tablecloth of the dining room table which normally seats six people. Small objects like a wedding ring or the top of a condiment bottle moved easily and rather quickly when she simply held her hands above them . . . Looking at a ring and moving her head slightly in a circular manner, she caused the ring to rotate on an invisible axis as it lay there on the tablecloth."

In one of the films taken of her,

Can metal be bent by thought? Uri Geller *may* have this gift and now others, like 17-year-old English girl June Charlton, seem to be able to bend cutlery.

Nelya actually managed to get a ping pong ball to levitate and hover in space for a few moments, before it fell back onto the table.

If we assume that psychokinesis exists, is there any rational explanation as to how it works? The obvious parallel is magnetism. Iron, when magnetized, is capable of defying the laws of gravity, by exerting an attraction sufficient to overcome it. Why, then, should scientists reject the possibility that there is a similar force which works by psychokinesis? The answer is not that the force cannot be demonstrated—it has been demonstrated countless times—but simply that it cannot be repeated to order. A few individuals appeared to have had the ability—D. D. Home, and more recently, Uri Geller. But neither of

them professed to be able to make their power work under any conditions, at any time.

If the force does come from the mind, though, there is no reason to expect consistency—rather the contrary. The assumption must be that it is only in certain states that the mind can act upon matter or upon other forms of life. The explanation most commonly accepted, by those who accept psychokinesis, is that—as the psychic researcher Hereward Carrington surmised early this century—the nervous force which actuates the body may, under certain exceptional circumstances, "extend beyond the periphery of the bodily frame, and exert an influence over the external, material world."

What is the Matter?

As popular author Arthur Koestler has showed in his recent books, it is a great deal less difficult today to reconcile orthodox physics with psychic phenomena. When the Victorians began "table turning" as a parlor game, the physicists understandably declined to believe that massive heavy mahogany furniture could be moved by the simple touch of a few fingers—or, sometimes, without being touched at all—because in those days it was assumed that the furniture consisted of "matter." But by the 1920s "matter" in that sense could no longer be said to exist.

As Sir Arthur Eddington wrote in *The Nature of the Physical World*, published in 1928, the writing desk he was using had a dual personality. On the one hand, it was the solid piece of furniture on which he leaned his elbows while writing; on the other, it was a mass of electrons whirling round their nuclei, with vast gaps of empty space between them, comparable to outer space. And this discovery of what "matter" consisted of proved to be only the beginning of the collapse of materialism.

Later nuclear physicists have demonstrated to their own satisfaction that an electron may be either an object, or a wave, or both at once; and that it may switch from one orbit to another, circling around its nucleus, without passing through the intervening space—as if, in Koestler's words, "the Earth were suddenly transferred to the orbit of Mars without having to travel."

In the light of these discoveries, psychokinesis becomes less incomprehensible—for the mind to move a mass of electrons sounds much simpler than for the mind to move a table!

Dave Bowyer

The outsider

Hitched, and—crash!—down comes the portcullis. Now it's just you two and the rest of your life. Outside connections are cut, the phone and doorbell cease ringing, friendship withers away. But how long will it be before you want to escape from your living-room prison?

A wedding day is the beginning of an entirely new way of life for a couple. The man and woman have formed a new social unit, and although they may be similar in many ways, there are sufficient basic differences of viewpoint to make some of the adjustments of living together difficult.

"Outsiders" can add to the friction which accompanies all processes of adjustment. For example, a marriage provides a link between two families, and the mixing of the clans of bride and bridegroom can be fraught with tension. It also brings together two sets of friends, or, to be accurate, it may do so if the couple decides to share their friends.

What happens often in practice is that the woman relinquishes her wider social circle in order to immerse herself in her husband's social life. During courtship, double dates with the man's friends are more common than with the woman's. So the joint friends of newly married couples are more often those coming from the husband's side, not the wife's. Often, after their marriage, the husband tends to keep his friends and to spend an increasing amount of time with them. Even in the case of joint friends, the woman may not be certain whether she is accepted and liked for herself or simply because she is "Tom's wife." This sort of conflict comes to a

head if there are marital difficulties and the mutual friends' loyalties are put to an awkward test.

Of course, there are many different patterns, different ways in which couples share friends or do otherwise. They may share some friends while they maintain special one-sided friendships; they may drop some or all close friends they had before marriage for a wider totally shared social set. Or there may be a withdrawal from all old pals. Some men continue to behave like bachelors after marriage, continuing with their chums on the old and familiar basis. Some do this with considerable insensitivity, giving so much time and attention to the friends that the only possible implication seems to be that their companionship is more valuable than the wife's. Not surprisingly she feels miserable and may well complain. Her resentment is quite appropriate to the rebuff which is implied in this behavior. Naturally she feels unhappy because her husband shares only a small proportion of his life with her. Marriage, after all, is always a sharing relationship—a commitment of two people to each other.

Like to Like

Men often forget that while they have a great deal of social contact just by going out to work and meeting different people there, their wives, if they are at home with young children, can pass the whole day without any adult company. The husband's homecoming really is an event. His wife is hurt if he leaves her to go out with his friends as soon as dinner is over each evening. Unfortunately, many women feel self-pity about this sort of situation, but make no effort to explain to their husbands how they feel. Other men go to the other extreme and drop all but their closest friends, gradually retiring from the "going out with the boys" routines.

But what should be done about friends in a marriage? After all, friendship is such a personal matter, a relationship which is based on voluntary and mutual choice. You cannot foist people on one another or "legislate" for mutual liking and attachment. When people are asked what it is about a close friend that makes for the joy of friendship, they emphasize the companionship, the sheer pleasure of the other person's presence, the fun of being with him. They also describe the relaxation of being able to be themselves with a friend, and of being able to unburden their most secret thoughts to him.

These complex elements, which combine to produce the mysterious chemistry of a good friendship, make nonsense of the question which people often ask: "Should a married couple share their friends?" Even if the answer was a wholehearted "Yes!" how could such an ideal be arrived at with anything like the emotional depth which differentiates real "friendships" from mere "acquaintanceships"?

Of course, in the process of sharing friends, in the narrowest sense of simply meeting each other's particular friends on many occasions, genuine friendships may be struck up. Indeed, on theoretical grounds, there should

be a predisposition for this to occur. The same principle called homogamy —"like attracts like"—influences the choice of partners in marriage and friendship. The partners in a marriage (being alike, in general terms) should be attracted to similar persons as friends. As the saying goes, "Birds of a feather flock together." But theory is one thing; practice is another! Homogamy, as a principle, has been shown to apply in group studies, that is, as a statistical tendency. This is no guarantee that it always obtains in particular cases. Sometimes opposites do attract each other! It is a very common observation that wives do not always like or approve of their husband's choice of friends and vice versa.

Derek's attitude to his wife's friends was like this. Before his marriage he was a person of few but intensely pursued interests. He was always something of a "loner." He had several friendly acquaintances, but only one really close friend. He loved the theater, read widely and was an interesting, if diffident, person to be with. Then he married Alice. This was after an intensely passionate courtship, during which there were many stormy partings and reconciliations.

After their marriage, Derek stopped seeing his friends, and Alice's friends, of whom there were quite a number, saw less and less of her. The few who persisted in trying to keep in contact were aware of an indefinable coolness in the atmosphere, a tension, which made them feel unwelcome. Alice did her best to be welcoming and relaxed, but all she managed to do was to present a rather embarrassing picture of artificial joviality. Derek was never exactly unfriendly, but neither was he particularly welcoming to them.

Possession Means Poison

Over the next two years situations arose in which the remaining friends found themselves having somehow "offended" Derek in ways that they could not understand. Alice would take his part and there would be an estrangement. Her closest and oldest friend persisted in the face of Derek's ill-concealed dislike, but gradually she found Alice less and less interesting to speak to and to be with. Neither Derek nor Alice expressed his or her own views any more, but always talked of "we." In the end she gave up, leaving them, as she put it, "to their symbiotic relationship, their submergence in each other."

This is a jealous and possessive

kind of love which leaves no room for unshared friendships. Some people may be happy without the friendship of other people, but most are not. And when they refuse to give up their friends there is often friction in the marriage.

Some of us might be disposed to criticize the monopolistic relationship Derek and Alice had. But do we have the right to do so, particularly if both choose such a pattern? It may be hard on the old friends but presumably the marriage comes first. Sadly, it is often one partner who decides to impose his preference on the other. As there is an asymmetrical distribution of power and/or dominance in many love relationships, one partner dictates (subtly or unsubtly) and the other has to submit.

Green-eyed Gremlins

With so many variables in play, can there ever be an answer to the question about the desirability of a couple sharing friends? When it comes to human beings, their behavior and their relationships, there is only one dogmatic formula that can be applied. It is enshrined in Bernard Shaw's aphorism: "There is only one golden rule—there are no golden rules." Sharing friends may be fine for some couples but not for others. Whatever pattern of friend sharing or maintaining separate friends suits the "temperament" of one couple may not suit another. Conflict only arises when the partners want different things.

A reasonable degree of emotional dependence contributes to a happy love relationship. But taken to extremes, dependence may undermine a long-term relationship. A marked feature of the emotionally dependent person who marries to find security is his or her acute need for the physical presence of the partner; the partner acts as a source of reassurance and alleviates the dread of being alone. If such a dependent person is courted by a lover who appears attractively strong, reliable and reassuring, but who, when the facade is penetrated, turns out to be insecure as well, demanding a suffocating monopoly of the partner's love and attention (to the exclusion of his or her friends and even relatives), the outcome is bitter disappointment and a potential source of tension in the long-term relationship.

A survey showed that half of the middle-class couples interviewed said they shared all their closest friends, whereas the remainder said that they

David Levin

This raises the question of defining a mature and lasting love relationship. A psychiatrist who is an expert on marriage states that the survival of every marriage depends on the capacity of the partners to meet the psychological needs of the other, which in turn requires a fair degree of maturity. He suggests that a mature relationship is based on mutual understanding and equality between the partners. Authority, power and decision making are shared. It has been suggested that today's happily married husbands and wives have the following characteristics: they are emotionally stable, considerate of others, yielding, companionable, self-confident and —to a degree which is not excessive— emotionally dependent.

Love and be Loved

Maturity is the aim of all development. Education and cultural influences lead to good judgment, the accurate assessment of other people's desires, and the resolution of conflicts between those desires and one's own. Love, too, develops in response to the love of parents, friends and lovers. In the early stages, as with the child, all love is self-love, demanding love. If stuck in this stage a person may become narcissistic, or will "love" only those who satisfy his desires, confusing those who proffer gifts with those who offer love. In the second stage a person may project his self-love onto others, loving only what *he* allows them to be. Unrealistically romantic love surrounds a real person with an ideal persona and must be either unconsummated or doomed. Excessive jealousy is often a sign of immature (and even neurotic) attitudes.

The wife (or husband) who resents what most people would think of as a reasonable amount of time that a partner gives to his friends is often simply jealous. Jealousy involves feelings which, at times, have to do with fear, sorrow, and shame, and at others with humiliation, anger, and suspicion. It might be considered the egotistical face of love. Jealousy has as its special aim the more or less exclusive possession of the loved object, whether this object is a man, another person, power, reputation, or property.

Karen Horney, the eminent psychoanalyst, has analyzed some of the neurotic components of love. She says we all want to love and enjoy being loved. It enriches our lives and gives us a feeling of happiness. But in the neurotic person the need for love is

So now she wants out from the marriage, but perhaps he has a strong hand and without friends there is no escape. The cards are stacked against her.

had some separate close friends. Those couples with the largest number of friends had both the largest number of mutual friends *and* the most separate friends, indicating that there is no necessary conflict between these two types of friendship. It has been shown, in fact, that happily married couples have more joint friends —friends in common—than those who become divorced. It could, therefore, be said that similar abilities for making human relationships underlie both marriage and friendship. Because of the companionship of happily married couples, they have more friends of their own *and* the opposite sex than unhappily married couples.

It has been shown over and over again by researchers into marriage that a web of friendly relationships buffers and protects marital stability. Marriage, or at least a good marriage, could be described as the most intimate and durable of all friendships; perhaps not surprisingly, it is usually the people who make friends most easily who make the best marriages. Individuals who have more friends of both sexes before marriage tend to keep them up after marriage and also make new ones. A successful marriage really does bring together their two sets of friends.

If a newly married man and woman are good at establishing personal relationships they gradually get to know each other's friends. A person's concept of love (and his need for it) has great influence on his attitude to the sharing of a spouse's affections with others.

increased. While it is important to the healthy person to be loved and esteemed by those he is close to, the neurotic's demand for love is compulsive and indiscriminate. It is insatiable and jealous. Love must be given exclusively and unconditionally, and the loved one must make every possible sacrifice to prove his or her love. In addition the neurotic shows an extreme sensitivity to rejection, either real or imagined, and, Karen Horney believes, a fundamental incapacity to give love.

Familiarity Breeds Contempt

It is one thing to be jealous of a man's attraction to other women, but why should his affection for his male friends be resented? In one way, of course, the gender of friends is irrelevant. If a woman feels that she is being deprived of companionship (a basic need in life and an all-important component of love) it matters little that her husband is giving all his confidences, his affection, and his leisure time to male friends. They are rivals.

At home she may see her husband laughing, talking, and joking with his friends, in a happy and relaxed manner that he seldom shows her any more. She sees him only tired and irritable. And he might talk a great deal about his friends, with obvious affection and admiration, while making little display of his affection for her. She begins to feel that he must value his friends more than he does her. Often the husband in this situation does not realize what his wife is feeling, and he would no doubt be surprised if she did manage to put her uneasiness into words.

It is very common for people who have been married for some years to begin taking each other for granted and to neglect the small gestures of love and affection which give each of them confidence in the other's love. It is this confidence which makes it possible for them to accept their partner's relationships with other people. If it exists, friendships are not seen as a threat to the marriage relationship. The stronger the marriage,

and the more emotionally secure the partner, the deeper the friendships which he or she can tolerate. And a network of outside friendships will help them both to preserve their individuality within marriage and ultimately make them more interesting and happier people.

The questions concerning sharing friends and why they are assimilated or rejected by the partners in a marital relationship raise a fundamental issue of the place of individuality in marriage. Novelist D. H. Lawrence, with his insight into the complexities of love, explores the extreme view, that held by Ursula in *Women in Love*. Ursula represents the romantic ideal—the dream of infatuated lovers merging their lives and isolating themselves from the rest of the world, having no need of further friendships. She, herself, knows that Birkin, when he asks her to marry him, does not want the total self-surrender that she does. For Birkin the idea of this close, exclusive intimacy is claustrophobic. He wants a cooler, more open, love

relationship, and he needs the friendship of other people in order to be happy.

There are obviously many types of jealousy. What is common to all jealousy situations is the threat to a person's self-esteem. It is the threatened ego which reacts with jealousy. Thus there can be two sources of threat. The man may injure the woman's self-esteem by the lack of attention he pays her compared with the amount of attention he pays his friends. Or the woman may be so insecure initially that even minimal attentions paid to friends may be perceived as a threat. (Of course, it may be the other way around.) There are two main categories of causes in this matter of possessive jealousy. One is social and the other is personal. In many ways this is a man's world. Women are at a disadvantage socially. And any society which places groups of individuals at a disadvantage because of racial, class, or sex distinctions, will be laying the groundwork for many jealous citizens.

When a man spends an increasing proportion of his time with his separate friends, it may suggest that there is something seriously wrong with the marriage. Often it merely reflects the general cooling of the romance and enthusiasm of the early months of the relationship. And this happens in almost all marriages to some extent.

Male Fantasy

If the marriage is to be a happy one the individual must understand and accept his or her partner's need to spend time with friends. If the wife does feel neglected and unhappy, she should make this clear to him. Like all problems in marriage it should be talked about. Possibly, her reactions are unreasonable. Up to a point separate friends and different interests are a good thing, and the woman may be envious of her husband's relationships only because she has a dull life herself. The problem will probably be solved if she spends more time with her own friends and cultivates her own interests. Her

Far left: Friends, it seems, are fine when they are the same sex as his wife. Now he can enjoy an evening out with the boys. Above: But when another man is around, she needs watching. No wonder his partner's wife is bored to tears.

husband is likely to have less need of his friends if she begins not just to take an interest in the things which interest him, but also to offer as mutual activities things which she has first explored on her own. Then their interests will be truly shared.

There is nothing inevitable about the drift away from companionship in marriage. Marriage is rich with the potential for growing love, understanding, and intimacy, if only people would work at it in the way that they work for other worthwhile things in life. The *sharing* of friends may go some way to helping a marriage stay alive. We can go a long way towards *creating* the possibilities for becoming friends with another's friends.

1161

J. Garrett

Going straight

He may be bent on straightening out, but if society takes a hand, who will pull the strings?

It has been suggested that prison and forms of criminal punishment exist to provide society with its pound of flesh. Society has been offended and believes itself justified in requiring some kind of retribution for the offense.

The label on that retribution—prison, remand, hostel, rehabilitation center —is of little concern; society sees no reason why it should be bothered further with the consequence of laws that have been made precisely to save itself that trouble.

But it is becoming increasingly clear that this pound of flesh is cut from society's *own* body. It is an old and unsatisfactory axiom that reasons, "If your hand offend you, cut it off." And since in medicine we have rejected this attitude, it would seem appropriate that we should reject it also in our social philosophy.

It is typical of our present attitudes to the criminal that we should discuss his punishment before we consider the consequences of that punishment, and often without giving a thought to the causes of his crime. We are safe from the criminal, we think, once he is behind bars or once he is in some kind of "care." Someone, somewhere is paid to keep an eye on him. But the bars have been put up too late. For the criminal already exists. To prevent his existence should be society's real concern.

In the relatively minor case of Barney, who threw a brick through a liquor store window, the reasons for his action should be of much more interest to those responsible for dealing with him than the sharp tap of retribution decreed by law. A doctor carefully diagnoses an illness; simi-

larly, a magistrate can only assign constructive treatment once he understands what he is treating.

Why did Barney throw the brick through that particular window? He was already drunk, or he was not drunk at all—either way he wanted some liquor. Straight theft. Or he had just had a row with a barman around the corner, who had refused to serve him, and wanted to show that he could manage without him. Or he was showing off to friends for a dare. Or he was aiming at something else, and missed. He liked breaking glass. He was expressing his strong disapproval of other people's drinking habits. He had nearly been run over by a liquor truck, whose label was blatantly advertised in that particular store. He was desperately lonely and wanted to draw attention to himself. His anger and frustration suddenly found an outlet in the nearest positive action to hand. It was a blow at his girl, who had accused him of drinking too much. The possible diagnoses are endless.

It was, society says, in any case an antisocial act that cannot be allowed to go unnoticed. Society means it should not go unpunished; what is more important is that Barney should not go uncared for.

Criminology is not merely a study of what crimes are committed and how the penalties are imposed; it is a study of human behavior and why men break the laws they themselves impose. Certain questions arise if we are to understand the so-called criminal mentality. Who is he? And why has he become a criminal?

Juvenile Delinqency

In general we think of the word "criminal" when referring to an adult. But criminal behavior is usually preceded by delinquent behavior. It is rare that the antisocial attitudes expressed by the criminal spring into existence unheralded by the influences and reactions of earlier years. The line of cause and effect goes far back, as Dr. Vincent Mazzola points out. "Juvenile delinquency is nothing more than the fruit which has grown from the seeds of parent delinquency, religious delinquency, educational delinquency, judiciary delinquency and municipal delinquency."

This may sound to our sensitive ears like an uncomfortable shift of blame onto our own blameless shoulders, a shift that society as a whole finds little time to tolerate. Most of us, we reason mildly, keep our hands clean. Is it not fair that everyone should be expected to do so? If anyone fails in their individual responsibility, then they should be shown that they have stepped out of line.

Most people, on both sides, whether arguing for or against reform, unapologetically try to apportion blame for the social rupture. It is an easy attitude to adopt. It has been adopted for centuries by those who deplore the criminal and seek to ostracize him; it is adopted in reverse by those who seek to apologize for the criminal and lay the blame soundly on society.

Society—that is, all of us—find it hard to accept either blame or responsibility. Our consciences may occasionally niggle and suggest that we should at least consider the matter. But what can we do about it? We see ourselves in the role of the injured innocent preyed upon by a deviant member. How can *we* stop him?

To most of us the criminal is an impersonal being, about whom we read in the papers. If we are unlucky, we might ourselves be burgled or conned or mugged. Yet, though the injury has then become very personal, the criminal often remains unknown.

The media foster this concept of the criminal as a man apart. So when the organizations devoted to the rehabilitation of the criminal and to the prevention of crime beat us about the head with admonitions that it is we ourselves who have caused ourselves to be robbed or conned or mugged, we find nothing reasonable in this argument and we resent it, tenderly rubbing our empty pockets or our sore heads. No wonder that criminal reform is such a social laggard, suppressed because of our inability to understand its necessity, our indignation at being expected to tolerate the blatantly unacceptable, and our strong suspicion that someone is trying to pull a fast one on us.

Whether blame is apportioned or not, there is no doubt about one aspect of the criminal that we need to understand before anything else: he is *not* a faceless individual. He is an integral part of society—ourselves. He may be lonely, he may have friends; he may have a family, he may have been rejected; he may work in the same job as ourselves, he may be out of work; he may have fantasies, he may be a coward, he may be ambitious, he may be kind. He may be all these and not a criminal at all. Preconceptions dissolve when the roots of criminal behavior are analyzed.

World without Love

None of us would feel flattered to be told that only our advantages keep us from crime. But this may well be true. It is a harsher but more realistic way of looking at the conventional point that the disadvantaged take more readily to crime. It is only when we have begun to rid ourselves of our preconceptions that we can begin to see more clearly what part of the social body turns to crime as a means of physical and psychological survival. Once we have accepted our similarities with the criminal, then we can ask: "What do we have going for us that others do not? What do we take for granted that others find it necessary to take by force or stealth? A home, a family, friends, money?"

It is wise to be suspicious of statistics, but when these are backed by innumerable case histories that bring the figures to life, they are worth paying attention to. Criminal attitudes

occur most frequently where there has been a breakdown of family life and disintegration of the social environment. Most of us, anxious to avoid the subject, would not think that "love" had much to do with the criminal.

To use such a word in this context may be enough to produce precisely that reaction of indignation and protest that is sparked off by implications of society's burden of responsibility for the criminal. If "love" raises the hackles and sets the sensibilities on guard, then read "affection," "security," the confidence of a family life—these are essential to a balanced attitude toward a socially responsible existence. And these are the aspects of life that time and again appear to be missing in the upbringing of many who turn to crime.

Bonds or Chains?

Who is then to blame? The parents, both out working to maintain a standard of living festooned with all the trappings of modern convenience? Or are they working simply to keep at bay one small circle of the inflationary spiral? The community environment, heartless in high-rise apartment buildings, partitioned, selfishly protecting its members from each other, discordant in competition? The classroom, where the teachers are too few and the pupils too many to receive anything richer than the minimal of attention? The impersonal confusion of the urban condition? Where these factors are present, there will be crime.

Deprived of an environment where the individual can be sure that he or she is wanted, deprived of the natural free and easy links between members of the community, deprived both at home and at school of any feeling of personal worth, the individual will naturally seek alternatives. It is no less natural that those in similar circumstances should seek each other out, creating their own form of self-contained community, providing their own interdependent bonds of reliance and affection. This is a simple way in which the delinquent gang can form.

Why delinquent, then? Gangs do exist without necessarily resorting to criminal behavior. Every child belongs at some stage to a local gang. But, when the child is emotionally deprived, every situation is distorted.

The internationally-known criminologist August Aichhorn has said that "children give up their instinctual demands only for love." Likening the delinquent and criminal mentality to that of a child, he postulates that the

Transworld

individual deprived of love from an early age knows only how to cry, hit out and grab with instinctive compulsion what it knows it wants. Failing to understand what it does want, then it will grab whatever is available.

Added to this, there are further layers of psychological incentive to crime. For instance, crime provides a convenient outlet for expressions of dissatisfaction with the society that has apparently rejected the individual. Crowded into anonymity by society's mass deployment, the individual draws attention to himself with criminal acts. Deadened by the drabness of the concrete horizon, he glimpses just a hint of glamour in crime. One sociologist even suggests that certain forms of delinquent behavior reveal expressions of creativity, commendable in the face of the almost overwhelming negativity of the individual's surroundings.

The existence of a group of similar individuals will certainly escalate the adoption of the criminal mentality. There is no stronger incentive to crime than the fear of ridicule. The group has an instinctive ability to make sure, in self-defense, that all its members keep up with each other. To avoid

rejection yet again, the individual has very little choice, with no support to fall back on if he feels hesitant about the new course he has adopted and wishes to step down.

Once begun, crime can easily become a habit—clever if you can get away with it, compulsive if you are caught. Once before the courts, once treated as a criminal, the individual follows a natural progression: people tend to act in the way that other people expect them to act. The man labeled "criminal" all too often will become a criminal for life. Returned from "care" to society, who in society cares where he goes? Back to his friends? Then he will certainly go back to his old habits. If he tries to strike out a line on his own, he will have no friends. No friends, no home; difficult to get a job because of his new label, difficult to get a cheap lodging; the only way out of the immediate difficulty is the way back in—back to crime.

So inevitable does this whole process appear from the very beginning that Harvard Professor and Mrs. Glueck, in the United States, have established what they call a Social Prediction Table. By tabulating cer-

tain information about an individual at a very early age, the Gluecks claim to be able to make a very accurate prediction as to the likelihood of that individual turning to crime at some stage in his life.

Using the formula in their table, they have claimed an 85 percent success rate in their predictions in Washington and New York—a remarkable record that should certainly be qualified by several factors that they do not seem to have been so ready to reveal. For instance it is questionable whether the sample was truly representative. All the same, it is frightening to consider the possibility that our criminal tendency might be predictable.

A danger lies in such prediction, too. It would be easy, taking things only one small step further, to prejudge and precondemn the individual. What might the state not feel empowered to do to protect society from the *possible* threat of an unproven and perhaps never-to-be-developed characteristic? The knowledge of your criminal potential may well lead you to fulfilling the prediction.

The truth of further prediction with regard to the proven criminal's progress and the roots of his disaffection

Above: A child discovers deception: his mother filches food, his father violates traffic laws and tells fishy stories. What about his future? Left: Coed prisoners learn fair play. This experimental prison in Fort Worth has proved successful. Right: A British bobby deals patiently with potential trouble.

is emphasized by some figures in Britain, where it is easier than in the breadth of the United States to give a whole picture of the situation. C. H. Rolph, former police chief in Britain, has estimated that one-fifth of all prisoners discharged annually in England and Wales are homeless. NACRO, the National Association for the Care and Resettlement of Offenders, puts the figure at one-quarter.

According to NACRO, 70 percent of Borstal (reform school) boys are reconvicted within three years of their release; 75 percent of prisoners discharged after more than 18 months inside return to the courts; 42 percent of men sent to prison have no job.

These are statistics. What, we complain, have they got to do with our pockets being picked, our homes being broken into and our heads being banged? If we are confused, it is not surprising. No one should feel that he has the solution, either to our questions or to these problems. Reformers through the centuries have believed in their own answers; today their efforts look painfully slight, as ours will doubtless look to future generations.

All you want to know about...

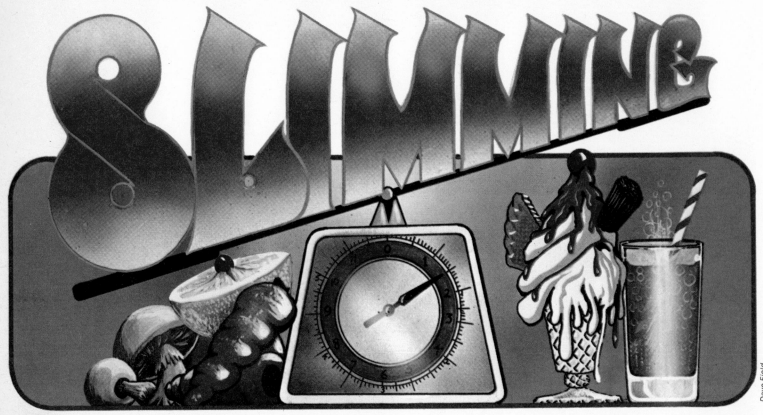

Dave Field

Q WHEN WE SAY SOMEONE IS OVERWEIGHT WHAT DO WE MEAN?

A We mean that he is carrying more fat—that is to say surplus stored energy—than he requires. The body is a biological machine, or to be more exact a complex of a number of different machines working together. Perhaps an even better analogy would be to think of it as a city with a large number of inhabitants, a great collection of factories and an enormous amount of general bustle and activity going on. To keep all this activity going, fuels of various kinds are required—coal and petroleum for the factories, electricity for the street lighting and communication systems, and so on. One way to supply all this energy would be to have constant pipelines and wires connecting the city to the outside world to ensure a running flow of energy, and many cities do receive some percentage of their supply in this way. On the other hand, cities, like most other complex organisms, tend to have cyclic energy requirements—street lighting demands go up at night, for example, but factories use far less fuel and the overall energy demand is low. Secondly it is not always convenient or economical for

all energy to be piped in from outside exactly at the moment that it is required. For this reason most cities set up fuel stores within their own boundaries which can be built up and tapped off when convenient. With every breath we take we draw in oxygen to the lungs—a kind of biological pipeline to the air around us which assures a constant supply of this life-giving gas. But it would obviously be horribly inconvenient if we had to take in food in a steady stream in the same way (though many simple animals such as amoeba do operate in this way). It is for this reason that most higher animals have acquired storage facilities within the body which will allow the creature to go days and weeks without food. All healthy people need to have stored energy, in the form of tissue fat, in their bodies, in an amount which is appropriate to their general build and physique. When the energy stores build up to an extent which is greater than the "recommended" level, we say that a person is overweight.

WHAT DO WE MEAN BY "NORMAL" WEIGHT?

This is an enormously difficult question to answer, for medical authorities and dieticians disagree to some extent

on what would constitute a "normal" reserve of energy. There are a number of factors to take into account. The first relates to the size or build of the individual. Here the city analogy is helpful again—the bigger the city the greater its energy requirement and the more prudent it would be to establish big fuel stores. The second relates to the working life of the city. The more active it is, the greater its energy requirement will be. A third factor might relate to the geographical location of the city. If it was on an island, say, which could only be visited by fuel tankers every month or so, and if monthly visits failed unpredictably, then the city would need to have absolutely immense fuel stores. Extending this argument to human beings, perhaps at one time in the early days of mankind, such fat stores were really advantageous when food was hard to come by and tended to turn up in great heaps. Nowadays of course the nearest supermarket is rarely more than a block or so away, and this excuse for fatness will no longer do! There is another side to the coin as well. Cities wanting to establish giant food stores merely have to extend their city boundaries a bit to do so and nobody really minds. People on the other hand do not welcome such bulges and expansions of their own "city limits." Furthermore, unlike the cities, people have to carry all this extra mass around with them. But bearing in mind that we have to take these three factors—size, general activity level and ready availability of food into account—we can arrive at some rough guides as to what constitutes an ideal weight.

HOW CAN YOU TELL WHAT YOUR IDEAL WEIGHT SHOULD BE?

Provided that you remember that there is considerable personal variation, the best way to decide what your ideal weight would be is to refer to the table (next page) drawn up by a dietician. The two important factors or "variables" are height (in bare feet) and frame or build. It is not difficult for you to find out your height, but there are obviously a large number of widely differing frames or builds. Try to decide whether you can best be placed in the "slight," "medium" or "large" frame category. If you find it difficult to do this yourself then ask a friend to do it for you. Now weigh yourself on reliable scales, naked, and check to look at your *ideal* weight (the first figure). If you are aged between 20 and 25, deduct two pounds for each year you are under 25. Variations of up to five pounds on either side of the first value are nothing to be bothered about either way. If you are slightly over this five-pound leeway, you have a minor problem which could build into something if you are not careful. However, if your weight exceeds the italicized figure alongside the initial figure, then you must count yourself as being definitely overweight. Even at this level it is likely to be only psychologically damaging. But if your weight exceeds the figure in parentheses, then you are seriously overweight to the extent that it may well be damaging to your health. Dieting and exercise, following medical advice, are recommended.

WHAT CONSTITUTES OBESITY?

Obesity is an unpleasant word which denotes an unpleasant condition, and for all practical purposes it refers to a state where surplus fat has built up to such an extent that it is literally harmful to the individual. A state of obesity is represented by the figure in parentheses given against the relative height/frame value in the table At this point it is worthwhile emphasizing the difference between obesity and simple "overweight."

Here an important factor which might be described as your "image of yourself" comes into play, which in turn leads on to a discussion of the various reasons that might make people want to diet and slim. For anyone classing themselves as obese by honest reference to the table, there can be no doubt that a course of slimming and dietary regimentation is essential. The more anyone's weight exceeds the stated figure for obesity, the more important it is to make a determined attempt to slim, though when a person is seriously obese this should only be done after receiving medical advice. In such cases the body is carrying far too much weight for its own good. At the level between "normal" weight and obesity, however, there is a kind of no-man's-land where the extra fat is not necessarily harmful to physical health, but may be psychologically damaging. The reason for this is that in our present society, and according to our present tastes, very small amounts of bulging surplus fat are unfashionable and aesthetically unpleasing.

WHAT MAKES A PERSON OVERWEIGHT?

With the exception of certain disease states, where massive weight gain takes place because, for example, the body retains far more water than it should, there is really only one way to become overweight. It is quite a simple way too and, in principle at least, is easily corrected. To gain too much weight all that a person has to do is to absorb in food more energy than is needed to supply the daily quota. Once this energy is in the body, it is released from the food by digestive processes and made available to the system as a whole in the form of simple "total energy" molecules. These are retained in various organs or float in the bloodstream, feeding muscles and nervous tissue and being used up as required. Those that are not used up get stored as fat and can be called up again at a later stage. But if on the next day another surplus of energy appears and work output remains level, the stores of fat begin to expand. There is no other way to become overweight, for fat is nothing more than stored fuel.

WHAT ARE THE VARIOUS WAYS OF LOSING SURPLUS WEIGHT?

There are only two ways of losing weight. The first is to increase the body's energy requirement by making

it do more work, mainly of a physical kind, and hence preventing the build-up of surplus stores. This can mean exercising in bursts now and again or simply raising the total level of activity throughout the day. The first is probably the most practical solution, but it takes a surprising amount of exercise to take off even small quantities of surplus fat. The second and ostensibly the easiest way to lose weight is to cut down the amount of energy taken in as food. As millions of us know, this is unfortunately far easier said than done.

WHAT ARE THE MEDICAL ARGUMENTS AGAINST BEING OVERWEIGHT?

If we are talking merely about being a few pounds overweight, the medical aspects are not too significant: small amounts of flab are more damaging to the psyche than anything else. With obesity, however, the problem moves out of the range of unkind comment and self-reproach into the area of ill-health and even a shortened life span. Insurance statistics now show, without any argument whatsoever, that obese people are far more prone to a whole range of serious ailments than are people of normal weight. These include the dreaded coronary thrombosis, which carries off thousands of people every year in what should have been the prime of their life; osteoarthritis, a painful and crippling bone disease; and chronic bronchitis and varicose veins. There is even evidence, surprising though it may seem, that obese people are significantly more likely to be involved in accidents of various kinds. Physicians and psychologists are still puzzled as to why this should be, but we can make a number of reasoned guesses. For example, obese people on the whole tend to have a balancing problem and may be far more likely to stumble and fall. There is also some evidence that their reflexes are slower, with obvious serious consequences in numerous aspects of modern life. The stress of such a common task as driving is more likely to affect very fat people, and there is evidence that their ability to shift attention is reduced. To add to this mournful list there is strong evidence that fat people are less resistant to disease than their slimmer brethren and are particularly prone to respiratory infection. The life expectancy of an obese person may be five or ten years less than that of someone without a weight problem. Excessive extra weight puts a colossal strain on a heart which is designed to move a much smaller body around. Being 20 pounds overweight may not sound too much of a problem, but translate it into a heavy briefcase or shopping bag which you need to carry around every moment of your life and you see the scale of the problem. If that does not sound too bad, imagine someone really obese—say 40 or 50 pounds overweight—and instead of a shopping bag you find yourself with a large family-size suitcase, and a full one at that! But even if the height and weight table reveals you are overweight or obese, do not despair. There are ways you can slim and come back to normal.

WHAT ARE THE PSYCHOLOGICAL ARGUMENTS AGAINST BEING OVERWEIGHT?

The principal one is that the fat person sees him or herself as being *different,* and different in an unpleasant way, from the majority of other people. Psychologists and sociologists have been aware for some time that in all human beings there exists a basic desire to be "one of the group." The origins of this desire lie very far back in evolution and are probably tied up with the fact that most animals survive better in a hostile environment when they live together. But being one of a group is not only a matter of living in close proximity with other people. A person must also be able to identify with others and feel that he is not only *with* them but *like* them. In many animal societies the eccentric or deviant individual is often rejected by the group and, when it is at the bottom of the pecking order, can lead a pretty wretched existence. Regrettably human beings are not always much kinder to each other than are animals, and members of a social group who differ in one way or another from the "ideal norm" often feel both unconsciously and consciously rejected. Even short people —particularly short men—tend to be aware of their relative isolation from the group and frequently try to make up for this (often successfully) by an aggressive, dynamic approach to life. Fat people fall into the category, cruel though it may seem, of social deviants and when they have real problems with obesity may suffer psychologically as a result. This in turn can lead to associated disorders, such as depression and paranoid problems involving jealousy.

The trouble is that fatness is something that is impossible to disguise either from yourself or from the rest of the world, and the overweight person is reminded of his or her problem agonizingly when trying to find clothes to fit a deviant figure. And fashionable clothes (which allow us to be part of the group) are never made in outsizes! One of the many rewards of achieving marked weight loss is the way overweight people cease to regard themselves as outsiders.

ARE THERE ANY ARGUMENTS AGAINST SLIMMING?

Only if a weight problem has been brought on by a physical illness of some kind or if a person is suffering from a heart condition which would be aggravated by sudden weight loss. For example, very fat people may develop heart trouble as the result of being overweight. One of the first things that the doctor will do is to put them on a careful diet to bring the weight down, but without inducing rapid physiological changes which might stress an already delicate heart. Vigorous physical exercise would never be prescribed in this situation. With these exceptions, sensible dieting and exercise can do nothing but good for otherwise healthy people whose weights put them in the "overweight" or "obese" categories. The critical word here, of course, is "sensible." Those who need to lose a lot of weight should always consult a doctor before embarking on any slimming program.

It's feeding time again (right), and just another snack to keep the wolf from the door. Eating is a consuming pastime—the bigger you get the more you think you need to keep going. OK, this is fine for starters— now what's for dinner?

CHECK YOUR WEIGHT

MALE

Height		Slight frame			Medium frame			Large frame		
		Ideal weight	Over-weight	Obese	Ideal weight	Over-weight	Obese	Ideal weight	Over-weight	Obese
ft.	ins.	(lbs.)	(lbs.)	(lbs.)	(lbs.)	(lbs.)	(lbs.)	(lbs.)	(lbs.)	(lbs.)
5	4	118	130	(142)	125	138	(151)	134	148	(164)
5	5	121	133	(145)	128	141	(154)	138	154	(166)
5	6	125	138	(151)	132	145	(157)	144	157	(173)
5	7	129	142	(155)	136	150	(164)	146	161	(176)
5	8	134	148	(162)	141	155	(169)	151	166	(181)
5	9	138	152	(166)	146	161	(176)	156	172	(188)
5	10	142	156	(170)	151	166	(181)	161	177	(193)
5	11	146	161	(176)	156	172	(188)	165	182	(199)
6	0	150	165	(180)	160	176	(192)	169	186	(203)
6	1	153	168	(183)	164	181	(198)	173	191	(209)
6	2	158	174	(190)	168	185	(202)	179	197	(215)
6	3	162	178	(194)	173	191	(209)	184	203	(222)
6	4	166	183	(200)	178	196	(214)	189	209	(227)

FEMALE

Height		Slight frame			Medium frame			Large frame		
		Ideal weight	Over-weight	Obese	Ideal weight	Over-weight	Obese	Ideal weight	Over-weight	Obese
ft.	ins.	(lbs.)	(lbs.)	(lbs.)	(lbs.)	(lbs.)	(lbs.)	(lbs.)	(lbs.)	(lbs.)
5	0	99	107	(117)	106	117	(127)	114	125	(137)
5	1	101	111	(121)	110	121	(132)	118	130	(142)
5	2	104	115	(126)	113	125	(137)	122	135	(148)
5	3	108	119	(130)	116	128	(140)	125	139	(152)
5	4	112	123	(134)	120	132	(144)	129	142	(155)
5	5	116	128	(140)	124	137	(150)	133	146	(160)
5	6	120	132	(144)	128	141	(154)	137	150	(165)
5	7	124	137	(150)	132	145	(160)	140	155	(170)
5	8	128	141	(154)	136	149	(164)	145	160	(175)
5	9	133	147	(161)	140	154	(169)	150	165	(181)
5	10	137	151	(165)	145	159	(174)	155	171	(186)
5	11	142	156	(170)	150	164	(181)	159	176	(191)
6	0	146	161	(176)	155	170	(186)	164	180	(196)

Coloriffic

Plumbing the depths

Water, water everywhere nor any drop to drink, but hazel finds the water by some mysterious link.

We normally think of a dowser, or water diviner, as a man walking across a field holding a forked hazel twig in his hands, looking for water.

Although it may look a little ridiculous, people are not quite so skeptical about dowsing as they are about other forms of extrasensory perception. Most believe there is "something to it," even if they do not have any idea how it works.

Nor do the dowsers themselves. It was once thought that hazel had some kind of affinity for water, so that the twig was attracted to the underground source in much the same way as a piece of iron is by a magnet. But this explanation has long since been dismissed. The point of the hazel twig does not necessarily dip *down* when the dowser is over water; it may tilt up or make spasmodic movements.

And in any case, there is no need to use hazel. Most accomplished dowsers can use any kind of wood; and often they employ a pendulum or more sophisticated type of apparatus. A gadget now used commonly consists of two L-shaped steel rods. The dowser holds the short ends of the "Ls" loosely in his fists, with the long ends pointing out in front of him as he walks along, and they give him the indications he requires.

It is not easy to separate the history of dowsing from the wider history of divination—the exploitation of second sight. In primitive tribes the witch doctor was expected to have this clairvoyant faculty, so that if drought dried up the streams and wells, he could tell the tribe where to find water—just as he could tell where to find game when food was short.

Above: When this diviner and his hazel rod find water, the twig will jump up and down in his hands.

But as man's apparent ability to use extrasensory perception in this way dwindled, witch doctors—and, later, seers or prophets of the kind familiar in the Old Testament—began to use aids of various kinds. They would throw pieces of stick or bone onto the ground, and from the pattern formed would advise the tribe—much as amateur fortunetellers use tea leaves. Or they would look into a bowl of water and "see" a picture of where the tribe should go.

Some of them used another method still found among some primitive societies. The witch doctor picks up two pieces of deer horn, and holds them out in front of him. The horns then appear to take over, as if they are moving him, rather than he moving them; and they lead him in the direction which the tribe should go. The process is similar to that which the present-day dowser uses. It is reasonable to surmise that dowsing is an evolutionary development from that early technique of divining.

The first recorded instance of the divining rod, it has been suggested, is described in the Old Testament in Exodus, when God commanded Moses to use his rod to strike the rock "and there shall come out of it, that the people may drink. And Moses did so, in the sight of the elders of Israel."

But though there are a number of other episodes which may or may not be considered as early examples of the art, it is not until comparatively recent times that the evidence for its existence becomes strong indeed.

According to W. F. Barrett—later Sir William Barrett, fellow of the Royal Society, professor of experimental physics in the Royal College of Science in Dublin—the first record of the use of the divining rod shows that it was used for mining purposes in Germany in the late fifteenth century. From there it spread to Cornwall in Britain, where it was used for locating tin. Only later was it used to find underground water.

It was first studied scientifically in the 1650s, by A. Kircher and G. Schott, who put forward the theory that the movements of the rod were due to unconscious muscular action. But scientists in general regarded the divining rod as bogus, and the church condemned it as diabolical (it was denounced by the Inquisition in 1701).

No further investigation is recorded until the middle of the nineteenth century, when the emergence of spiritualism, which aroused curiosity about the behavior of objects during seances —tables tipping, for example—led to renewed interest in the behavior of the divining rod.

A great deal of often amateurish experimentation followed in the second half of the nineteenth century, some of which is described by Barrett in his book *On the So-called Divining Rod*—the qualification "so-called" giving some indication why so few orthodox scientists were prepared to interest themselves in the subject: "divining" was a dirty word. Characteristic of their attitude was the derision poured on water diviners by Professor Fiske of Harvard in his *Myths and Mythmakers*. Fiske believed that he had shown the art to be a fake, because when *he* used the divining rod, nothing happened.

However, there have been countless stories of how dowsers have found water in improbable places—in some cases rescuing their comrades by doing so. One often-told incident happened during the Gallipoli campaign, in World War I, when British troops which had landed found themselves unable to advance. The sun beat down and the water supply began to run out.

Sapper Kelly offered to find more; and with the help of a makeshift divining rod constructed out of copper wire, he claimed he had found an underground spring beside Divisional

Left: The dowser tries to locate water by the indoor method of swinging his pendulum over a map. Right: Diviners can use a variety of rods in their searching work.

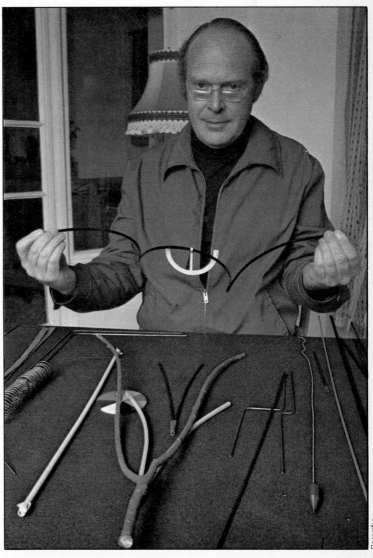

Colorific

HQ. Skeptically, Divisional HQ authorized the sinking of a shaft, and the result was a supply of fresh water at the rate of 2,000 gallons an hour—not enough to meet the needs of all the troops, but enough to make Sapper Kelly's reputation, so that he was transferred to water-divining duties and soon found another 30 sources, sufficient for their needs.

In many parts of the world, local authorities employ dowsers as a matter of course, as do some major commercial firms. But orthodoxy still rejects the possibility that dowsing can work except through ordinary sensory clues, given by "the lie of the land," or the color of the grass.

Oddly enough, the managing director of one of the world's biggest mining corporations is a dowser. When buying a site for his holiday villa on the Mediterranean, he went over the ground first with a divining rod to make sure he could sink a well on it, in case of drought. But when his directors heard about it, they begged him not to let his prowess become known. They were worried that investors would be frightened away if it became known that the company's surveys were conducted with the help of a forked hazel twig.

There is some excuse, though, for the skeptics, as dowsers rarely perform well when they are being tested. In *Water-witching USA*, published in the late 1950s, the authors Evon Vogt and Ray Hyman had no difficulty in producing evidence which showed that whenever diviners had been subjected to any kind of scientific controls, their performance suffered.

The dowsers explain this by saying that the controls which are imposed are often calculated to inhibit the dowsing faculty. For example, no test over natural ground is allowed—because the dowser might cheat through local knowledge. He is expected to demonstrate his technique in laboratory conditions; and it is not surprising that he should fail. Nevertheless, most dowsers allow themselves to be tested, hoping one day for the breakthrough.

An attempt at a serious trial of dowsing was made in connection with a television series, Margins of the Mind, presented in Britain in 1966. The producers decided to ask John Cohen, professor of psychology at Manchester University, to set up the experiment in such a way that it could reasonably be described as scientific.

A dowser is apparently able to find the answer to his question—"Yes" or "No"—by the direction in which his pendulum swings.

After considerable discussion, a scheme was agreed upon which would make it impossible for anybody connected with the program to divulge information to the dowser who was being put on trial.

Six identical cans were filled with water, five of them having salt added. The cans were then sealed and buried in a gravel patch. The gravel was raked over, and a dowser was invited to try to find the cans, and to identify the one which had fresh water in it. He also had the opportunity to see if he could find three cardboard boxes which had been buried, two containing absorbent cotton and pebbles, the third containing a kitchen knife.

The dowser, Norman Leftwich, went over the area—it was about 100'×150'—with his divining rod. He had been told what he was to look for, and the rod duly indicated six places where, he claimed, the cans were buried (though he expressed doubt about one of them). His method was to wait until the rod's movement indicated "something curious down below" and then ask himself "Is it a can of water?" and "Is it fresh or salt?" Then he walked over the raked area where, he was told, the cardboard boxes were buried. He pointed to three places and named the one where the box with the knife could be found.

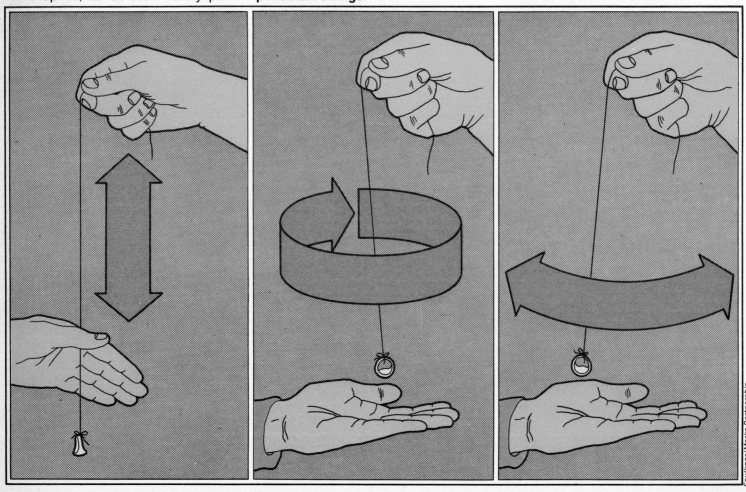

Faulkner/Marks Partnership

It was. So were five cans, at the places he had marked; and the one he had said would contain fresh water did contain fresh water. The sixth, which he had been uncertain about, turned out to be a massive stone.

Up to this point Professor Cohen, who had supervised the arrangements in such a way as to make it impossible for the dowser to detect the presence of the buried objects except by extrasensory perception, had been resolutely skeptical. Now, he had to admit that there was apparent evidence for the dowser's ability. Accordingly he set up another test, this time in a plot of wasteland near his university department, where Leftwich was asked to find five buried cans of water. He duly pointed to five places—only to be told that it had been a trick experiment; only one can had been buried—and he had not found it.

Magic Wand

So the final result was inconclusive. Yet the evidence from the gravel patch seemed striking enough. And it could be argued, in Leftwich's defense, that the test in Manchester was no real test. But conclusive proof of the dowsing ability was not established, and it has continued to be elusive.

Dowsers are ordinarily associated with the search for sources of water, and that remains the task for which they are most commonly employed. But just as Leftwich located the knife, so many others soon find their rod will guide them in other ways, with a little practice.

One of the best-known British dowsers, Major-General J. Scott-Elliot, made a list of some of the things he had found by dowsing:
a lead pipe laid under the lawn
a Roman ditch outside a camp
the healed fracture in a man's leg
a piece of metal in a man's back
the end of a duct buried under earth in a grain-drying kiln
the latitude and longitude of a ship in the Mediterranean
Scott-Elliot's particular speciality has been the discovery of Roman remains in Britain. There is no shortage of them; the trouble is not finding where the remains of a Roman camp lie under the earth, but in selecting the precise places to dig up, to avoid wasting the archaeologist's time and the landowner's patience. Scott-Elliot's method is to try to visualize the camp's perimeter—a ditch or wall—and then to approach it from the outside, marking the points where his divining rod gives the appropriate indication, until he has a rough idea of the dimensions of the original site. It is then possible to "ask" his rod individual questions to pinpoint where the remains are.

A look at the membership list of the British Society of Dowsers discloses a number of other retired senior army officers, as well as Scott-Elliot. And this is less surprising than it may sound, as guarding the "far-flung British Empire" before World War II continually put army officers into strange places where water for drinking and for ablutions was scarce.

The description by Colonel K. W. Merrylees, of how he came to be a dowser is probably typical. He was an army engineer and, until he was posted to an Indian unit, though he had heard of water divining, he had never seen it and knew nothing about it. Then one day in a frontier province he saw another officer wandering around with a forked hazel twig, which was performing strangely. Merrylees did not know him, and did not care to interrupt. But when he had finished, Merrylees decided to try for himself. "Peculiar things happened. I could not hold the twig still when I walked in certain areas, or rather on certain lines; it was something which seemed quite peculiar." Peculiar though it seemed, Merrylees was convinced there must be something to it. And he became a dowser on his own account.

Water Holes

How can the dowsing phenomenon be accounted for? It used commonly to be believed that there must be some extension of a known sense, like hearing or smell, which was capable of picking up the existence of an underground water course—in much the same way as some individuals and many animals can pick up sounds ordinarily not recorded by the human ear. But dowsers point out that this theory is untenable, because they can get indications of where a stream runs by using a pendulum or other device over a large-scale map. Not all dowsers use this technique, but many do, and they claim that the instrument, when held over a map, gives them sufficient indication of where to look, even though they may be many miles away from the place.

Dowsers now commonly attribute their ability to what they describe as "resonance." When the dowser mentally asks the question "Is there water here?" and there is, his projected thought-form unites in some way with the water radiations present in the area to produce the characteristic movement of his divining rod. If there is no water, his thought-form finds, as it were, no target, and there is no response from his instrument."

There is one aspect of dowsing which could easily be investigated and about which there is no dispute: the actual movement of the implement used, whatever it may be. Whether or not there is a watercourse down below, there can be no question that a dowser's hazel twig dips or makes other movements as he is holding it. How? What is the force involved?

Mystery Movements

On this issue the dowsers themselves are divided. One theory, which still finds favor today was originally elaborated a century ago by the great French naturalist M. Chevreul. Chevreul had watched spiritualists using a pendulum for purposes of divination, asking it questions and getting the answer "Yes" or "No" from the way the pendulum moved. Most scientists of Chevreul's standing assumed that the spiritualists were simply faking such movements; but he became convinced that the movements were involuntary. The explanation was that the movement of the pendulum was dictated by the spiritualist's thoughts —though they were not aware of this, believing that the information came from the spirit world.

In those days the concept of the unconscious mind had not been popularized; but as soon as it was, it was put forward as an explanation for dowsing. The hazel twig is responding to messages from the mind, transmitted through the muscles, though the dowser, unaware of how the mental process works, can only offer terms like "resonance" to explain it.

The trouble with this theory is that, though it can be used to explain the movements of a pendulum, it is much less satisfying as an explanation of the movements of a hazel twig. True, for some dowsers there is what appears to be a muscular movement— notably for those who use no implement at all, just their bare hands, which may twitch. But others find that the movement of the twig is apparently unrelated to any physical act on their part. People who hold the ends of the twig loosely between crooked forefinger and thumb may find it turning round and round; and if they try to stop it by tightening their grip, they may find it actually takes the skin off the finger, as it continues to move.

1173

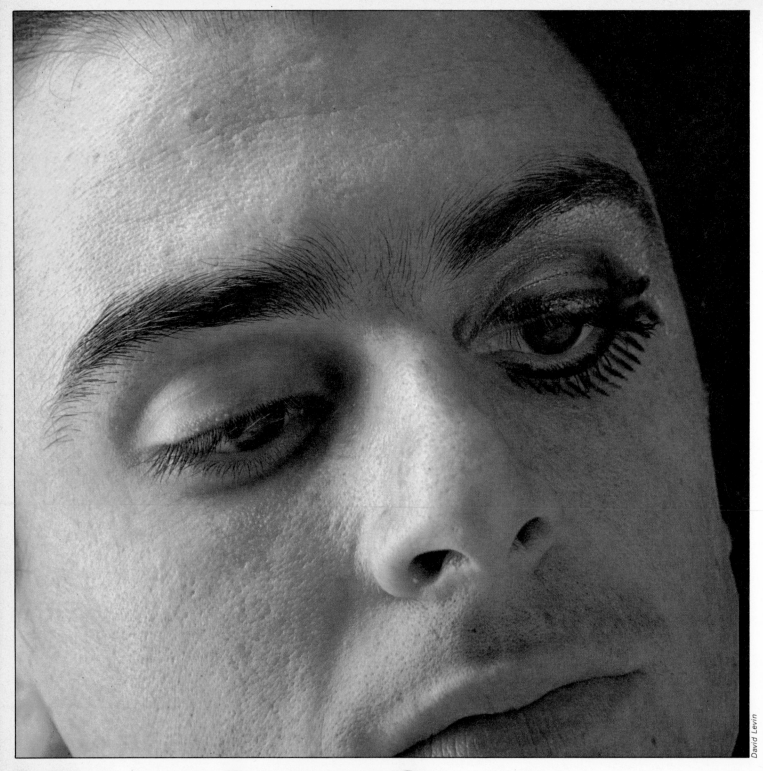

David Levin

His or hers?

A man in a bra is without doubt bizarre. What's more, this fancy dress is a dreadful drag.

Every man in the room was dressed in women's clothing and a feminine wig. They were transvestites—people who like to dress in clothing of the opposite sex—meeting at their club.

The men were particularly masculine in appearance, mostly from lower-class backgrounds and with manual occupations. Their faces and bodies were broad and chunky. They dressed either in a matronly way or rather like tarts; and they looked embarrassingly unattractive. Their muscular legs were encased in flimsy stockings, often with fancy motifs running up one side; their artificial breasts sat uneasily between their broad shoulders and heavy waists; their wigs were dressed in extreme styles. In their deep male voices they talked energetically about tights and bras and skirts, and the difficulty of getting them in large sizes.

Only two males present looked anything but bizarre. One was only 17

Ron Haywood

years old—he was slightly built and his face was still smooth-skinned. The other, an engineer, had a fine-boned, narrow face—the sort of face commonly associated with intelligence or sensitivity. In this case, the association seemed accurate. He spoke more thoughtfully about his transvestite practice than the others. He claimed that there was no sexual activity involved in transvestism, for him. The satisfaction arose from merely being in female dress.

Putting on the Agony

When asked if he found his "cross-dressing" satisfying, he became depressed. "*Sometimes* it satisfies me. Sometimes I just feel a fool," he said quietly.

The causes of transvestism are a matter of considerable doubt and argument. Most of the men at this transvestite club put it down to an early-childhood episode, sometimes sexual, more usually involving their mother or her female friends dressing him in their clothes in play. Some researchers and therapists have thought that transvestism is a mark of an immature personality—one interpretation being that the man wants to revert to the time when he could, in play, don his mother's clothes and in so doing become a part of her, as he had been in the womb.

It is probable that the desire to reenter the more secure, less demanding phase of his life may contribute to the transvestite's compulsion. Many societies classify the preadolescent boy as a sort of female—putting women and children into the one category. In fact, in most tribal societies, adolescent boys are required to undergo initiation tests before they may be accepted as men. Unlike a girl, who achieves womanhood effortlessly, merely by menstruating, a boy has to "prove" his manhood.

If he fails, he is in a most unenviable position—even if his disability arises from his being disabled. Failure means that he will not only *not* be acknowledged as a man, but that he may be classified as a *woman*: a "man-woman." In a sense, a young man who

In the study of transvestism, a strange phenomenon has come to light. It appears that the majority of men who dress up as women come from the laboring class, where there is less opportunity for creative work than there is, say, for a photographer or doctor. Can it be that transvestites are working out a repression?

1175

fails to achieve manhood in the way prescribed by his community may be said simply to have "remained" an immature female—as much a "child-woman" as a "man-woman."

Certain tribal societies impose a peculiarly punitive mark of disapproval on such gender anomalies, as sociologist Michael Banton points out: "Among some such peoples a young man who, because of physical infirmity or lack of courage, cannot pass the test must wear women's dress for the rest of his life."

Such "men-women" cannot marry: they must live as women. Some are homosexual: transvestite homosexuals. "In some societies," Banton writes, "homosexual males are permitted to dress and live as women after going through ceremonies analagous to marriage"—marriage, that is, to another man. The transvestite homosexual among Plains Indians was not subject to social scorn, although, strangely, his "husband" *was.*

In Western society, the transvestite is usually heterosexual and married with children. Sexual relations with their wives are more or less normal—that is, very successful or partially successful or very poor, just like ordinary heterosexual men.

Putting on the Style

Transvestite practice varies: for some the act of dressing is itself the pleasure; for some it is the exhibitionist thrill of going out in public in full female dress from time to time. Some wear one or two feminine articles of underclothing all the time; with some, sexual emission may occur spontaneously when dressing: with most, the "cross-dressing" is invariably associated with the act of masturbation. Finding a safe place to secrete the feminine garments (if they are not borrowed from a wife or mother or sister) and washing them or getting them cleaned may either add to the excitement or reinforce the anxiety states that usually accompany transvestism.

The misery caused by transvestism —the fear of discovery or the humiliation and anxiety felt by wife and family

Shakespeare's female characters were always played by boys dressed as women, and traditionally in slapstick comedy men dress in girlish attire. These cases are, however, essentially different from men who dress in drag for their own sexual titillation. Transvestism is a deviant practice and is often accompanied by states of anxiety.

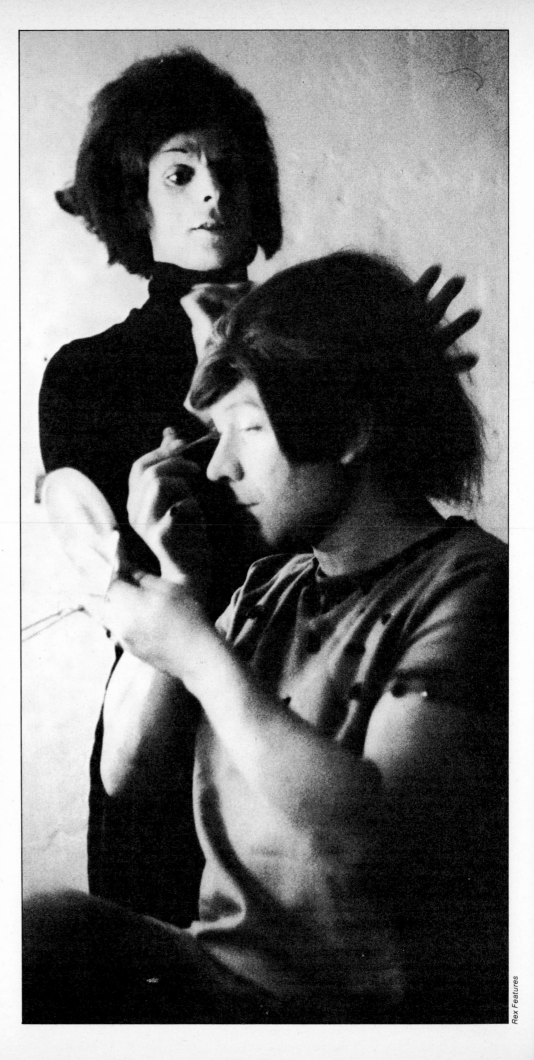

—seems disproportionate to the pleasure involved. Extraordinary tolerance of discovered transvestism is sometimes shown by wives.

"I have seen a strong, burly man who was an Air Force officer, played football, and mixed normally with other men. He showed a normal interest in women, yet he liked to wear female clothes when he had intercourse with his wife and did not obtain satisfaction unless he did so," writes Clifford Allen (*A Textbook of Psychosexual Disorders*). "His wife was kind and sympathetic and allowed him to do this although it distressed her that he was so abnormal." (Dr. Allen does not mention how it affected the *wife's* sexual enjoyment.)

Petticoats and Pickaxes

Many psychologists assume that transvestite homosexuality is quite distinct from transvestism, that it is a form of homosexuality, not a form of transvestism. Research indicates that the nonhomosexual transvestite tends to be an emphatically "masculine" man. Since transvestite activity tends to be spasmodic and/or secret, estimates of numbers or types of transvestites are highly speculative.

Most scientific and medical knowledge of transvestism is drawn from limited groups—transvestites who have sought treatment; neurotics or psychotics whose transvestite practice is discovered in the course of treatment of a different disorder; transvestites whose deviance has become so public and exhibitionist that they are prosecuted and committed to prison or for treatment; and people who join a transvestite club and do not object to inspection by journalists or researchers.

One psychologist found that about half of the group he studied were in manual occupations; a quarter were scientists and engineers; another quarter were in other professions and businesses. Few had clerical jobs; and even fewer were in artistic or creative occupations.

His sample consisted of people who had been referred to him for treatment at the hospital in which he worked, plus people from a club for transvestites. This means that he dealt only with people who had chosen to be "cured" of transvestism and the sort of person who would join a transvestite club. Neither category can be said to offer "typical" transvestites.

But if transvestism does occur among just that type of man in whom one would least expect it—the most "masculine"—there could be many

The logical extension of transvestism: Christine Jorgensen underwent surgery to become a woman, and still looks pretty good at 50.

reasons for it. The boy who has been brought up in a very masculine lifestyle, in which books and art and music may be considered effeminate, may feel the need for some expression of the more "feminine" aspects of his personality and choose the most superficial and obvious source of "femininity"—clothes.

Or the enforcement of masculinity may be so great that fear makes him react in a deviant way, as sociologist Margaret Mead *(Male and Female)* writes: "Fear that boys will be feminine in behavior may drive many boys into taking refuge in explicit femininity." Fear of the apparently complex difficulties of the masculine role—in child or adult—may similarly prompt deviant behavior.

All children at some time have some anxieties about their sexual characteristics. All human beings are partially bisexual—even anatomically this is so: every man has rudimentary female organs and every woman has certain masculine characteristics. It is obvious that there will be different norms of masculinity accepted by

different people—for instance, differences between norms pertaining in the household of a truck driver or car salesman and in the household of an artist or university professor.

Sexual norms also differ, and if parents' responses to normal sexual play in a child are too repressive, deviant behavior may result. Deviance may also be caused by a mother who treats a child like a doll, paying excessive attention to dressing it, and, perhaps disappointed at not having a girl, dressing a boy in demonstrably female clothes.

Many transvestites cite childhood memories of this kind. We cannot rely too much, however, on the childhood memories of adult deviants. Adults may easily give a sexual interpretation to nonsexual childhood acts; or they may rationalize the precipitating factor of their deviance in an inaccurate way. A transvestite who has an early memory of a delicious session of dressing in his mother's silkiest or frilliest clothes may have "forgotten" a traumatic event occurring about the same time—perhaps his father suffering a terrible accident at work or being summarily dismissed from his job or being refused a long-sought promotion. This may have persuaded him that the male world is a frightening one, the female world playful, luxurious and safe.

While dressing in women's clothes is generally practiced as a solitary erotic act, a few transvestites may prefer to assume permanently a feminine identity. They may seek hormonal treatment that will change secondary sexual characteristics, or even surgical alteration of primary sexual characteristics. This normally puts them out of the transvestite category and into the transsexual one.

Sex Switch

Transsexualism is understood to be quite separate from transvestism. The transvestite is sexually attracted to females and wants only partially to identify with them. A transsexual believes that he *is* female and wants his masculine body changed into a female's. He is sexually attracted to males, but does not find homosexual sex appropriate. He wants to live entirely as a female, among females, relating to men only as a female. He is capable of union with a woman—a number of transsexuals who have undergone chemical and surgical alteration have previously been married with children—but he feels that he is the wrong "half" of the union.

A few transsexuals may be the result of a genetic gender fault of some kind. Although this possibility is very attractive to a lot of transsexuals (and to some homosexuals and transvestites), the likelihood is slight: such cases are exceedingly rare.

A very few babies are born with ambiguous sexual characteristics, and the decision about which sex to attribute to them may be in the hands of a fairly uninformed doctor. They will usually receive some treatment to eliminate the ambiguity. Scientific advances which make it possible to measure innate masculinity or femininity sometimes prove that an individual has been brought up in the wrong sex after the "wrong" sexual characteristics begin to appear at the onset of puberty.

If such an error is discovered, it is then difficult to decide on the correct course of action. It depends on the age of the child and the family environment. In a small child, a switch to its true genetic sex, with appropriate hormonal or surgical treatment, may work successfully.

But an older child may already have been so strongly conditioned toward belonging to his attributed gender that it would be damaging to allow or compel him to join the sex to which he naturally belongs. A "boy" will be too conditioned to a striving commanding, muscular, male-bonding role—as opposed to a nonstriving, submissive, male-dependent role to make a change. But if the family is well-educated and very liberal, and the child has not been strongly conditioned towards absurdly disparate gender roles, the alteration may be feasible.

Different as transvestism and transsexualism are, however, they may well have similar triggering factors. The treated transsexual Jan Morris, who was previously James Morris, an historian and travel writer, wrote a best-selling book about his experiences called *Conundrum.* Although he seems to deny its relevance, he admits that he was the youngest of three brothers and that his mother had wished for a daughter when he was born ("but I was never treated as one"). He writes of his middle-class, high-church upbringing—Eton collars, the fluttering gowns at the choir school of Christ Church, Oxford. His family did not, however, make strenuous gender-role divisions: they did not reject arts and music as feminine, for instance. But his father, who died when he was young, had been "ravaged" by war.

"Had I decided that I would rather grow up to be a woman than a man? Did some fearful legacy of the Great War, which ravaged and eventually killed my father, make the passions and instincts of men repugnant to me?" he wrote.

Female Fantasies

For twenty years he told nobody of his belief that he was female, not male. He "cherished it as a secret." In spite of a comparatively educated and artistic background, however, the girls he dreamed of emulating were the American film stars Deanna Durbin and Sonja Henie—both excessively cute, Hollywood-film-starrish girls: in Sonja Henie's case, habitually dressing in frilly, provocative skating costumes and blond curls.

It is characteristic of transvestism (and to some extent of transsexualism) that the transvestite has his own interpretation of "femininity"—and that it is often "tarty" or extreme. Necessarily to do with the superficial aspect of femaleness, transvestism is often also concerned with negative or "desired object" aspects of being female. (James Morris did not enjoy homosexual sexual acts at his school but very much enjoyed being chased and kissed and admired and sought after by homosexuals there, and he assumed that this was what being a girl would be like.)

The transvestite is not concerned with any of the frustrations and difficulties of being female: his female role playing emulates not an individual and complete woman but a fantasy woman. He is playing the role of his young mother, his sister or his wife or a prostitute or any sexual-fantasy woman—submissive, permissive, fetishist, sadistic, or whatever he fancies.

Skirting the Issue

It is for this reason that transvestites feel uncomfortable about "unisex" fashions. They do not want ambiguous fashion, they want unmistakably female clothing and, usually, erotically fanciful female clothing. They seem indifferent not only to the lifting of social prohibitions against long hair, frilled or flowered skintight shirts, velvet trousers and so on, but also to the moderate tolerance of male fashions that are, in Western eyes, extremely feminine: like Arabian and oriental kaftans and flowing robes.

It is, however, strange that there is considerable resentment expressed by transvestites towards the greater "permissiveness" of female fashions: women are "allowed" to wear trousers, but we cannot wear skirts, they complain. It is as though they supposed that the new freedom for women to wear trousers to work—rather than just for leisure—were a bid for masculinity rather than a matter of comfort and freedom of movement (and to some degree of fashion).

It is possible that the very masculinity of many of the men who resort to transvestism indicates that they are sometimes men who, by reason of upbringing or occupation or both, could be expected to condemn the wearing of unmasculine male clothes as "hippy" or "artistic."

Some psychologists believe that transvestism is invariably accompanied by other abnormalities. In any case it is generally found that an increase in mental stability will reduce the compulsion. Whatever form of therapy is used, treatment must be prolonged to be effective.

Although some liberal opinion suggests that therapy for sexual deviance is an intrusion on the privacy of the individual, there seems little doubt that transvestism *should* be treated by therapy, if the subject has the slightest wish to be cured: both for his own sake, in the long term; and for the sake of his relationship with his wife and family.

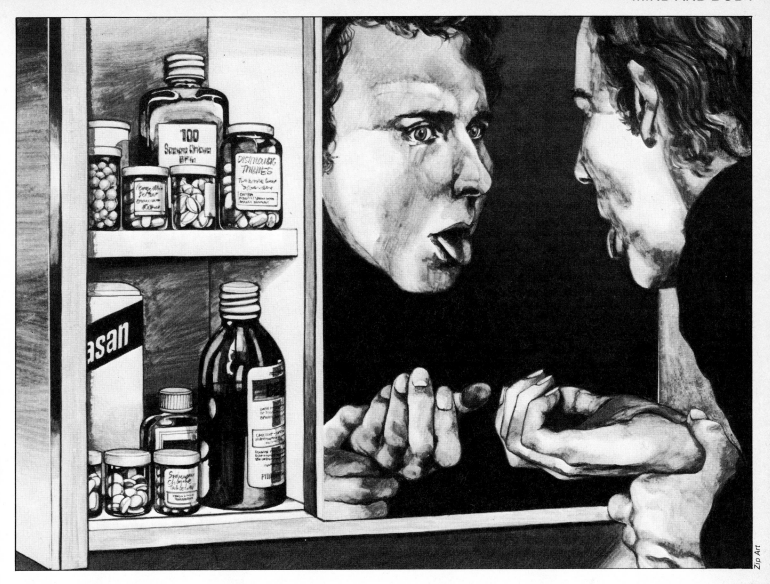

All in the mind

When the face in the mirror greets you with a shudder and your pulse feels like a tribe of Indians on the warpath, perhaps a cupboard full of pills is not the best place to look for a cure. Could it be that the source of your sickness is the troubles on your mind?

Psychosomatic diseases are bodily disorders or illnesses which are influenced by the mind. This definition covers an enormous range of conditions, from minor rashes to actual death. The most simple form of psychosomatic condition is the reddening of eyes and cheeks seen after prolonged crying. Crying is stimulated by an emotional upset, and there are undeniable physical results on the facial skin, so a true psychosomatic condition exists.

Most psychosomatic disorders are much more obscure in origin. To take the opposite extreme—death can result from autosuggestion. This is the so-called "bone-pointing" syn-

drome, best known among Australian aborigines, who may literally will themselves to death after being cursed by a witch doctor. But between these two extremes lies an enormous range of diseases classed as psychosomatic. They can be loosely divided into three categories.

First are those diseases with known organic causes, such as viruses, bacteria, or protozoal infections. Mental attitudes are not thought to play a significant part in the origins of these conditions, which arise by normal disease processes. The mind may, however, influence the subsequent course of the disease, by lowering the resistance of the patient. The body is

then less able to combat the infection, and recovery may be prolonged or followed by relapse.

The second group are more mysterious diseases, the exact causes of which are uncertain, but which are thought to be influenced by psychosomatic processes. The autoimmune diseases fall into this category—the diseases in which the body reacts against itself. Some forms of cancer are thought to be of this type, but the theory is unproven as yet and remains very controversial.

The final group is comprised of a wide range of "stress diseases," the typical psychosomatic diseases. Best known of these are heart disease,

1179

hypertension or high blood pressure, peptic ulcer, bronchial asthma, migraine, and some types of skin rashes.

Because of their association with the mental condition of the patient, many psychosomatic diseases respond well to psychiatric treatment. Some will respond to simple suggestion. Diseases most frequently benefiting from faith healing, laying on of hands, and religious pilgrimages are those of psychosomatic origin. In many cases, although the disease itself may remain, painful or incapacitating symptoms often seem to disappear after such unorthodox treatment.

Sham Symptoms

Hypnosis has also proved effective in the relief of psychosomatic conditions such as asthma and can also be used to demonstrate the actual formation of a psychosomatic condition. When a suitable subject is deeply hypnotized and informed that the experimenter is about to apply a red-hot iron to his skin, the subject's skin will obligingly turn red and blister when touched with an ordinary pencil. The physical effects closely resemble a real burn, but the damage to tissues is more like that of a poison ivy rash. However, this pseudoburn is just as painful as the real thing. The mechanism of this reaction is not clear, but as there is a two-way passage of information in the nervous system, from skin to brain and from brain back to skin, the solution is probably to be found in neurophysiology.

Yet another related phenomenon is the appearance of stigmata, or wounds, on the hands, feet, or head of certain Christian mystics. These wounds mimic Christ's wounds at the crucifixion and are well attested scientifically, although regarded with suspicion by many religious skeptics. They are usually regarded as being of hysterical origin and consist of shallow, inflamed wounds on the skin, which sometimes ooze blood. These wounds are said to arise spontaneously, although some persons with stigmata have been seen to pick at them with their fingernails while asleep. However, even if stigmata are brought about "artificially" in this manner, they should still be regarded as psychosomatic since the process is worked by the unconscious mind.

Some psychosomatic diseases seem to be mechanisms of escape from distressing or intolerable circumstances. Religious stigmata characteristically appear in extremely poor, intensely religious communities.

Possession of such miraculous wounds confers a welcome degree of importance to the stigmatized individual, and this is often reinforced by the formation of local religious cults, headed by the stigmatic.

Similarly, hysterical paralysis or blindness, which was common among soldiers in World War I, often occurred under battle conditions. Curiously, this physical condition has almost vanished and is replaced by the fashionable "nervous breakdown" or "battle fatigue"—a clear indication that it was of psychosomatic origin, rather than a pure physical condition, though it does not mean that the patient consciously willed the disease.

Fainting is a psychosomatic reaction to distressing circumstances. In the Victorian era, women swooned or were overcome by "the vapors" at the least provocation, whereas the hardier females of today reserve this ultimate defensive weapon for escape from the sight of blood or a mouse in the kitchen. The stimulus required to trigger this reaction is conditioned by the mental make-up of the individual and the standards of society. In the twentieth century, most of us are conditioned *not* to respond by fainting at the sight of violence or at foul language. But if we do faint, and if the crisis was traumatic enough, severe shock may follow, and subsequent circulatory collapse could even lead to death. The unfortunate victim would have been quite literally frightened to death.

Fight or Flight

In this case, what should have been a protective reaction has run out of control. This is also the case with many of the stress diseases of modern society. In an effort to cope with stressful conditions which the body is not equipped to withstand, physiological changes take place inside the body which can result in serious psychosomatic illness.

Even emotions can have a marked effect on the functions of the body. This can be demonstrated quite dramatically in both animals and man. If a cat is given a barium meal, which shows up on X-rays, and the shape of the stomach is observed on an X-ray monitor, the normal churning movements of peristalsis can be seen as the digestive system gets to work on the "food." But if a dog is suddenly brought into the room, a dramatic change takes place in the shape of the cat's stomach. The valves controlling the entry and exit of food to and from the stomach close firmly and peristal-

sis ceases, letting the stomach sag as it relaxes. This results from the liberation of adrenaline into the bloodstream: part of the "fight or flight" reaction which readies the animal for violent exertion.

An almost identical reaction can take place in the human stomach at times of stress or emotion. This was clearly demonstrated by study of Tom, a man living in New York who, because of an accident, had a blocked esophagus and could eat only through a gastric fistula, an artificial aperture in his abdomen leading directly into his stomach. The reactions of his stomach to emotional stimuli could be viewed through this aperture.

Purely in the interest of science, Tom was told, quite untruthfully, that he was to be fired from his job. Understandably, he became extremely angry, and his facial reaction was mirrored by that of his stomach wall, which became reddened and swollen and even bled at the lightest touch. When the trick was explained and Tom calmed down, his stomach quickly returned to normal. If Tom was in a depressed or subdued mood, his stomach wall became gray and limp, covered with mucus.

Placebos Please

Surely here are the beginnings of the businessman's ulcer, with continual frustration or anger causing inflammation and eventual bleeding of the stomach wall. The actual formation of a peptic ulcer requires an additional predisposing physical condition though, as only about 10 percent of people respond in the same way as Tom. Probably the sagging, gray-walled stomach which results from depression is the cause of much dyspepsia and many other digestive difficulties.

Emotional disturbance may produce psychosomatic disease with no physical symptoms, in the form of pain of a psychic origin. Pain resulting from surgery or from malignant disease can be relieved in about one-third of patients by giving them a placebo, or medically inert substance, rather than the usual pain-killing drugs. Placebos are even *more* effective than ordinary drugs in treating psychosomatic diseases without a known physical cause, and it is thought that they work in a similar manner to hypnosis and faith healing.

Bronchial asthma is one of the most common and most debilitating psychosomatic diseases which, until the beginning of this century, was thought to be purely mental in origin. Recently, however, severe allergic

Marshall Cavendish

A common psychosomatic condition is the puffy face and pink eyes after a good cry. Crying is caused by emotional upsets, and it is primarily the emotions which cause red blotches on the face.

reactions have been shown to play an important part in triggering an asthmatic attack. After being exposed to a normally harmless substance a number of times, the body may suddenly become sensitized and will react violently on the next exposure. This sometimes occurs after a person has been stung repeatedly by wasps or bees. It is a very severe form of allergic reaction, and when it occurs in the lungs as a result of inhaling an allergen—or sensitizing substance—the small air tubes or bronchi contract so much that it becomes very difficult to breathe. In an asthmatic attack,

breathing may be so difficult that the muscles of the chest and back must be used in an attempt to force air in and out of the lungs, often resulting in total exhaustion.

However, an attack is *usually* brought on by emotional factors. More than two thousand years ago, Hippocrates noted that rage could cause an attack, and later physicians recorded how even pleasant emotions could trigger seizure. Laughing or crying have all been known to start an attack, and oddly, also to stop one. But asthmatic attacks do not always follow strong emotional episodes; a combination of precipitating factors must be present. Such apparently unrelated factors as the presence of allergens capable of precipitating a reaction, emotional disturbance, genetically determined susceptibility, and the presence of minor respiratory

infections may all play a part in inducing an asthmatic attack.

Persons who suffer from bronchial asthma have a genetic tendency towards the disease, but by no means all the people carrying the gene or genes responsible for it will actually develop asthma.

Attacks of asthma are usually treated by physical means, such as the use of steroid drugs, or by inhaling substances which relax the spasm in the bronchi within the lungs.

Antibiotic treatment is often given, as mucus trapped in the lungs often becomes infected and could start a fresh attack. Another promising avenue of research is desensitization, which is a technique for reducing the allergic reaction against inhaled substances. A particularly powerful allergen is present in all houses. This is the dust mite, a microscopic creature which feeds on shed scales of human skin. It is found in huge numbers in bed mattresses, where warmth, food, and humid conditions are particularly favorable. Desensitization is achieved by injecting the patient with progressively stronger extracts of dust mite, or any other allergen, until the body learns how to cope with the foreign substance in it.

These physical treatments are often successful, but resistant cases may need psychiatric help. A psychiatrist may recommend a change of employment or a more prolonged period of psychotherapy.

Heart disease can also be psychosomatic. Heart attacks are a form of this disease which are often brought to a critical point by emotional factors. Men are known to be particularly liable to heart attacks, and faulty diet, stressful occupations, and lack of exercise are all known to contribute. But the actual attack is usually precipitated by an emotional crisis or a period of overwork. Attacks may also occur during sleep, perhaps as a result of disturbing dreams.

As with most psychosomatic diseases, there may be an inherited tendency towards heart disease. A high blood cholesterol level is known to run in certain families, and it is the deposit of this fatty substance on the walls of arteries supplying the heart muscle which ultimately impedes the blood flow sufficiently to cause angina, a full heart attack.

Raised blood cholesterol levels have been associated with certain personality types. Canadian researchers have attributed dangerous cholesterol levels to persons with exaggerated social ambition, those

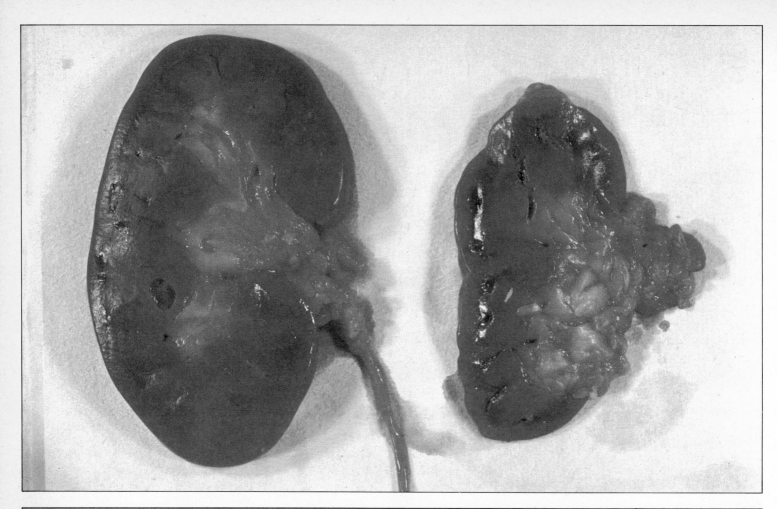

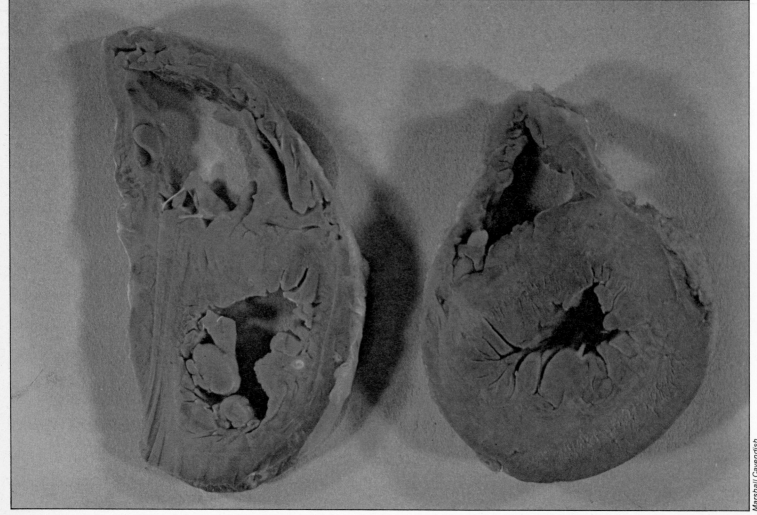

who may be generally dominant, aggressive, hostile, and inflexible. Many studies tend to confirm this view, which should permit identification of susceptible persons *before* they have an attack or suffer permanent damage to the heart. Regular health checkups can detect the accumulation of cholesterol, and proper diet and exercise will slow the process. But avoidance of stress is probably the most important single factor in staving off a heart attack.

Peptic ulcers (either *gastric* ulcers, in the stomach, or *duodenal* ulcers, in the duodenum) affect about one in twenty people in the Western world at some time in their life, and currently cause more than 10,000 deaths annually in the United States. The studies on Tom, the New Yorker with the window in his stomach, demonstrated how the stomach can become highly sensitive as a result of emotional stress. Further tests showed that if part of the mucus layer was removed from Tom's stomach wall, ulceration resulted. This mucus is the fragile barrier which separates the stomach from its corrosive contents, and when this is removed, the stomach simply begins to digest itself, producing an eroded area, an ulcer. Peptic ulcers are extremely painful and once formed may take a long while to heal. They may bleed or even perforate, and this frequently proves fatal.

Executive Monkey

Ulcers are often thought of as a slowly developing condition, but animal studies have demonstrated that they may appear very rapidly. For example, if rats are painlessly immobilized by clamping their tails, they develop gastric ulcers within 24 to 36 hours. Predictably, if they also receive mild electric shocks, the ulceration is more severe. But when shocks are administered to some rats at regular intervals and to others at random, those receiving random shocks have much worse ulceration than the other group. Apparently the uncertainty and anxiety of waiting for the next unpredictable shock is the factor which intensifies the ulceration.

Illness brought on by stress falls into the psychosomatic category. In stress diseases what should have been a protective reaction runs out of control and physical changes take place. Left: A kidney (above) and a section of a heart (below), severely affected by hypertension, beside larger, healthy organs.

An excellent parallel in man is the uncertainty and stress of executive life, causing ulcers in the businessman.

Similar results have been obtained in experiments on monkeys. The more severe the task given and the more anxiety it provokes in the animal, the worse will be the resulting ulceration. An even closer parallel with man resulted from experiments with "executive monkeys." Monkeys were yoked together in pairs and given mild electric shocks, which could be avoided if the "executive monkey" pressed a lever. After several weeks, it was found that the rate of ulceration was much worse in the decision-making "executive monkey"—once again proclaiming a clear message to busy executives.

Sleep Treatment

Ulcers are usually treated by physical means and by modified diets, avoidance of alcohol and smoking, and other means designed to reduce further inflammation of the damaged tissues. In the Soviet Union, however, treatment is aimed more at the emotional factors precipitating the condition. Russian scientists have observed that perforation or bleeding usually follows an emotional disturbance. Accordingly, they often treat ulcers by sleep treatment, sedating the patient for as long as 14 days to allow the nervous system as well as the stomach to rest. Unfortunately, in both the United States and Britain, psychiatric treatment for peptic ulcers is usually given only when other psychiatric complications are also present.

Migraine and other forms of headache have been associated with a wide range of physical and emotional causes. Muscle tension, spasms in blood vessels supplying the brain, and the toxic after effects of alcohol can all cause headache. Migraine is the most acute form of headache, often combined with complete physical prostration, vomiting, and interference with vision in the form of patterns of lights. It is thought to result from constriction of the blood vessels supplying the brain and scalp, provoked by the presence of histamine. This substance is produced during allergic reactions, and sometimes the antihistamines used to treat hay fever will relieve the pain. But like the other pyschosomatic diseases, migraine is brought on by a combination of factors. Migraine sufferers tend to be tense perfectionists, and when exposed to stress such persons be-

come progressively more tense, until an attack results.

Skin irritations are a minor, though very common, form of psychosomatic disease. In a susceptible person, an itching may be felt, without any visible rash, as a result of psychological stress. Lesions are then produced by scratching, and if the source of tension is removed, these will quickly heal. But if emotional tension continues, scratching produces extensive sores, which may become infected. These unsightly sores lead to self-consciousness and embarrassment, increasing the nervous tension, which in turn increases the itching, and so on. A vicious circle is established. This condition is particularly common in adolescents and is usually treated by steroid ointments to relieve the itching and by an attempt to relieve the source of the environmental stress which began the cycle.

Anorexia nervosa, one of the most devastating of the psychosomatic conditions, is confined almost entirely to adolescent girls and can lead to eventual starvation. It apparently results from a conviction that the sufferer is overweight, and this is followed by severe dieting. Having reached the target weight, however, normal eating habits are not restored. The sufferer continues to be obsessed by her "excessive" weight and may stop eating completely.

Obsessive Slimming

When well-meaning relatives or friends begin to comment, she will hide her progressive emaciation beneath loose, bulky clothing, and if persuaded to eat, she will secretly vomit up the food later. Eventually, menstruation ceases, hair begins to drop out, and death from starvation may follow unless there is effective medical treatment.

Anorexia nervosa is extremely resistant to treatment. A high calorie diet is given, and the patient is watched to make sure that it is actually eaten. Some anorexic patients are extremely ingenious at hiding food or secretly vomiting it up, and for this reason they are usually hospitalized. Psychotherapy is an important part of the treatment, usually together with tranquilizers. Some extremely resistant cases have been treated by specialized forms of psychosurgery, with varying degrees of success. A woman recovered her appetite after surgery but did not lose her fear of putting on weight. She was so horrified at what she saw as her repulsively fat body that she killed herself.

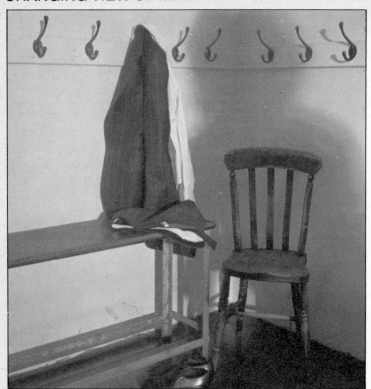

David Levin

Quality of mercy

Mercy, Shakespeare wrote, "is twice bless'd; it blesseth him that gives and him that takes,"
and where the sword of justice is not contained by the scabbard of mercy, no criminal or country
will have a chance to set the record right.

In Britain the custom of boiling criminals alive ended in the fifteenth century. Not only did it fail to deter crime but it was thought to have a degrading effect on those watching.

However, it could be safely assumed that the onlookers were less concerned about this possibility than the disappointment of being deprived of their entertainment. For in 1633 the diarist Samuel Pepys recorded that he was compelled to pay for an extremely uncomfortable hour on a cartwheel waiting with 13,000 other people to see a man hanged.

The deterrent effect of capital punishment on the criminal himself was, at the same time, equally questionable. It was thought that others would be frightened by traitors' heads being exhibited on the ends of poles. But the theory failed in practice, as witnessed by the number of active pickpockets among the crowds watching the executions, when pickpocketing was itself an offense subject to the death penalty.

Today's reformers question the morality of meting out extreme punishment to one individual in order to deter others from similar crimes, as if the one was being punished for the potential crimes of all. In this century capital punishment has been largely confined to the crime of murder. Society agrees that murder is unacceptable. But has capital punishment acted as a deterrent?

In those American states which have abolished capital punishment, the incidence of murder has not risen in any marked way, nor is it any higher than in those states which have retained capital punishment. If the ultimate deterrent does not deter—if we are merely using the criminal as an example to others—then we are getting no nearer to the roots of the problem: why has the murder been committed and how do we eradicate the causes of murder?

Most countries have now abolished the death penalty. One government made this statement: "In our country the lesson has been learned that respect for human life is best inculcated by the state itself refraining from taking life in the name of the law." This attitude is reflected by Howard Jones, author of *Crime in a*

Above: An empty room with a wallet carelessly left lying may be enough to push someone into crime. But when it comes to judgment, will we be prepared to take some blame?

Changing Society, who writes, "How a society treats its offenders is an index of its basic attitudes towards human personality."

The arguments of reformers and reactionaries rage around capital punishment, not only because it is the ultimate retribution. Death can teach the offender nothing, nor can it entertain any error of judgment. Now that life sentences have largely replaced the death penalty, the arguments continue. Society slowly is diluting its own revenge ethic. In the age of psychiatric dissection, the criminal's mental state at last speaks for him, not against.

Society must still protect itself against the threat of violence but now it has a choice, whether to send the murderer to prison or to hospital. Is the offender capable of *deliberate* wrong? Is he responsible for his own actions? The Soviet Union understands that mental illness may deprive a person of his free will. But in several of the American states and other places, including Canada, New Zealand and Western Australia, the law dictates that the criminal is responsible for his own actions unless he is under such delusion that he believes something that, if it were true, would make his act excusable.

Nothing Deterred

But what could make murder excusable, however mentally deluded the murderer? Not if he killed his wife merely because he suspected her of poisoning his prize plants and vegetables. However, if he imagined himself on the point of being murdered by his wife, then his reaction might be excusable on the grounds of self-defense. Since it is presumed that the murder in both cases is carried out under purely deluded provocation, and since to a sick man the first delusion might well seem more provoking than the second, the distinction may seem unsatisfactory.

If deterrence through punishment does work, then it would seem worthwhile providing a system of penalties which, made clearly apparent to all potential offenders, would stop them from committing the offense. But if it can be shown that this kind of deterrence has no effect, then society is using the offender as a scapegoat. Knowledgeable "experts" contest both sides of the argument equally vehemently. But what can no longer be argued—for the figures in every country speak clearly against punishment in this case—is that punishment will never *cure* the offender. Only unlimited care can do that.

On the subject of deterrence, George Kirchwey, a well-known advocate of reform among American prison administrators, wrote—maybe too skeptically—in 1911: "It [punishment] cannot deter the mentally defective, they cannot appreciate their danger.

It cannot deter the insane, their minds are too distorted to reason. It cannot deter the antisocial, they are at war with society and the danger only adds pleasing zest to the contest. It cannot deter the thoughtful and deliberate for they have no intention of getting caught. Nor can it deter the impulsive, for impulse is always quicker than reason. Whom then will it deter? Why just you and me—who have high standards and much personal pride, and who are law-abiding anyway."

But why are most of us law-abiding? "High standards and personal pride?" —these are not very convincing arguments. A criminal may take pride in the high standard of his work. What Kirchwey refers to, it seems, are the

The last public execution in England took place in 1868. This cartoon produced a year earlier made the point that the gory spectacle merely evoked further violence among the onlookers.

advantages of good fortune and proper upbringing. Are these all that keep the majority of us from crime? It is well worth considering what does prevent us: to understand this might bring us nearer to an understanding of the criminal himself.

Maybe we cannot be bothered to commit a crime. Then we are clearly well enough provided for not to need to do so. Maybe we have been brought up in an environment so alien to the concept of crime that the very thought of even aiding or abetting a crime would not enter our heads. Once again, we are lucky.

Resisting Everything but Temptation

And maybe we *are* deterred by the thought of punishment, just a little. If we knew that we could steal without any fear of being caught, perhaps more of us would try our hand. Think carefully. It is easy enough to succumb to temptation, once the opportunity is provided. We all know that. How much easier, then, for the disadvantaged to slip something into their pocket, to reach through a car window for a camera left on the seat, to take the car itself if someone has been foolish enough to leave the keys. Once successful, how easy, too, to repeat similar offenses and subsequently more ambitious ones.

Think again: if you found it so easy to hoard a gallon or two over the legal limit during a gasoline crisis, if you were able to congratulate yourself and boast to your friends on bringing in a couple of extra bottles of scotch through customs, if you managed to slip an extra pack of cigarettes onto the pile that had already been passed through the checkout counter at the supermarket—if you suddenly found yourself in profit at no cost to yourself, would you not be tempted to have another go?

Take it a stage further: who has not said, "I could *kill* that person?" Without meaning it, of course! "If only I could get my hands on so-and-so." Naturally, you would not *do* anything. You are controlled, you are sensible, you know that it is wrong. You have been brought up to abhor such violence. Yet you hear of it all around you. You know that it *is* possible, that people do let themselves go. You yourself get so angry sometimes that you scarcely know what you are doing. Would it not be very easy to let go just once? If you knew that you could get away with it, maybe you *could* kill.

There are, of course, plenty of people who could never behave like

this. But there are plenty of others who might—without the deterrence of law or social stigma (and this is far more important)—just *might* find it quite easy.

Perhaps luckily, we do not question that murder should be considered a crime. The very fact that capital punishment is used less and less implies a higher value on human life and in consequence greater abhorrence of death. To condone murder would put us all in peril. So it is with other crimes and offenses: to condone theft would put our possessions in peril; to condone fraud would put our business dealings in peril; to condone blackmail would be to lay ourselves open to threats of all kinds. In each case laws exist to ensure the survival of society as we have molded it.

We think we know what we mean by "crime." We mean everything that threatens to break up the structure of our society, with its emphasis on both social and private protection. The law fulfills the needs of society: to protect it from itself.

But there are many circumstances —probably we all have our favorite ones—in which the law seems absurd. Or it seems absurd that there is a law at all. But the process of erasing certain "crimes" from the statute books is a slow and steady progress. Sociologists and criminologists are urging that this process, in certain areas, be speeded up. Should, for instance, desertion from the armed forces be a criminal offense? Should a drunkard be regarded as a criminal?

Give Them a Chance

The word "criminal" is now frequently dropped in favor of the tag "offender." But only when the label of "criminal" or "offender" has been dropped from the social vocabulary might it be possible to turn our unbiased attention to finding out why the individual has become an alcoholic, why the thief who wants to go straight finds himself unable to do so, or how, if not to stop prostitution, for example, then to ensure that it offers no foothold for physical disease, coercion or violence—the only real social ills the profession might foster.

The National Association for the Care and Resettlement of Offenders now emphasizes that what offenders need is not the severity of the law but affection and attention; that it is the responsibility of the community and not the law to divert the offender from his disaffection.

NACRO believes that teachers should

work with the community to instill a sense of worth and an attitude of fairness and honesty in their pupils; that doctors should use their position to spot the first signs of social and family stress; that the police should rebuild their local knowledge to the advantage of the community; that social workers should act constructively and continuously, not only in a crisis; and that press and radio should present a realistic picture of crime, not only the ugly face of it which frightens the community into rejecting the offender. All this is what criminology is about. There is an enormous amount of work to do and a huge responsibility for everyone in the community. From the neighbor who lends a hand to resettle the man who has found himself in trouble, to to the employer who is prepared to take the risk and offer a job, to the friends who have the patience to keep listening and talking and to the landlady who is happy to provide a home.

Self-protection

And we still need the law, even if only to protect us from those who truly are like "ourselves." The antisocial acts that are committed by the advantaged, in the full knowledge of what they are doing, without social or legal deterrence—these are the actions the law should be aware of, the ones it should seek to control.

The whims and profits of the wheeler-dealers of the stock market can have repercussions of a devastating nature on the small-time saver; the political machinations of vote seekers can disproportionately affect the local trader and the private consumer; the misleading panegyrics of the advertiser can, even within the restrictions demanded by the law, lead the average person into errors of judgment that may well produce considerable difficulty and hardship.

In the final analysis we must realize that if we are to be protected from ourselves, and from our fellows, we should consider very carefully exactly what it is we need to be protected from, and whom among us we need to protect.

A man leaves prison with his belongings hoping for a future of freedom within the law. But what are the odds? Once tagged "ex-prisoner," there will always be those who are not prepared to give him a second chance. Perhaps work and accommodation will be hard to find and so all that's left is a return to crime.

All you want to know about...

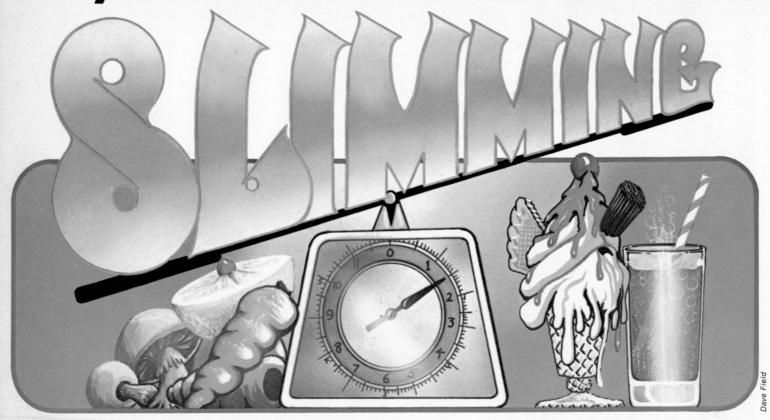

Dave Field

Q WHAT IS COMPULSIVE EATING?

A Most people get themselves into a weight problem for one or both of the following reasons. Firstly, their enjoyment of eating—which is after all one of the major human pleasures—develops slowly but surely into a hobby. Secondly, they generally have too little understanding of the raw materials of the foods which they eat, and often they do not really know which foods are fattening and, almost as important, *why*. Add these two factors together and what you get is a person steadily increasing his daily quota of energy—measured, of course, in calories—and remorselessly building up reserves of stored fat. This might be described, for want of a better phrase, as "normal overeating," the penalty we pay for our general affluence and the delicious foods available any time we want them. Compulsive eating is quite another matter. Here the individual is seized by a craving to eat which is quite out of proportion to hunger in the accepted sense of the word and even to the taste or quality of the food being eaten. In its milder forms, most people, if they are honest with themselves, will recognize that they have had bouts of compulsive eating, or "stuffing" as it is sometimes rather crudely called. For apparently no reason at all sometimes we feel a pressing desire to consume really large quantities of food, often of a particular kind, and for a short period at any rate our appetite seems almost insatiable. There are few of us who have not on occasions gone through a whole bowl of peanuts in a matter of minutes, or devoured large quantities of potato chips, ice cream or bread, butter and jam! Such bouts, if they are at all frequent, do horrible things to the figure, but the damage can often be eliminated by one or two days' restraint. Compulsive eating on a grand scale—when huge meals may be eaten and vast quantities of snacks consumed throughout the day—is a tragic and dangerous habit, often requiring treatment from a psychologist rather than a physician. At the origins of the condition there generally lies an anxious and disturbed personality, whose anxiety finds momentary relief in the act of eating. Psychologists tend to believe that the "stuffing" serves as a substitute for affection and attention—an unconscious wish to return to the security of the infant's feeding bottle or the mother's breast. A slightly different theory suggests that eating bouts are related to childhood when adults comforted the distressed or crying child with candy and tasty foods. To this extent compulsive eating is a habit of long standing. Probably the true explanation lies in a combination of the two theoretical approaches. Certainly the act of putting things in the mouth and chewing or sucking them does suggest an association with the oral gratifications of childhood reflecting one of the primary instinctive drives, the sucking reflex. It is interesting to note that smoking—another habit which tends to increase under conditions of stress or anxiety—is also orally based.

WHAT IS COMPULSIVE FASTING?

As its name implies, this is more or less exactly the opposite of compulsive eating. This condition, which is sometimes known as anorexia nervosa, is also largely psychological in origin. Typically it affects women only, and in particular girls in their late teens who are often just leaving home, starting at college, or in their first job. In many cases the girls have had a tendency to overweight or obesity, and it seems as if their natural concern about this condition becomes amplified in a horrible way at some critical time in their life. It generally begins with a neurotic and quite excessive preoccupation about the figure, with the girl sometimes spending hours of the day studying herself in the mirror. Often what is merely puppy fat is built up in the imagination so that she believes that she is hideously obese. From here extreme dieting in an effort to remove the fat begins, and this in turn may be transformed into a total loss of appetite and a possible loathing of food of any kind. Attempts to take food on the advice of worried parents or friends may be followed by vomiting and other unpleasant symptoms. All fatness soon vanishes, of course, but unfortunately this seldom satisfies the sufferer from anorexia nervosa, who still sees herself as fat and bloated. All evidence of scales, the mirror, the pleas of family and so on are disregarded. Compulsive fasting continues and may even do so, almost unbelievably, until death takes place from malnutrition. This complaint, which is not all that uncommon, is at present poorly understood but is probably related to the colossal significance which is ascribed to a "slim figure" in our society and to the enormous anxieties which are characteristic of late adolescence. The girl becomes so horrified at the thought of being fat that her judgment of her condition is warped beyond reason. Anorexia nervosa is a dangerous psychological disorder and needs the most careful and sustained medical attention. Occasionally, it is seen in later life and often follows an obsessive preoccupation with dieting and "figure consciousness."

WHAT PART DO CALORIES PLAY IN SLIMMING?

Calories are units of energy and are useful to the would-be slimmer principally because they allow him to label the energy content of food and hence its potential for fattening. If more calories are ingested in the course of the day than are burnt off through working, then a person will put on weight. It is worth remembering here that, contrary to what many people seem to believe, calories are not *things*—that is, packets of energy themselves—but only a *measure* of energy. Much confusion arises out of the careless use of this word. Now the amount of energy which a body needs is dependent upon its size and, of course, the amount of work that it does. For this reason, since people vary so enormously in size and general activity, it is not really possible to give

an exact figure to indicate the number of calories which are needed for the "average" person in any one day. A useful guide, however, would be to begin with a housewife of medium build, not physically very active and who tends to drive a car rather than walk. A rough average for her daily requirement would be 2,000 calories. For a man working in an office, who again does not take a great deal of exercise, 2,500 calories would be a useful round figure. But a highly active woman, who exercises an enormous amount and leads a bustling, busy life involving a good deal of physical work, might use up as much as 3,500 calories a day, while a man engaged in really hard manual labor might require 4,000 calories a day, or even a little more. These figures are for a person of medium frame and need to be adjusted up or down by (roughly) 500 calories a day if the frame is slight or large. Once again the inflexible rule for weight watchers becomes apparent: take in more than your daily requirement of calories and you will gain weight. Take in less and you will lose weight.

DO OVERWEIGHT PEOPLE NEED MORE ENERGY TO KEEP THEM GOING?

It depends on what is meant by "keeping going." Remember that the larger your frame, the more calories you require to keep that frame (that is, to keep your weight constant). A fat person is in some respects equivalent to a person with a large frame, at least inasmuch as they have about the same amount of body mass. Now to keep their mass constant (that is, to remain fat) they *do* need a greater amount of calories, and hence comes the unfortunate increase in hunger which often accompanies being overweight. The trouble is that if a person tends to overeat a little anyway weight tends to creep up remorselessly, with appetite increasing and the weight problem getting steadily worse as the result. People on a successful diet in which their total body weight is reduced often find that in due course their appetite declines because their remodeled body no longer requires so much energy to keep its weight constant.

CAN YOU INHERIT A TENDENCY TO GET FAT?

The two *principal* factors which determine overweight are the amount of physical work which the body is put to

and the total amount of energy which is absorbed in the course of eating. When the amount of energy used up by the first process is less than that taken in by the second process, then a person will put on weight. But there is also a third factor which intervenes to complicate this otherwise simple equation—the process known as the metabolism. Metabolism is just a technical word which refers to the biological machinery which breaks down food into its essential components—carbohydrates, proteins, vitamins, and so on—and then makes use of the by-products to form the microstructure of bone, nerves, and muscle tissues. The breaking-down process is known as catabolism, the building-up process as anabolism, and the two put together are called metabolism. In these terms the efficiency of a metabolism would be a measure of how quickly and how well food products were catabolized and how quickly and how well the components were anabolized to build and repair the body. Now it so happens that while our bodies use the same general processes, there is considerable difference from person to person in the efficiency of the metabolism in general. Those people with highly efficient metabolisms will handle the raw materials more rapidly, more effectively, and with less waste than those with comparatively inefficient metabolisms. Such people have a definite edge as far as keeping slim goes, for their bodies can take in more in the way of energy-rich food, make use of it more effectively, and hence be far more resistant to weight gain. There is good evidence that a super-efficient metabolism is something which is inherited. Conversely, so is a sluggish metabolism. For weight watchers these facts are good or bad news depending on whether they are fortunate enough to have had parents with high or low metabolism. Often when two women of equivalent build and weight set out to diet, and both stick strictly to the same food intake and manage roughly the same amount of exercise, one will find it harder to lose weight than the other. It is tough luck on one of the pair but nevertheless a fact of life. Incidentally, this does not mean that a person with a low metabolism will be unable to diet successfully. It merely means that it may be a little more difficult to do so. The metabolism is at its most efficient during the years of maximum growth and begins to slack off a bit in the early twenties. This is why it is often so much easier to keep a constant weight until about the age of 25, after which the first psychological and physiological problems of overweight tend to appear.

WHAT CULTURAL FACTORS AFFECT THE WEIGHT?

It is not only through genetic inheritance that family and family background can affect your weight. There is now very good evidence that cultural factors, particularly the example that parents set their children, are of very considerable significance in determining the relative ease or difficulty which a person will have in keeping his weight down to a reasonable level in the course of his life. It might even be said that fat people tend to come from fat families. Of course metabolism *can* play a major part in bringing about weight problems, and this is almost invariably a hereditary factor. But it is also by no means the most important factor, and overweight people who sit around blaming their parents or grandparents for their inheritance are really ducking the fact that the *main* reason for carrying excessive poundage is eating more than the body needs. There are three principal cultural factors, the first a rather simple and obvious one, the other two somewhat more subtle and therefore more insidious. The first relates simply to bad eating habits set by the parents themselves. If a mother and father are preoccupied with food, eat large quantities of it, nibble snacks between meals and are themselves overweight as a consequence, it is no surprise that their children will come to accept this pattern of overeating as "normal" and fall into a similar groove themselves. Unfortunately, habits of any kind established in the early years tend to be difficult to unlearn, and the chances are that a child who has been brought up on careless eating habits will retain them for the rest of his life—or at least until obesity in middle age pulls him up with a jolt. The remaining two factors have more to do with ignorance than carelessness. There is still a surprisingly widespread belief that sugar is essentially a good thing, a nutritious food in one form or another. Also enormously rich in calories are cooking fats of various kinds. Bread and potatoes are also heavy in calories, though not as much as many people think. But it is generally the *combination* of two types of energy-heavy foods that do the worst damage. A slice of bread on its own may contain a hundred calories, but when spread generously with butter its calorie content will double. Three slices of buttered toast therefore will bump you up 500-600 calories, and the sin can be compounded with jam or jelly, to bring this wicked breakfast up to about 750 calories—a quarter of what a man might require for a whole day. The trouble is that toast, butter and jelly are good to eat, and here lies one of the most unhappy pitfalls to successful dieting: so many of the most delicious foods are also the most fattening of all.

WHAT ARE THE FOODS THAT HELP YOU SLIM?

All foods contain calories of some kind, so everything that you eat is fattening to some degree. There are no foods which actually *take off* weight, despite one or two myths to the contrary, like one that concerns the so-called "grapefruit diet." The grapefruit has acquired a reputation as a slimming food, the implication being that some magical ingredient in it actually helps to burn off energy and reduce excess poundage. This is, unfortunately, complete nonsense, for the average grapefruit contains about 40 calories, which means that when you have eaten one you have 40 calories more than when you started. The grapefruit myth does in fact have a kind of foundation, for if a large number of them are eaten in a day, the appetite for other foods tends to be depressed—but only because your stomach is full and not because of any special property of the fruits themselves. You would not last very long on an exclusive diet of grapefruits. They are rich in vitamin C but contain little else, so while you would lose weight very rapidly you would also suffer nutritional deficiencies. What you can do is to stack your diet with low-calorie foods in the hope that your appetite for the high-calorie alternatives will be reduced. You end up with the same number of mouthfuls, which is psychologically satisfying, but less energy coming into the body will promote weight loss.

HOW EASY IS IT TO LOSE CALORIES THROUGH EXERCISE?

Any kind of exercise will burn up energy, and for this reason exercising is a helpful adjunct to any slimming course and also to keeping weight constant once it has reached an ideal level. The trouble is that calories are very easily taken in and not all that easily burnt off, and really effective exercise needs to be something more than just doing two or three push-ups a day or wiggling the legs in the air for a minute or so in the morning. To make any real contribution to preventing or eliminating surplus fat, exercise needs to be sustained and regular. But just how easily the good effects of even vigorous exercise are destroyed by careless eating, particularly of the "tasty snack" variety, can be seen by looking at some of the relative values of different foods and then the energy requirements of different activities. First it is important to establish that just to keep the body ticking over—the basic metabolic processes and the operation of heart, lungs, the various organs and a certain amount of gentle body movement—uses up about 1500 calories in a whole day, or about one calorie a minute. General pottering around the house might raise the level to 2 calories per minute, and about the same amount would be used up doing routine light office work. Walking would use about 4 calories per minute and cycling about 6 calories. Exercises of the bending and stretching variety use about 4 calories per minute, and swimming about 10, which is almost exactly the same figure as running briskly. A fast game of tennis will use up about 7 a minute, and squash a little over 10. From this it can be seen that *sustained* activity of this kind will bite into calories. But if we look at the debit side and consider how much exercise of various kinds would be needed to eliminate the calories taken in with some of the common "death to slimmers" snacks, the picture is not so rosy.

1. *A chocolate-covered cookie*—this contains approximately 100 calories and, while eaten and swallowed in a matter of seconds, would require nearly half an hour of typical slimming exercises to work off.

2. *A spoonful of ice cream with a covering of chocolate sauce*—this could contain as much as 200 calories, for which you would need to substitute 30 minutes of hard work digging or nearly 10 minutes' fast running up and down stairs.

3. *A favorite cocktail of generous size*—250 calories. This means 45 minutes' fast cycling or half an hour's steady swimming.

4. *A 2-ounce chocolate bar*—325 calories. A six-mile walk or nearly two hours of slimming exercises.

While exercises *can* help slimming, it is clear that they are no substitute for a restrained diet.

Use your body

Once you have accepted your body and come to enjoy it, you will certainly WANT to be more active. Instead of the drudgery approach to fitness, you will be ready to take up positively some means to improve your vigor. What you choose will depend on your body-type, your lifestyle and your personality.

How Fit are You?

Have you ever had eight hours' sleep, yet still felt tired next morning? Have you ever gone to your doctor for a checkup, feeling vaguely out-of-sorts, only to be told that you were in good health? Have you ever looked back with amazement to the days of physical ease and suppleness of your childhood?

Few of us feel as well as we would like all of the time. Every now and then, we resolve to do something about it—to exercise, stop smoking, cut down on food or alcohol. What fun is that? We get the impression that being healthy means living a

Try it: plant feet firmly on ground with knees rigid — now touch toes while looking back between legs.

monastic life. Who wants to do that? Yet you know that you need to be reasonably fit to enjoy life to the full. Is there an answer?

Before you work out a possible program test what your body CAN do. From these simple tests, you will find out which aspects of your body performance need attention.

Test Your Stamina

1. Take your pulse in a reclining position. Do not do anything strenuous beforehand, and rest quietly for a few minutes before you count. The average heart rate for a man is 70-75 beats per minute; for a woman, 73-78. Tension, smoking, or coffee drinking can raise it by 15 beats per minute.
2. Now run quickly on the spot for 20 steps. Take your pulse again. If it has not gone up or is only slightly faster (2 or 3 beats more per minute) your stamina is excellent. An increase of 5-15 is average. Above 15 indicates low stamina—you are not fit enough to sustain any strenuous activity over an extended period of time.
3. Take your pulse again after three minutes. It should have returned to normal. If it has not, you should engage only very gently in any fitness

program until you have built up your strength.

Test Your Flexibility

1. Stand with your back against a wall, making sure that your back, hips and heels are touching the wall. Raise your arms straight above your head with the palms turned forward. Can you touch the wall with your wrist bones? If you can, your flexibility is good. If you can get up to six inches from the wall, your flexibility is fair; more than six inches away shows a lack of flexibility.
2. Sit on the floor, legs apart in front of you, toes stretched outwards, hands clasped behind your head. Gently twist your trunk to the left and try to touch your left knee with your right elbow. The closer you can get, the better your suppleness. Now try with the left elbow and the right knee. Are you more supple on one side than on the other? If so, you need to develop your weaker side.

Test Your Balance

1. Stand on one foot with the other knee raised and bent against your body. Stretch your arms out on either

Camera Press

side. Close your eyes and try to hold your balance without moving for a count of 15. If you make it to 10, your balance is fair. Less than 10 (do not cheat by counting fast!) indicates poor balance.

2. Try the same exercise, but this time balance on your toes and keep your eyes open. Again, 15 is good, 10 is fair and less than 10 is poor.

Test Your Speed

A simple test of reaction time is to hold a pencil by the point with one hand, at shoulder level, keeping the other hand open an inch or two below the end of the pencil. Then release the grip of the upper hand and catch the pencil as it falls with the lower hand. Try with each hand. If you are very fast, you will catch the pencil at the bottom end. If you manage to catch it at all without falling on the floor yourself, your reaction time is fair. Letting it drop shows slow reactions.

These simple exercises will give you an indication of the present condition of your body. If you found some of them difficult, practice them for short, regular periods of time until they become easy.

What is Your Body Type?

No two people, even identical twins, are exactly alike in body structure. But three basic types are discernible. Can you identify yourself?

The Ectomorph—the skinny type. Relatively little flesh, muscles over-tensed, uses up energy without restraint. People like this are often the objects of envy because they find it difficult to put on weight however much they eat. Body density is high and being underweight can be a serious problem. If this is your type, you should concentrate on relaxing activities rather than very demanding ones. Breathing techniques can help you control your energy to better effect.

The Endomorph—the chubby type. Body contours rounded with soft, perhaps even flabby tissue. Body density is low, and food tends to be slowly metabolized. Often overweight and vulnerable to heart and chest disorders. If this is your type, forget about starvation diets and strenuous keep-fit programs. You will not stick to them and you will feel miserable. Moderation is your watchword. Find some activities that you enjoy and make them a regular part of your life. Toning-up exercises and the gentle, all-round stimulus of walking are much better for you than pushups.

Whatever you do, start gently then increase until you reach your optimum level.

The Mesomorph—the athletic type. Rather square in build, usually vigorous in activity. Body density is balanced. While this type is active and body weight is constant, in middle life, with the lessening of exercise, overweight can occur. If this is your type, you probably enjoy hard physical exercise. You need a well-balanced program as you may tend to overdevelop some muscles. If you have put on weight, start gently until your fitness is recovered.

How Do You Feel About Fitness?

Besides your physical characteristics, your attitude to activity is an important factor in your well-being. Check your feelings about fitness.
1. Given a free afternoon would you
a. stay at home and read or watch TV?
b. get out for a walk or exercise of some kind?
c. catch up with chores?
2. If you go to a party do you usually
a. want to dance for most of the evening?
b. drink a little too much on your own or with one or two others?
c. head for the most interesting group of people in the room?
3. When you need a few things from the local stores, do you
a. walk?
b. take the car?
c. wait or get someone else to do it for you?
4. If you want to lose weight or stop smoking would you
a. join a club?
b. cut down on your own?
c. worry but achieve little?
5. If your partner likes a particular sport, would you
a. feel resentful about the amount of time it takes up?
b. join in?
c. go and watch occasionally but fail to understand what he or she sees in it?

What You Can Do

Any activity that you enjoy will do you good. There are many available, and the following are only suggestions.
Swimming—an activity that can be social or solitary. Particularly good for the overweight as you feel lighter in water and become more agile and free-moving. All the muscles are used, but particularly the shoulders and chest.

Dance—not exclusively for women.

Dance can be as strenuous or as gentle as you like. Good for social mixing, it increases your suppleness and grace. You can release emotional tensions and dance out pent-up feelings.
Yoga—good for those who like to be on their own or for busy people who need to get away from time to time. Develops bodily awareness. It can be as simple or as difficult as you choose.
Love-making—if no other activity appeals, this is almost sure to! Make love more often, more vigorously. It can be as active as the hundred-yard dash and much more fun. Don't stick to one or two positions; don't always wait till the end of the day, when you are tired. Sexual activity turns lethargy into exhilaration and energy, melting away mental and physical tensions. As with all other activities, practice brings improved performance and enjoyment.

How Do You Rate?

16-20—you are probably an extrovert, enjoying company and exercise. But you need to guard against dissipating your energies. Sometimes, you may push yourself to exhaustion then need a time to recover. Make sure that you have enough rest and food as well as exercise, and take up relaxing as well as demanding activities.

9-15—you tend to be hard-driving. You probably try to keep fit, but as a kind of duty. Try not to cut yourself off from physical pleasure. Use your drive to develop a body that will make you proud and let yourself relax.

0-8—you take little notice of your body and prefer to make as little physical effort as possible—until, of course, your body protests. Then you feel a nagging sense that you should do something about it, but the thought of competitive sports have appalls you. Competitive sports have little appeal for you, but there are many things you can do on your own. The important thing for you is to enjoy what you do. The more luxurious aspects of body care—massage, sauna baths, and the caressing effects of mild exercise in water—will attract you more than spartan regimes.

Your Scores

1. a.1, b.5, c.3.
2. a.5, b.1, c.3.
3. a.5, b.3, c.1.
4. a.5, b.3, c.1.
5. a.1, b.5, c.3.

1192

Make that interview

It has been shown, many times, that the interview is a far from perfect method of selection. Interviewers know this. Yet so strong is the belief of most people in THEIR own good judgment that interviews form an important part of job and college selection. A successful interview is like playing a game. You must know the rules and be prepared to take some risks.

Is the Job Right?

If an ad asks for an experienced man there is seldom much point in an inexperienced woman applying for the job, though unlikely things do sometimes happen. To be sure of getting an interview, you should have at least some of the qualities demanded. A well-written, well-presented application, with just a touch of individuality, should help you to get as far as an interview. Once there, your first concern is to project the right image.

Dressing the Part

You will have about twenty minutes to create the impression you want, so you need all the help you can get from aids like clothes and grooming. People often jump to conclusions about character and abilities from such illogical clues as hairstyle. Silly? Yes, but employers often are prejudiced and you must take likely biases into account.

You are making life difficult for yourself if you go to a conservative firm with freaked-out hair and a "Jesus Saves" T-shirt, or in a neat dark suit to a hip recording company. Before your interview, go and have a look around the office or college; what seems to be the norm? In any case, clean hair, nails and clothes will look better. You will feel uncomfortable if you try to be too different from your ordinary self (but if what you really are is SO different from what they want, are you sure you want to go there at all?) so extend your usual style in the desired direction.

Conquering Nerves

Experienced interviewers expect candidates to be nervous and are ready to make allowances. Keep this in mind. Being well-prepared will improve your confidence. Find out as much as you can about the organization, its aims, its history, its current position. A favorite question is "Why did you want to come HERE in particular?" Be ready with an answer that shows some knowledge and interest—most places like to think that they are unique and a little flattery goes a long way, provided it is not too obvious.

Find out, too, as much as you can about the job or course. A useful ploy is to have some question in mind, so that, if you are asked at the end of the interview, "Is there anything you want to ask us?" you can sound thoughtful. Avoid questions about time off, holidays or getting home early—they will not create a good impression. However it is perfectly in order to ask about opportunities for advancement within the organization.

Those Terrifying Questions

Some interviewers are downright sadistic. They have trick questions, designed to test your nerves or capacity to think. If you meet one of these, take your time. You could be asked, "If you had $500 to spend on a work of art, what would you choose?" Possibly you know something about the art market, but what the questioner is after is some indication of your cultural tastes. Don't be tempted to dishonesty in order to impress. If you pull a name out of the air, you could be questioned further until your lack of knowledge is shamefully revealed. Instead, tell the truth. "I don't know what $500 would buy, but what I would like to own is . . ." Or, "I don't approve of private ownership of works of art. I'd rather give it to a gallery." Or even, "I wouldn't buy any work of art. I'd rather have a new stereo-cassette recorder." Then be ready to explain your choice.

It is often a good idea to watch news broadcasts for a few days before your interview and read a quality newspaper. Questions about current affairs are often asked as an indication of intelligence and awareness. Be ready, too, for those standby tests about what you do with your leisure time. Don't lie, just make the most of the truth. If you don't read much, say you prefer practical interests. Most places want a well-rounded personality, so use whatever you can about yourself to display liveliness and interest in life in general.

You could be asked about something of which you know absolutely nothing. Don't bluff, and don't be too apologetic. Admit that you haven't thought about it before, say something if you can, and if not, say honestly, "I don't know enough about it to answer that."

The interviewee who makes the worst impression is the one who lets all the questions fall flat with the simplest yes-no answer, giving no room for development. The opposite trap is overconfidence. Show willingness to think things out, to be flexible. Give the appearance of considering any point of view put to you by the interviewers, but you do not have to agree with them.

Group Dynamics

Interviews are often conducted by more than one person. It can be terrifying to step into a room with a circle of strangers sitting around, waiting to judge you. Remember that they are only human and that most of them have been in your place at some time. You will probably be introduced to them. Try to remember their names; at least look each one in the eyes and smile as pleasantly as you can.

Each interviewing group has its own dynamics. Generally, there is one more-or-less sympathetic person. If you feel very nervous, glance at this one for support from time to time. Look directly at whoever addresses a question to you. There is usually one tough person per group, too. Stand up to him. This is what he wants, and a seemingly fearless, but not aggressive, response will gain you a little sympathy from the others.

Answer the questions asked. That sounds too simple, but a very common mistake is to ramble in answering questions or attempt to shift the ground to something else. If you do not understand, say so. Speak clearly and keep your head up. If you impress a majority of the group, you have a good chance of success.

If You Fail

It is difficult to judge your own success at an interview. You may feel that you have been halting and stupid yet get the job, or you may feel that it went pretty smoothly only to be disappointed. This is because many other factors come into play. Internal politics may have assigned the job to someone already, and the interview is little more than a blind. Pressure for some kinds of job is so great that there could be more qualified applicants.

Occasionally, you will be told why you have not succeeded. If possible, learn from your experience. Check off the following possibilities: lack of knowledge, lack of relevant experience, underconfidence, overconfidence, views insufficiently thought out, views in conflict with the interviewers'. If you honestly felt it was a good interview, other factors are probably operating. Do not lose heart—the more interviews you have, the better you will learn the techniques.

Appreciating music

A tune from the past, and you are transported—total memory is recalled. Nothing is such a powerful influence on mood and memory as music. We probably depend more on vision than on hearing, and certainly a larger part of the brain is given over to handling visual information, but even sight is less stirring than listening to rhythmic patterns. One psychologist suggested that this is because we can close our eyes but not our ears!

What Music Can Do
Music is the universal language, speaking to our deepest emotions and at the same time to our intellect. It is appreciated by everyone. You may know very little about the mathematics of music, but it does not matter. If you can hear, you can enjoy music, a much greater range of it than you may use at present.

Filmmakers, supermarkets, and even dentists have found out how to create mood by appropriate choice of music. (Mozart diverts and soothes nervous patients in the dentist's office.) You can create, enhance or change mood with music. A record can be more relaxing than a nap, more stimulating than a martini.

Some people claim that animals and even plants respond to music. Cows that have music in their sheds are supposed to yield more milk! An eccentric millionaire in Britain has a speaker on the roof of his country house so that he can play Beethoven to his trees—which are magnificent!

Music in Your Life
How much music do you hear now? Certainly there is a lot around. If you listen to the radio on your way to work or as you go about your chores, if you watch movies or television, if you or someone in your household owns a record player or tape recorder, many of your waking hours will have a musical background.

Most of it you do not really listen to; the first step in developing an appreciation of music is to pay attention to what you hear. Then you will begin to sort out what you like. Keep an open mind—many different kinds of music can offer you different experiences and suit different moods.

When to Listen
Music can make you feel livelier in the morning, a good way to start the day. If you work at home, get into the habit of playing music as you tackle chores that do not demand all of your mind or make too much noise. Take your ironing to wherever the record player is and give yourself a concert. When you relax, make music part of the pleasure. For the first time in history, everyone can have a private minstrels' gallery to help woo his lover. (Be careful, though, of pieces with a definite beat; it can be disconcerting!)

Music for Different Moods
Some of the less obvious classics may be new to you. When you first listen, let the music sweep over you. It will take several hearings even if your musical memory is good before the whole structure takes shape in your mind. It is often a good plan to listen to one new piece in a selection already known to you. Too much novelty interferes with attention. The more often you hear something that is good, the richer your response to it becomes. This is one way of distinguishing really good music; it will not pall nor become thin and unsatisfying.

Try listening to some of these selections. Even if you do not like them all, they will give you some indication of the variety available.

Moods of nostalgia and sadness
Segovia—Platero and I: guitar music, gently sad.
Brahms—Violin Sonata in G Major: tender, searching, introspective. Also try his four symphonies if you do not already know them.
George Gershwin—Rhapsody in Blue: a marriage of jazz and "serious" musical forms. Listen to this if you know Gershwin only by his songs.
Vaughan Williams—Fantasia on Greensleeves: haunting variations on an old English song, believed to have been composed by Henry VIII.
The music of your youth is always nostalgic; explore it in depth. Blues, of course, is a form dedicated to the expression of sadness. If you listen to sad music, you will find that after you experience the feeling a kind of resolution comes, a peacefulness.

Cheerful moods
To enhance or create cheerfulness, try these pieces. Lots of popular music is cheerful, with catchy tunes that are easy to pick up. In more complicated music, the emotion is less on the surface and needs more effort to grasp.
Sousa—any of Sousa's marches will liven you up.
Beethoven—Opus 18, Symphony No. 5 in A Major: despite the dry title, this string quartet is lively and appealing, not at all heavy. Try, too, the Fourth and Eighth symphonies which are buoyant and serene.
Mozart—Eine Kleine Nachtmusik: bright, jovial, perfectly constructed. You will never get tired of hearing this.
Elmer Bernstein—The Great Escape March: a lot of good modern music is written for films. If you find film music that attracts you, it is usually possible to buy it on record or cassette.

Moods of excitement
Missa Luba: an extraordinary piece, a sung Mass in Congolese, full of vitality. None of the music was written down and a Belgian priest, Father Guido Haagen, thought that it was too good to lose, so he formed a choir of 45 boys, Les Troubadours du Roi Baudoin, whose European tour immortalized the strong rhythms and soaring songs.
Orff—Carmina Burana: not the easiest of operas to like on first listening, but worth hearing several times.
Sibelius—Karelia: if you know Finlandia, this may surprise you. It is much lighter and livelier.
Ballet music is often exciting. Try Stravinsky's Petrushka, The Firebird and The Rites of Spring, a recreation of pagan Russia that can be ferocious.

Peaceful, idyllic moods
Beethoven—Sixth Symphony, the Pastorale. This symphony is a hymn to nature.
Debussy—Prélude à L'Aprés-Midi d'un Faune: a tone poem about the faun, half-man, half-goat, who tries to remember if he really has been visited by three lovely nymphs. Full of sensuous warmth.
Aaron Copland—Appalachian Spring: one of the most attractive ballets by America's best-known composer.
Smetana—The Moldau: a nationalist piece, describing the progress of the chief river of Czechoslovakia.
Rimsky-Korsakov—the Festival of Light and the Sea, from the ballet Scheherezade: recalls peaceful evenings at sea.
De Falla—Nights in the Gardens of Spain: portrays the gardens of the Alhambra; hot Spanish nights with just a touch of melancholy.

Learning More About Music
The more you hear music, the more you will begin to notice its patterning, the characteristics of different instruments, the styles of different ages. Whenever you feel interested or curious, find out. If you are content to enjoy without knowing much, that is fine, too. Start with pleasure then move on to information. That way, music will stay alive for you.

Making music

Did you suffer music lessons as a child? Or have you had no training of any kind in playing an instrument? In either case, you have probably decided that making music is not for you; it may seem too difficult, too specialized for you.

Perhaps you feel, with Freud, that creative people are different from the rest of us: "One may heave a sigh at the thought that it is vouchsafed to a few, with hardly any effort, to salve from the whirlpool of their emotions the deepest truths, to which we others have to force our way, ceaselessly groping amid torturing uncertainties."

This is not true. Effort accompanies most artistic endeavors, and yet, as far as music is concerned, we are all endowed with some ability.

Music is one of man's most natural modes of expression. We are born to rhythm—in the heartbeat, breathing, pulse, all our movements. We distinguish tone and pitch in speaking and all the other sounds around us. However unmusical you think you are, your own body provides you with the basis of patterning sound which is all that music is.

Test Your Musical Awareness

1. You are at a friend's birthday party and you are asked to start singing "Happy Birthday to You." Do you
a. refuse because you cannot sing?
b. comply without shyness?
c. sing only if the rest sing with you?
2. When you listen to music, do you find that you beat time with your hands or feet?
a. always
b. sometimes, but if you stop to think of it you have difficulty in keeping time
c. never
3. When you listen to music, can you distinguish some of the instruments by sound, even if you do not know their names?
a. easily
b. occasionally
c. never
4. You find yourself in the middle of a party where the music is loud and everyone is dancing. Do you
a. stay close to the bar and long to get away?
b. wait until someone drags you into the dance?
c. join in immediately and dance until you are exhausted or the party breaks up?
5. Have you ever been able to pick out from memory a tune on any kind of instrument?
a. often
b. never tried
c. no
6. Do you whistle or hum to yourself?
a. often
b. sometimes, if no one is around
c. never
7. Can you remember a tune after one hearing?
a. usually
b. pretty often
c. only vaguely
8. Have you had a fantasy of singing or playing before a huge audience?
a. often
b. only as a child
c. never

Make the Most of your Voice

Most people have no idea of the true sound of their voices. Shyness constricts the throat and chest so that the voice is distorted. Your first task is to loosen up your voice and discover the range in which you sing.

When there is no one else around, lie down and bellow as loudly as you can. Play music if it helps you feel less inhibited. Let the sound roar, but try not to force it. It sounds awful but feels great. Do this until you feel easy about making a noise.

Rhythm

When you listen to music, beat out the rhythm. Try variations on the basic beat. Make your own instruments—cans half-filled with dried beans or improvised drums covered with rubber stretched tight. Simple percussion instruments, like the triangle or tambourine, will all help to develop your appreciation of rhythm.

Simple Instruments

If you are a beginner, try a xylophone, or the larger glockenspiel, to pick out and invent tunes. Recorders or tin whistles are the easiest wind instruments and will give a pleasing effect after very little practice. At this stage, you may want to learn to read music, but it is not strictly necessary. Musical notation is of much more recent date than music itself. Many musicians today cannot read music, but it does not stop them from playing and composing. New methods of teaching music dispense with those boring hours of playing scales—you can learn the principles of harmony and counterpoint through improvisation. If you like to sing and accompany yourself, try the guitar, ukulele or banjo. Simple chords can sound good.

Making your own music will add pleasure to your life, introduce you to others and give you emotional release. You may not hit the big time, but you will have a lot of fun.

28-40—your musical awareness is high. You may have some previous training, or your natural gifts may have been left reasonably free to grow. Do not stop where you are. If you play one instrument, take up another. Get together with others and discover the fun of putting different sounds—vocal and instrumental—into more complex patterns. Borrow a technique from encounter groups: have everyone start off quietly singing anything they like, gradually increasing the sound. The larger the group, the more impressive this sound can be—more like the sea than traditional choral singing. Go beyond academic music; listen to natural sounds—recordings of birdsong and whale music may inspire you.

17-27—your musical awareness is average, but you are limiting your potential. You could be a secret singer, in the shower or tub. Perhaps you lack the confidence or training to play and sing in front of anyone. It would give you great pleasure to make music; you may even have a talent for inventing your own. Start in private—sing in the tub, but see how high and low you can go; vary the volume; try running out of breath. Build up your sense of rhythm and start on a very simple instrument.

0-16—your musical ability appears to be low. If music plays any part in your life, it is probably as a background that you scarcely hear. Perhaps you were told at one time that you had no ear or could not sing. You are stuck at an early stage of musical development. Even if you are tone-deaf (and very few people are) you can improve your discrimination of sounds. Start with rhythm—you do not need to worry about tunes until later. Hand clapping and simple percussion instruments will develop your skills.

How Do You Rate?

Musical Scores

1. a. 1, b. 5, c. 3
2. a. 5, b. 3, c. 1
3. a. 5, b. 3, c. 1
4. a. 1, b. 3, c. 5
5. a. 5, b. 3, c. 1
6. a. 5, b. 3, c. 1
7. a. 5, b. 3, c. 1
8. a. 5, b. 3, c. 1

Just good friends

In the war between the sexes, can there be fraternization between male and female combatants? Or will friendship always fall to the extremes of love and hate?

Friendship involves a deep affection. We speak of loving our friends; we often know them intimately and the relationship is lasting. But it is a special kind of love. Nonsexual or "platonic" love is the kind prescribed by social norms for the bond of friendship. Friendship is generally defined as a relationship between those (usually members of the same sex) who are bound by common purposes other than the satisfaction of sexual drives. Why is it necessary to add the phrase "usually members of the same sex"? *Most* close friendships are, in fact, formed by members of the same sex. Of course, people tend to have a mixed circle of friends of varying degrees of intimacy and closeness, and, in the case of married couples, mutual friends of both sexes. But can individual men and women form close friendships in the conventional framework and meaning (that is, nonsexual) of the term "friendship"?

We know that strong and genuine friendships *do* frequently arise between men and women, contradicting a popular adolescent and even adult view that any cross-sex tie must involve romantic or sexual love. Nevertheless, for reasons of appearances (and for other reasons) friendships between members of the opposite sex tend to be relatively rare compared with friendships of members of the same sex. Certainly the joking answer to questions about the intimacy of a relationship between a man and woman—"We're *just* good friends"—suggests that the world puts a chaste interpretation on the literal word "friend," but a skeptical, not to say cynical, view of the likelihood of a nonsexual friendship between the sexes. This disbelief would be particularly marked if the friends

Above: Once he gave her comfort, but then people began to talk, and soon the pressure was on them to make it something else. When his parents began to nudge each other, it was just too much. But bed was a disaster. Is this the end of a beautiful friendship?

were young and physically attractive. The fact is that we usually seem to find it necessary to qualify the friendship between a man and woman with the term "platonic," to bring it into the same category of friendly relationship as those between persons of the same sex.

The argument seems to go something like this: How could there be a long-lasting friendship between a man and a woman without sex entering it? A friendship involving confidences and intimacy between a man and woman normally have only

Dave Webster

one logical conclusion . . . bed. A nonsexual relationship between men and women can be difficult to achieve in our society, even when it is desired —unless the people concerned are preteens or in their dotage. Indeed our somewhat salacious society tends to *imagine* that when men and women "go out" or spend evenings together, there "*must* be something in it."

This thesis tends, in mixed company, to give rise to a heated debate about the meaning and nature of love, friendship and sexual relations. Women are more likely than men to attack this thesis as derogatory to the female sex in particular and degrading to the notion of human choice in general. Lawyers trying to prove "cohabitation" in cases of alleged fraud of social security benefits by young widowed mothers who have men friends, provides a neat example of the cynical attitude to the possibility of men and women enjoying nonsexual relationships.

Before exploring the problems of friendships between the sexes, we need to look at the main question again, and at the notions of friendship and sex that it raises. The concept of a platonic friendship derives from the doctrine of Plato concerning what he thought to be the noblest form of

relationship, namely a friendship— devoid of sensuous desire—between men. Nowadays the term refers mainly to the relationship between members of the opposite sex. To ask if there is such a thing as a platonic friendship is simply a polite way of saying, "Must friendship between men and women always lead to sex?" The answer to any question with the word "must" in it, when it concerns human relationships, is a categorical "No"!

Love without Sex

Human relationships are infinitely varied and can encompass a multitude of possibilities . . . and improbabilities. Let us take the relationship broadly described as "friendship"; it is inclusive enough to cover a multiplicity of relationships, certainly too broad and rich to be confined to some conventional definition. One might ask why it should exclude a "physical giving" to one another when it includes emotional sharing? Nevertheless, we are stuck with the conventional definition. Anything else is a "love affair"!

Dr. Fred McKinney tries to distinguish the relationship of friendship from the more sexually orientated relationship of, say, courtship, in the following way: In an ordinary friend-

ship we are more concerned with the activity in which we and our friends are engaged, rather than with the friend himself and his intimate relationship to us. We normally enjoy our friends, but we do not show a strongly possessive attitude toward them. Of course, we like to help them and even to make sacrifices for them, but these sacrifices are not the result of our desire to have this friend intimately dependent upon us.

Even when we stick to the nonsexual definition there are many degrees of friendship, ranging from a casual acquaintanceship to a deep, long-standing relationship which can mean more than many so-called love affairs. Many practical examples show that platonic friendships between the sexes are possible. Good friendships are often struck up between heterosexual women and homosexual men (and vice versa) where the homosexual friend could no more think of initiating or receiving sexual exchanges than flying, even after years of loving and intimate friendship.

Then there are individuals who, while not being homosexual, have a low sex drive so that a desire for sexual contact with the friend of the opposite sex is no more likely or appropriate than his initiating an incestuous relationship with his sister. A point to make here—one we tend to forget in this post-Freudian age—is that we do have choice! Choosing may be difficult, but we can make friendship just what we want it to be.

Erotic Overtones

Having mentioned Sigmund Freud, we have to admit that it is probably difficult for many men and women to banish entirely the possibility of a sexual component entering their interactions, especially in the case of a long-standing, close relationship. The sparks of electricity—of physical desire—between a man and a woman cannot be ignored. Indeed, friendships in general (according to Freud) are tinged with erotic overtones, and this applies to friendships with members of one's own sex which have no overt manifestations of sexuality.

Freud defined sex far more widely than the narrow popular notion of genital sex, and he would suggest that there are homo- or hetero-erotic elements in all close friendships. As the psychologist Derek Wright observes, in some friendships it is not difficult to discern features like mutual wooing, emotional overevaluation of the other and increased body contact —all of which hint at a degree of erotic involvement. The erotic component, however, is marginal and covert. Sometimes, explosively, this component breaks into consciousness.

The trouble is that, as human beings, we like to categorize our experiences, sort them into neat conceptual pigeonholes. Friends do this, but *not* that! They love each other in this way, but *not* that! They should not have sexual feelings toward each other! And so on. But complex phenomena like friendship, love and sex are too big to be contained in our precise little boxes. They overflow our conventional constraints, stray into areas in which they are *not* expected or remain aloof from places in which they *are* anticipated.

"Of course there is no such thing as

For the young, friends of the opposite sex provide another point of view which is vital for a mature outlook. If men and women see each other only as sex objects, half the world will pass them by.

Marshall Cavendish

platonic friendship between men and women!" How many times have you heard this dogmatic view—usually propounded by a man? Again, the answer to the question "Does friendship between the sexes lead to love and thus to sex?" depends on what you mean by friendship and what you mean by sex and love. But we cannot even begin to define these terms with any accuracy.

Creative Relationship

Poets with intricate metaphors and scientists with precise and dry, technical language have tried to capture the elusive meanings of terms like sex and love. But phenomena like sex and love have so many facets and mean so many different things to different people that no satisfactory definitions have been ever achieved. Often they are referred to as if they were synonymous.

After all, sex is the compelling force which is the logical conclusion to being in love and which results in an act of creation—the formation of a new life. It has been the inspiration behind artistic creations—great works of literature and art. It can be urgent and sensuous, purely erotic, or it can be a spiritual force which transcends the pleasures of the flesh.

At another level, sex is simply a universal biological urge which ensures the preservation of a species, its only function being to bring about the union of the male sperm and the female ovum. It has a violent and negative side, often being allied with cruelty or sadism. Where it *can* be a joyous and liberating force, it can also be a sad, furtive and shameful act; where it can be an act of love, pride and fulfillment, it can also involve feelings of inferiority, fear and humiliation. Can it be that sex is such an emotional imperative that the forging of any relationship whatsoever between a man and woman is bound to go beyond the confines of the platonic into the sexual?

There are many gratifying ways of expressing and sharing love, and our own means of finding this emotional satisfaction often blind us to the possibility that others may get just as much pleasure out of different ways. It may be impossible for two people who have a physical relationship to understand how love can ever be as intimate and full if the sexual union does not take place. But we have to accept that for some people a physical union would detract from their emotional enjoyment of each other. There are joys to be found in giving sym-

Camera Press

pathy or sharing interests and conversation, which can also give a feeling of very close union. Emotional needs can even be satisfied by devotion to God or in service of one's fellow human beings. It would therefore seem that some people have little need for a sexual outlet.

The trouble is that sex is usually classified as one of the instincts. Because it is seen as a biological

As men and women age, friendship, not sex, must be the bond to hold the two together. And in the gathering years, what better to bring harmony and happiness than a ripe and rich relationship?

need, like hunger and thirst, we are made to think that a denial of sexual gratification should lead to an increase in need. The notion leads us to assume that it is emotionally un-healthy, perhaps even dangerous, not to have regular outlets for our sexual energies. And this makes some individuals seek many sexual conquests in relationships with the opposite sex with compulsion and urgency that looks like some aberrant physical instinct.

But what does science tell us about sex being an instinct, that is to say, an emotional necessity in the absolute sense? There is no denying that inbuilt or innate physical factors such as hormones and brain mechanisms are important in the sexual behavior of animals and humans. Of course, biological factors do influence sexual behavior in quite a large number of ways. But the scientific story also suggests that the wide differences in sexual behavior between individuals are less a consequence of biological influences than of learning experiences and environment.

A distinguished researcher into sexual behavior, Professor F. A. Beach, states that the evidence shows that it is misleading to see sex in human beings as a simple reaction to biological needs. It is more valid to view sex as an acquired appetite or taste. And this appetite is a product of each individual's experience—his unique cultural, social and personal milieu. What we inherit is the capability for sexual arousal and orgasm, but the forms and patterns that sex takes are like other appetites or tastes —they are habits and emotional preferences which have been learned. The emotional needs, situations and circumstances which make for sexual arousal and satisfying relationships can vary infinitely.

Physical Longing

By extension it can be argued that *some* men and women can love one another in nonerotic ways within the framework of friendship as it is widely thought of. Having said this, it must be obvious that the social taboos which mark off fairly clear-cut boundaries in the development of emotional and physical intimacy between friends of the same sex, are not so strong between friends of the opposite sex. Thus, it is very easy for an emotional warmth with natural sensuous overtones to deepen into a more explicit sexual attraction.

Friendship provides the atmosphere of trust and mutuality in which love of a more complete and three dimensional quality, involving physical intimacy, is likely to flourish. This is why society does not take long to label a friendship between young men and women as a "courtship" which can be expected to lead to sex in married life.

There are "dangers" in such an occurrence and they are at their height when the friends are lonely and depressed, at a point in life when they feel existence is meaningless and empty. A physical longing for comfort, relief from pain, or diversion, may be translated into a sexual approach. The togetherness of two bodies, intimately clasping each other, momentarily chases away the specter of loneliness. Identity can be reaffirmed in the attraction one's body has for another and in the pleasure it can give you both.

Something in Common

It is in this situation of alienation that sex can become an emotional imperative—there is something peculiarly satisfying about sexual intercourse. It is, after all, the closest of human embraces and the physical parallel of an emotional bond—a form of bodily conversation in which two people meet and become part of each other in both a psychological and a physical sense.

Interestingly, individuals who have more friends of *both* sexes before marriage tend to keep them up after marriage and also make new ones. It is often the people who make friends most easily who make the best marriages. And a successful marriage not only links the couple's two families; it also brings together their two sets of friends. In a study concerning this topic, half of the middle-class couples interviewed said that they shared all their closest friends, whereas the remainder retained some separate close friends. Those couples with the largest number of friends had both the largest number of mutual friends and the most separate friends, revealing that there is no necessary conflict between these two types of friendship. It has been shown, in fact, that happily married couples have more joint friends—friends of both sexes in common—than those who become divorced. It could be argued that similar skills in making human relationships underlie both friendship and marriage.

Whether cross-sex friendships exist in the social circle of the married couple or outside marriage, there are those who feel a sexual attraction for a woman or man friend but suppress it because they cannot or do not wish to become lovers—a possibility which would, in their estima-tion, alter the special qualities of their friendship which they cherish. Trouble, of course, arises because many of us are not good at forseeing "danger" or coping with it when it does inevitably arrive.

Many of these cross-sex friendships begin with a love affair but continue on a warm, confiding platonic basis when the physical attraction burns itself out or is found to be unful-filling. Some friendships develop between colleagues at work. And many people of advanced age find (as in the case of the widow and widower) mutual solace and a defense against loneliness in friendship with one another. They may have met in the park or at an old people's club. The friendship is sufficient; it needs to be taken no further. A genuine friendship can be struck up between an employer and, say, his secretary, quite devoid of the affair anticipated by the snide expectations of convention. Working in close proximity, united in a "conspiracy" against competitors and rivals, giving mutual support: the ingredients are there for the development of a good friendship. Young men have struck up friendships with mature female colleagues who have helped and sheltered them in their anxious introduction to their profession or business.

Sexual Sharing

The ways in which these bonds are forged are many and various, and they exist for all the reasons that most of us require friends: the need for sympathy, mutual support, a confident, appreciation and love. It cannot be denied that such a relationship—generating, as it does in some people, intense feelings of love and gratitude and sharing—could lead only too easily to sexual sharing, especially in those who do not rigidly compart-mentalize their sexual behavior from other aspects of their life.

It would seem, then, that the question "Is there such a thing as a platonic friendship?" can be answer-ed "Yes" most emphatically in friend-ships between individuals of the same sex and "Yes" (but less emphatic-ally) in the case of individuals of different sexes. There is in our mono-gamous society a self-preserving tendency for friendship between adult men and women to take place within marriage and to be relatively rare out-side it. When such a friendship does take place we tend to be uncharitable or charitable (depending on the view-point) and say that they are not friends, but lovers.